THE LABOUR
AND
THE WOUNDS

A personal chronicle
of one man's fight
for freedom

MASSIMO SALVADORI

Trovatello Press 2017

ISBN: 978-0-9906459-4-8

Printed by CreateSpace, an Amazon.com company.
Available from Amazon.com and other bookstores.

To my friends who died
so that liberty should not die.

CONTENTS

'Say not the struggle naught availeth
The labour and the wounds are vain.'
— Arthur Hugh Clough

FOREWORD

by
Clement Salvadori

History is too often forgotten, and the same mistakes can be made, leading to the same unfortunate results. I am writing this foreword to a new edition of my father's World War II memoirs, more than 70 years after that war was over, because it is necessary to keep that history alive. The events that led up to that conflict are still part of the life of today; simply put, it was essentially the economic frustration of many Italians that led to Mussolini's being voted into office in 1922.

My grandfather saw the dangers in this new fascist government, and was quite outspoken on the subject. In 1924 he, and his 16-year-old son Max, were severely beaten by the Blackshirts, as the para-military fascists were known, and had to leave the country. The family went to Switzerland, but my father returned to Italy in 1929 to do his obligatory military service — and to join a growing underground resistance called *Giustizia e Libertà* (Justice & Liberty). My father's code name was 'Speranza' (Hope), and hope is a keyword in his memoir. When the world is looking dark and bleak, the notion of hope for a better future can sustain a person. And he believed that individuals were important in this fight against fascism, and, while hoping, one must also act in order to bring about change.

My father was betrayed in 1932, and subsequently spent a year in prison and confinement on the island of Ponza, before managing to escape from Italy. After the war broke out he joined the British army and became a member of SOE (Special Operations Executive), the British equivalent to the American OSS. He was in the Italian section, and involved in activities behind enemy lines. After Mussolini was ousted in 1943, Papa was offered a position in the new government that would run the country; however, he chose to continue the military battle because he understood the power of the courageous individual.

Parachuting into enemy-occupied northern Italy in early 1945, my father made his way into Milan and effectively organized the resistance in that city forcing the fascists and Germans to retreat. For his bravery he was awarded Britain's second highest medal, the Distinguished Service Order, and Milan's mayor gave him "the keys to the city".

And now many western countries seem to be again indulging in excessively right-wing political machinations, possibly leading the way to more fascism and dictatorial leaders. And individuals must stand up to these anti-democratic forces.

When I returned home from my first trip to Vietnam in 1966, I told my father this American involvement was a colossal mistake which could only end badly. And said I would like to fight in a war which mattered, like WWII. His reply, "I hope you never have to."

AUTHOR'S NOTE

This book perhaps needs an explanation. Soon after the first world war, I happened to be close to people who uncompromisingly opposed fascism in the country where it was born. These, for twenty years, were the people I lived and worked with. They opposed Italian fascism and all other dictatorships because, though their political and social creeds varied, they were liberals – that is to say, believers in liberty and supporters of the institutions evolved during the last three hundred years by the North Atlantic democracies. They knew that liberty is the autonomy of the individual, man's right to live his own life as long as he respects the other fellow's rights. They recognized that a nation is free not just when it is independent, but when power is distributed fairly evenly among the citizens, when opposition and dissent can be expressed and government is through representative institutions. They, unlike others, the communists for instance, were unflinching enemies of all despotism and all privilege because it was despotism and privilege.

— ⧗ —

Many of my contemporaries were indifferent to liberty. To me, it was never the confused concept which has often led people to bondage in the name of real or of greater freedom. There were a number of reasons why liberty meant much to me while I was still in my teens. I listened to the conversations of my parents; I read; I saw with my own eyes some of the events leading to despotism; I shrank from the violence of fascists and nationalists; I was repelled by the injustice that could be seen so clearly everywhere. A little later, as a university student, followed a reasoned conviction that liberty is the greatest good not for what benefits it may bring, but because only a free man is fully a man.

Although man has an inherent capacity for freedom, the concept of liberty and the institutions through which that concept becomes the practice of free societies, are the result not of laws of nature but of conscious creative efforts. What man creates, man can also lose. Those who are convinced that liberty is good and necessary have no right to sit back and let things go when free institutions are threatened.

This, man's conscious struggle for freedom, is the thread connecting the episodes in this book. But why write about one individual's small part in the conflict between despotism and liberty? Why an autobiography mostly in the third person? Who cares what happened to an unknown man, or what he did?

We should not forget that behind masses and their movements are always individuals, their experiences and their actions. One life reflects thousands or millions of lives. Historians and philosophers write about liberty, but it is through the actions of individuals that ideas become the practice of everyday life. In many countries there would be no liberty today had there not been hundreds of thousands of people whose efforts translated the idea of liberty into free institutions.

That is why the book was written.

— ⧗ —

The struggle for liberty is clearly not over. Far from it. The threat to liberty is greater than it was forty years ago, because of the fanatical passions searing the hundreds of millions who are abandoning traditional ways of life and looking for a better future.

Most states today are ruled by dictatorships, some old, many new. It is easy for people in free countries to talk about uprisings and revolutions, to relax while waiting for popular agitation to express itself and overthrow dictatorships. The twentieth-century experience shows that within a country ruled by dictators, a few may feel the moral duty of standing for liberty; but that the work of conspirators rarely achieves its aim unless those who live freely in free countries give a helping hand.

The personal experiences described in the book are small, even insignificant. They achieve dignity through being woven into the tapestry of great events. In Petrograd at the end of October, 1917, a few thousand Red guards carried out a *coup d'etat* which grew into the communist revolution. At the end of October, 1922, a few thousand black-shirted *squadristi* [1]carried out a march on Rome which grew into the fascist revolution. The two events were connected. A terrific storm had swept over Russia. Millions had been killed. Millions of exiles found shelter in other

---

1 Members of fascist 'action squads'.

countries, and fear grew everywhere on the Continent. The war had weakened individuals and nations, and in Italy, which had weakened most, fear begat fascism.

Few people had foreseen in 1917 that the communist revolution would be a turning point; that the centuries-old march towards liberty would be halted; that despotism, in a fresh guise, would seize the initiative. In 1922 still fewer people foresaw the consolidation of fascism in Italy as anti-communist totalitarianism, its expansion outside Italy, the growing fever of individuals and nations who, under the pressure of fear, had abandoned the path of reason. No one foresaw the vastness of the conflict started by the agreement of August 23rd, 1939, between fascism and communism: the millions of dead, the ruins spread over three continents. No one foresaw that, by 1941, most of the European and non-European nations won over to the cause of liberty since 1790, would have reverted to despotism.

What bolshevism did forty years ago on the European continent, Soviet and Chinese communism are doing today all over the world. Then it was the Russian nation in convulsion and the Italian nation afraid. Now it is the gigantic, well-organized communist bloc which is growling like a hungry bear ready to devour the little, weak, terrified nations that are clutching at an America afraid both of Russia and of her tremendous new responsibilities. Through fear of bolshevism, millions of Italians lost their heads and became fascists. Through fear of communism, millions all over the world may repeat the Italians' tragic error.

It is not the materialism and collectivism of communism which are a threat to us. The menace is the despotism of a perfected autocracy, the establishment of the totalitarian state controlling all citizens in all their activities, destroying the autonomy of the individual and turning human beings into puppets. What matters now, as then, is the destruction of liberty. One does not promote the cause of liberty by turning, for hatred of communism, to fascist, nationalist or traditional despotism, by calling those countries free which are ruled by Latin-American, Mediterranean, Middle Eastern and Far Eastern dictatorships. If the choice were really not between liberty and tyranny, but between leftist and rightist tyranny, communism would win in the end. No greater help can be given to the communists than to support a dictatorship of the right.

— ⌛ —

My original plan had been to write the book anonymously. Names always mean little and as years go by they mean even less. In the Italian edition, published a few years ago, most people were indicated by initials or pseudonyms. For reasons of accuracy, and as a tribute to those – the living and especially the dead – who contributed to the struggle for liberty, some of the real names are given here.

Massimo [Max William] Salvadori-Paleotti
[b. June 16, 1908 — d. August 6, 1992]

ACKNOWLEDGMENTS

The author's mother, Contessa Giacinta Salvadori-Paleotti, translated the Italian edition, *Resistenza ed Azione*, into English. The translation was revised and adapted for the English edition published by Pall Mall, London, England, and explanatory notes added, with the help of Adeline Hartcup and Joyce Pawle Salvadori.

This new edition remains true to the original English translation with the addition of the foreword by Max's son, Clement Salvadori.

CHAPTER I

The Widening Horizon

A bright, smiling summer's day, gaiety in the air, crowds milling in the streets of Florence, young and old singing *Tripoli, bel suol d'amore* (Tripoli, fair land of love): that was the first remembered impression of the outside world, of events happening beyond the family circle.

The child, as yet small, did not know what the song and gaiety meant; it was the summer of 1912 – Italy had won the war against Turkey[1] (then an empire), had conquered Libya and occupied Rhodes. He had seen soldiers marching by, gallant and gay, behind bands which blared loud, stirring music. Vaguely he heard, then and later, talk of other wars and battles in strange, far-away countries, as fascinating as fairy-lands. There seemed nothing odd about it; why should there be? He had seen bigger boys playing with lead soldiers. It was natural that their elders should amuse themselves in the same way.

He lived in a world where everything seemed to happen with the regularity of things eternal. Breakfast and lunch, tea and dinner. Kindergarten on weekdays during

---

1 The war between Italy and Turkey started on September 29th, 1911, and was concluded by the Treaty of Lausanne of October 18th, 1912. On that day began the first Balkan war of Bulgaria, Greece and Serbia against Turkey, ended by the Treaty of London of May 30th, 1913, and followed by the Second Balkan war of Greece, Serbia, Rumania and Turkey against Bulgaria, begun June 29th, 1913, ended by the Treaties of Bucharest and Constantinople. August 1st, 1914, saw the beginning of World War I.

the autumn, winter and spring. Walks in the parks and tree-lined avenues on Sundays. In summer, the excitement of a railway journey, a few weeks' (or was it months?) holiday in the mountains or at the seaside. Now, new awareness began to enter his mind. Somewhat withdrawn by nature, the child had the habit of looking and listening – even if he did not always understand what he saw and heard. His thoughts lingered at times on scenes which did not seem to fit into the normal pattern of the days, months and years; over phrases and words which formed the pieces of the puzzle he later put together. He was like a traveller in a foreign country who stops at a busy crossroads, an onlooker who stares and observes, not yet understand a world so different from his own.

Even before he had learned to read, he used to enjoy looking at the many illustrated books that were in his home. The pictures showed people of other countries and other ages. They suggested that the world was a many coloured place and that it was always changing, that it was not true that things had always been as they were now, or that they would remain so. Atlases, with their patchwork pages, held a special fascination; he spent hours at a time looking at the colours, learning to recognize continents and oceans, mountains and plains, learning to distinguish the different regions and countries. In the atlases, Italy looked small. Evidently there were many other countries quite different from Tuscany and the Marche, with the well-tilled hills and dried-up river-beds he knew so well. Before he was old enough to go to school he saw newspapers with huge headlines spreading over two, four even eight columns, which seemed to tell of nothing but violence:

MAX AS A CHILD
sketched by his mother, Giacinta Salvadori.

wars, murders, revolutions. It seemed that, outside his peaceful little circle, great and tragic events were taking place. The name of one newspaper, *Concordia*, often cropped up in grown-ups' conversations, alongside the words 'war', 'neutrality', 'Germans', 'Austrians', 'Trieste', 'Allies'.[2]

The summer of 1915 came, and instead of being sent as usual to the mountains or to the sea, he stayed with an uncle in a city which seemed to be all steep narrow streets and old palaces (it was Perugia, one of the hill-towns of central Italy). His uncle had a beautiful house with a large garden; among the many relations staying there that summer was one of his aunts, a young woman dressed in black. Black meant death – he had often seen the Brothers of the Misericordia[3] in their mournful black robes. Nobody spoke of death, but, by piecing together chance remarks, he gathered that her husband had been killed far away in the mountains, only a few days – perhaps no more than a few hours – after firing had started at the front.

Two years later, for reasons which were not explained (actually it was because of the shortage of food in the towns), the child's summer visit to his grandfather at the seaside was allowed to drag on. Summer turned to autumn, autumn to winter, and the house, which had always before seemed gay and full of sunshine, became sadly grey now that the days were short and the rain drizzled monotonously. One evening at dinner an aunt suddenly

2 Between July 1914, and May, 1915, politically-minded Italians were divided between a majority which wanted Italy to remain neutral (but favourable to the Allies) and a minority favouring intervention on the Allied side. Pro-Germans were few. *Concordia* was a newspaper advocating neutralism.

3 Professional mourners at funerals, in Florence and other places.

4

burst into tears. A cousin, a cavalry officer who had come home on leave in a fine blue cloak admired by all, suddenly left. For days on end the grown-ups spoke of nothing but Caporetto.[4] People he had never seen before began to turn up in the village. There was something different about them; they were taller, they held themselves straighter than other people, they wore dark clothes. These were the refugees from the Friuli who had been driven from their homes by an invasion painted in the darkest of colours, a manifestation of the Spirit of Evil.

Winter wore on. One day he stood watching at the garden gate for what seemed to be hours, while an endless stream of soldiers and horses, wagons and guns went by. The sky was heavy with black clouds. Fine, icy rain was falling. The wind blowing from the sea brought with it the chill of far-off, snow-covered plains. Not a soldier sang. They were marching northwards towards the front. War must indeed be a grim affair if all these men must set out in the depths of winter over muddy roads to go and fight.

During the summer the house filled up. Relatives, whom he had never seen before, arrived. Among them was a great-aunt with white hair, a sad face and a kindly word for everyone. She never talked about herself or her family. Once again the child pieced together scattered fragments of the conversation and learned that her husband and her only son, both regular army officers, had been killed up yonder in the mountains. She was convinced that there was another life beyond this one, that it was possible to get in

---

4 At Caporetto, the Austrians inflicted a severe defeat on the Italians in October, 1917, and occupied, besides other provinces, the Friuli, eastern district of Venetia.

touch with the spirits of those who had been everything to her here, and she spent hours on end sitting in a chair with closed eyes, living a life that was no more than the fabrication of a sick imagination. But she seemed – indeed she was – a poignant symbol of grief and suffering. Niobe was not dead, she was alive, here in the house.

One morning the bells of the nearby churches rang their most joyful peals. It was a cool day, but the sun shone down on the walls as if it wanted the bricks and stones to share in the universal happiness. "Armistice! Armistice!" he heard people cry over and over again, with tears in their eyes. That moment marked an end to the tension and to the endlessly nagging anxiety which had lasted so long that they almost seemed a normal part of everyday life. Flags were flown from the windows, faces beamed, guns and rifles were silenced, and their silence brought with it the transformation of the world he had known.[5]

Now he heard other people, other events discussed – the Fourteen Points, Versailles, Orlando, and Fiume.[6] One name in particular kept cropping up in conversations – Wilson, President of the 'America' which had, all of a sudden, lost its fascination as a mysterious land bounded by gigantic cities, with hordes of redskins inland, and had become instead a near-at-hand, friendly country which took an interest in what was happening in Europe. It

5 The armistice between Italy and Austria was signed on November 4th, 1918.

6 V.E. Orlando, a leading Liberal, was then Prime Minister of Italy; Fiume, a city on the shore of the North Adriatic, was claimed both by Italy and by the newly-established state of Yugoslavia.

was said to be a country where people grew rich quickly, as anyone could see from the houses of the *Americani* – Italian emigrants, back now in Italy with the fortunes they had built where before there had been nothing but open fields. It was a country where, so people said, everyone could do as he pleased, where there were neither peasants nor master, no poor, no beggars (until then he had taken it for granted that these all were part of the natural order of things everywhere).

The horizon was widening to the east as well as to the west.

— ⧗ —

Once again it was summer, the relations had come back, and so had the holidaymakers in their hundreds. On the beach the swarming crowds sweltered under the July sun. Among them one could hardly help noticing a plump woman of about fifty, who always wore dark glasses and had a shock of thick red hair. As she passed there were murmurs of 'spy' and 'Bolshevik'. For all who lived in those parts a Russian signified – no doubt quite incorrectly – all that was then happening in the distant country none of them had ever set foot in. Who could say what reasons the woman had for coming to live in a place where foreigners were unknown, where summer visitors never came from further afield than other parts of Italy? The newspapers told of 'Reds' and 'Whites', of massacres in which human beings perished by the thousand, of murderous battles, of wars in which nothing escaped devastation and destruction, of people with curious names like Lenin, Trotsky, Chicherin and Kolchak. The child had read in books, and had heard at home, that the Tsars were hateful because they killed their enemies or sent them to die in distant cold lands, or threw them into prison. Were they then better or worse than the Tsar? Or were they just about the same? On the maps, the part which used to be all one colour from Germany to the Pacific now became a many-coloured patchwork, and every patch represented a new country and a new nation – Finland, Poland, the Ukraine, the Don Republic, Georgia...

He heard people saying how difficult it was to make ends meet. There was *polenta* (corn meal mush) for breakfast now instead of bread. Sometimes he accompanied his mother on her shopping expeditions, and stood in queues – endlessly, it seemed – outside the shops. He was struck by things he had not noticed before. He began, for one thing, to be aware of the economic side of life. For years at the seaside he had known Gennaro and Filomena, two old market-gardeners. They lived in a one-room hut made of mud and straw. They had no table or chairs, nothing but a sack of maize husks to sleep on and two bowls to eat from, and they set off several times each week to sell their garden produce at a market ten miles away. They left on foot during the night, one pushing and the other pulling the little hand-cart with its load of vegetables. They reached their destination at daybreak, sold their goods, and set out on the return journey in the heat of the day, taking turns to push the cart and ride in it. The child would not have cared to trudge for hours in the dust under the scorching sun. Why did the old people have to do this, and not he? Both of them were always good-tempered and kind, they always had a friendly smile for him, and spoke quietly and with dignity.

The peasants walked barefoot, many of them lived

in mud cottages, a little larger than that of the two old market gardeners, but just as bare and uncomfortable. Their children had no toys. When he happened to be with the peasants or fishing people in their homes at meal-times, he noticed that they ate only bread and green salad, with a glass of the vinegary *vinello* that he knew came from the grapes after the juice had been pressed out to make wine. In his grandfather's house there were at least three courses to every meal. The contrast didn't make sense. He remembered things he had never bothered about before – such as seeing an old labourer, Stefano, eating a sandwich made of black bread with a filling of white bread and a slice of onion. One day the old man did not feel well, soon afterwards he died, and someone said that he had died because he had not had enough to eat. In the heart of the city, too, the boy noticed narrow alleys, dismal houses, dark, dank stairways and decrepit doorways disgorging squalid men and women and barefoot children. And everybody looked thin. Clearly something was wrong with it all. In the evenings his father used to read from the Scriptures; the New Testament precepts seemed to contrast strangely with the suffering and inequality of which there was so much evidence all around.

Nearly two years had passed since the end of the war. Then, once again, though nobody actually spoke of it, there was tension in the air. It showed on people's faces, particularly when the conversation turned on the 'general strike'.[7] By now the child was eager to discover what was

7 Tension in Italy had been growing since the end of the war. Socialists and syndicalists agitated and demonstrated. The general strike of September, 1920, was the climax of socialist and syndicalist revolutionarism. It failed, but left a wave of fear in its wake. The communists had not yet split from the socialists.

happening in the world around him, and he explored the towns and countryside. A lot of people, he noticed, were wearing red carnations or red neck-ties. One day he came home and found in the garden a group of strangers whose leader seemed to be the man wearing a broad black tie and a wide-brimmed black hat; he and his companions were chatting animatedly together, planning how they would one day turn this house and garden into a holiday-home for working people. But that was not what they had come for. They had come to ask for ten barrels of wine to distribute among the people of the village. They were given the ten barrels, then they left.

It was a long time before he understood the full implication of this little episode. After all, what were ten barrels of wine from an estate of over a thousand acres, worked by some thirty peasant families? The clue to the puzzle was fear. The danger of a revolution had passed but the dread of it lingered. The extortions of the Red revolutionaries (socialists at the time) had cost the boy's grandfather ten barrels of wine. In his alarm and eagerness for revenge, the old landowner provided the stable-boy – a lazy, irresponsible good-for-nothing, who was appropriately known as Mustafa – and his equally idle and troublesome brothers, with the use of a car. Mustafa and his brothers formed their own 'action squad', and used the car to travel round the countryside, villages, and towns, beating up – whenever they were sure that their victims were outnumbered and unarmed – various so-called 'subversives', and raiding socialist clubs and trade-union offices. The old gentleman who lent the car and gave the money had indeed forgotten his own and his family's traditions – his great grandfather who had helped to introduce the principles of the French Revolution into the region in 1797, an uncle who had been a Member of Parliament in the short-lived Republic of the United Provinces in 1831 (and for that had been condemned to death – the sentence was not carried out), and even the part played by himself and an older brother in the events of 1860 in Naples and Sicily.[8] Mustafa and his gang used their bludgeons freely, with no thoughts beyond their delight in being in positions of power at last, in the luxurious life which had suddenly come so easily to them, and in the sound of terrified screams from defenceless people. Thus money and hooliganism together gave birth there, as elsewhere in Italy, to fascism.

— ⧗ —

Back to Florence. Back to school. Greek now as well as Latin. One afternoon the boy grew tired of studying at home and went out into the street. Although he saw no one about, once more he had the feeling of tension in the air, of uneasiness, fear and violence. Presently he heard distant shots and explosions, which seemed to come at first from San Frediano, the working-class district, later from the centre of the town. There were sounds of shots from revolvers, rifles, machine-guns. Every so often he heard the sharp explosion of a mortar shell, echoed by the

---

8 During the 1831 revolution a republic was formed, with its capital in Bologna, by districts of the Papal States and the Duchy of Modena. In 1860, Garibaldi's Thousand ended the Kingdom of the Two Sicilies and the Kingdom of Italy came into existence through the unification of northern Italy, achieved in 1859, and of southern Italy.

surrounding hills.

Bullets came whistling through the air and buried themselves in the wall of the house he lived in. The white plaster crumbled, leaving the bare, red bricks. The sky was dark and rain began to fall. The noise of firing died away. There was not a soul to be seen in the streets. An armoured car sped across the broad square in front of the city gate and disappeared towards the town's centre. The *Piazza del Duomo* was crowded, but not with the usual milling mass of people going about their business, passing on their way to or from work, stopping to rest or chat with friends. Everywhere small groups of people were talking excitedly. A white-faced peasant spoke in gasps, as though his emotions were choking him: "But I saw him myself! He'd had his brains blown out!"

That day at least a dozen people had been killed by the blackshirts, and many more wounded.

— ⧗ —

At school, too, there was tension. Strikes – which meant not going to school – had become customary. One day he went to a public meeting where a school-teacher was giving a loud harangue. "She used to be a communist, and now she is a fascist," he heard people say.

A classmate explained to him one day how his mother, a war-widow, had high hopes of a man who was going to save Italy. This was the first time he heard the name of the future dictator mentioned. It sounded ridiculous, reminding one of a well-known bandit, Musolino, and of the epithet '*messicano*'.[9] He could not quite understand what Italy needed to be saved from: the blackshirts were the men who went about killing people, so how could the leader of the blackshirts claim to be a saviour? The boy was not impressed by the reverence, almost adoration, with which the name of the future dictator was mentioned. His immediate reaction was one of aversion, perhaps because he felt the injustice of inequalities, so that servility towards higher-ups was as distasteful to him as was arrogance towards the peasants, the fishermen and the poor who lived in the slums. Every day now the papers gave news of fresh outrages, of buildings burned to the ground, of men and women killed and wounded. Squads of young men in black shirts marched along singing, making their way back from exploits which they attempted only when, like Mustafa and his gang, they were certain that their enemy was outnumbered and that they were protected by a government made weak by its members' lack of sense of responsibility. There were no more red carnations or red neck-ties to be seen anywhere.

The boy read foreign news avidly. He knew that the reign of violence was not confined to Italy. The civil war was over in Russia but the murders and massacres still went on. There were revolutions and attempted revolutions in Germany and in the countries which had won their independence through the Allied victory. There were wars in the Near East. One day he read that during the struggle between Greeks and Turks a great city had been set on

9 Musolino was a famous outlaw in southern Italy before 1914 (no connection between the Mussolini family and Musolino). Admiration for Benito Juarez, the Mexican hero, had led the future dictator's father to give that name to his son: but to Italians, *messicano* epitomized disorder, violence and inefficiency.

fire, thousands of people had perished in the flames and hundreds of thousands had been made homeless. That night he lay awake for hours. In his mind's eye he saw the flames leap up, the walls crash down. He heard the screams of the panic-stricken crowds, and smelled the acrid tang of burning human flesh.[10]

Calls to violence, demonstrations, and strikes multiplied and followed each other in quick succession. In most of northern and central Italy the action squads spread their activities from province to province, killing, burning and plundering. The fascists were particularly violent in Tuscany, where the boy lived. He heard bitter complaints against the successive coalition governments (in which moderate liberals prevailed) for allowing such outrages, but he had doubts that the blame was being put where it belonged. Was it not Parliament – rather than the Cabinet – which was inadequate? And as Parliament represented the citizens, was it not on the nation as a whole that the responsibility for the lawlessness and violence lay? The constitutional monarchy of 1860 had grown into a parliamentary democracy; it was right, he felt, that this should have happened. The boy thought a good deal about these things. He knew that parliamentary institutions rest on two foundations – the will of the majority and respect for the rights of minorities. The first of these foundations had already failed, for there was no majority; there was nothing but minorities, many of which (revolutionary socialists, communists, clericals and nationalists, just to mention a few) had not enough common sense and decency to make it possible for different parties to join

---

10 Smyrna had been taken by Turkish nationalists in August, 1922.

together in a government capable of maintaining order and of guaranteeing the liberties of the citizens. Right- and left-wing liberals, democratic catholics, republicans, radicals and social-democrats – those who stood for free institutions – were all well-intentioned, but incapable of handling a critical situation effectively. No individual or single group was to blame for the paralysis of Parliament, but all shared in a common collective responsibility.[11]

He read the accusations and insults politicians hurled at each other. He followed the story of Don Sturzo's veto, of Turati's refusal to assume Cabinet responsibility, of Giolitti's failure to form a Ministery. He heard talk of fascists and communists, of Russian money and bourgeois reaction. But who was really to blame? Who allowed the enemies of democracy to assault it? Surely it was just those very people who should have been its foremost defenders. He had read in ancient, medieval and modern history of occasions when a general, a party leader, a demagogue or a rebel attacked Parliament, suppressed it and imprisoned and killed its members. But now Parliament was not being attacked by physical force. There had been free elections both in 1919 and in 1921. It was the members of Parliament themselves, the deputies, the representatives of the people,

11 Before the seizure of power by the fascists in October, 1922, the largest plurality went to Liberal candidates, hopelessly divided in many groups (followers of Giolitti, of Salandra, of Nitti). Republicans and Radicals were small groups. Political Catholicism was divided then between a strong 'clerical' minority – usually allied to authoritarian rightist groups – and *popolari*, led by Don Sturzo. Socialists were divided into a small social democratic group willing to co-operate with non-socialist parties, a larger democratic group, led by Turati, unwilling to co-operate, revolutionary socialists (*massimalisti*, corresponding today to Nenni's socialists) led by Serrati, and communists (organized as a separate party in 1921).

who were failing in their task. It was their conduct which paralysed Parliament and Cabinet, leaving the field clear for the trouble-makers who seized their chance of gaining an advantage. The conviction grew in the boy's mind that it was not just fascism which threatened freedom: unless the citizens developed a firm conviction that freedom was good, and had strength of character enough to face crises, there would be a tyranny of one kind or another.

One autumn afternoon the boy and his father saw a crowd in the big *piazza* by the station. It grew minute by minute, until soon the square was full of laughing, shouting people. It was a dark-coloured crowd, not because people were dressed in their winter clothes, but because so many of them were wearing black uniforms. An open car, surrounded by blackshirts in full military array, advanced slowly into the heart of the wildly cheering crowd. It was a few days after the March on Rome.[12] Standing in the car was a thick-set man of medium height, with coarse features and a heavy jaw.

"Looks like a gorilla," said his father. The name stuck.

He was to see the 'gorilla' again twenty-two years later, a few days before his body was left hanging from a lamp-post in the *Piazzale Loreto* in Milan.

— ⏳ —

"This will last ten years," he heard a friend of the

---

12 At the end of October, 1922, about 8,000 *squadristi* gathered in Perugia and other localities to march on Rome. On October 28th the King entrusted the formation of a new Cabinet to Mussolini.

family say a few days later. The friend was an influential member of the catholic Popular Party, and he spoke pessimistically.

"No," came the reply. "It can't possibly last ten years. We aren't living in the days of the dictators. This is just a bad dream, soon we shall all wake up."

No one then expected that the dream – for many a nightmare – was to last over twenty years. They could not know then that there would be ten years of war, foreign intervention, two military occupations of the country and a cruel civil war before the dictatorship could be brought to an end, that after aggressive wars and massacres in Africa, Spain and the Balkans, would come a world war taking a toll of hundreds of thousands of Italians, bringing destruction everywhere in the peninsula and the islands.

Every day brought fresh evidence of the the fascists' dictatorial aims. But most of the country's political leaders still lulled themselves in a comfortable optimism.

"We've already seen this kind of thing with Crispi and Pelloux."[13]

"Let them have their fling. Soon they'll be satisfied, and then things will settle down again."

"We'll be back to normal again in a few months.

"Here we are, trying to think how we can bring these madmen to see reason, while really they are being quite useful in putting the Reds in their place and bringing back law and order. Meanwhile, a growing number of influential politicians, who had called themselves liberals, radicals, democrats and socialists at a time when no risk

13 In the 1890s and at the turn of the century, repression under the premiers Crispi and Pelloux followed periods of workers' agitation.

was involved, now pinned the fascist badge on their lapels and promised their allegiance in return for some portfolio or other, for a seat in the Senate, or merely for a decoration. However, the foundations of an uncompromising were being laid by a few men conscious of the gravity of the situation and of the necessity of making a desperate effort to save, if not liberty, at least the idea of liberty.

The 'gorilla' and his supporters were busy consolidating their position. The fascists murdered and ordered murders, escaping punishment for their crimes through the demoralization of the judiciary and the complicity of privileged groups. Many citizens – too many – applauded. Once again liberty was bartered for order, for economic security and prosperity, for promises of better times to come. Schoolboys reflected the tension that was gripping the country. On May 24th, Italy's entry into the Great War eight years before was commemorated at school with the usual speeches and flags flying in the courtyard under a blazing sun.

"Get out!"

The words were angrily hissed in the boy's ear by a schoolmate well known as a *squadrista*, a member of a fascist squad. On his rare appearances at school he was always swaggering about with a dagger or revolver, bragging of exploits he had taken part in – assault, murder, and arson.

It would have been pleasant enough to escape the morning ceremonies. The boy was there only because the whole class had been told to be present in the courtyard to hear the pompous oration of the history teacher, whose task it was to make the speech of the day. But this was a threat . . .he was not going to be bullied.

"Mind your own business. I'm staying."

"I'll be waiting for you when you come out."

Nothing happened in the courtyard. The speech droned to an end, the pupils clapped, and all went back to their classrooms. Later, when lessons were over and the boy was running down the steps to the street, he was struck a violent blow on the head from behind. His arms were pinned down by the assailant's cronies before he could hit back . . .; then other boys appeared, the *squadrista* made off, and he went home with a sore head.

Why had this happened? At school, pupils turned from their Greek and Latin, science, history, modern languages and mathematics to discuss the events that were transforming the country's life. To mark the Easter holidays they had been given the usual task of writing an essay on the meaning of Easter. It was easy for the boy, brought up as he was to listen to his father's lucid commentary on the nightly Bible reading, to make a comparison between the violence of nineteen centuries earlier with what was taking place every day now; in his essay he criticized the spirit of violence guiding those who were posing as the architects of a new Italy, the spirit which led to fresh disputes and bloodshed every day. The essay was read aloud in class; a few days later it was answered, in another essay, by a classmate who extolled the martyrdom of the young fascists dying, as many did, in the genuine belief that they were helping to end all that was corrupt in Italy, all that hindered its progress and expansion or weakened its influence among the nations. The class listened while each essay was read, and soon the news of this unusual debate – resulting from a routine classroom task – spread throughout the school.

The incident was negligible. Yet, in miniature, it reflected what was taking place throughout the whole country: the use of force to reduce people once more to a flock of docile sheep, as they had been during the dark centuries of foreign and native despotism, until the last sixty years. Of thirty pupils in the class, most of them already politically minded at the age of fourteen or so, only four others were opposed to fascism: one committed suicide several years later; another took refuge in the academic world where he could search for truth without talking about it; a third lost himself in the demoralizing grind of bureaucratic life; the fourth later took the line of least resistance, joined the Fascist Party, and sang the praises of fascism both in Italy and abroad.

Months passed. Far from returning to normal, the situation grew even more strained. Many people had recovered from their bewilderment at the easy success of the *coup d'état*, while others were shedding the foolish optimism which had caused them to stand passively by in October, 1922. Only the blind still failed to see that the operetta had elements of tragedy. It was easier, now to see where the blame should lie. True, the root of the trouble was the political feebleness of liberals, democratic socialists and democratic catholics; but it was equally true that the parliamentary paralysis had been exploited by left- and right-wing authoritarian agitators, who hated the free institutions which had been in precarious balance since 1860. There were nationalists dreaming of the grandeur that was Rome and coveting the wealth of the hated Western powers; sindicalists identifying Parliament with capitalism; capitalists identifying Parliament with capitalism; capitalists identifying Parliament with threats to property, strikes and – worse – collectivism; there were generals disliking the 'bourgeois'; and a monarch forced by parliamentary deadlock to protect a constitution to which he was bound by his oath, though he had never had any love for either Constitution or Parliament.

To restore democracy in Italy and bring back the liberties now being destroyed, it was not enough to lament past history, to sit in judgment on oneself or on other people, to inquire where the blame should be laid. Quite a number of people were beginning to be convinced of the need for action, but shrank from the logical conclusion: the need to use violence. In critical situations violence is needed to end violence, two enemies are not fairly matched if one fights with the written word and the other with a club. A brave few began to make active opposition against the tyranny of the new régime; due to their influence there were signs of awakening among the very people who, by their failure to agree among themselves before the *coup d'état*, had brought about the paralysis of the Parliament.

Late one afternoon, it was April 1st, 1924, the boy – now in his middle teens – stood waiting for his father in front of the *palazzo* which housed the Fascist Party headquarters. The *palazzo* stood in a small square by the river (in the centre of the square a monument commemorated the dead of Italy's Risorgimento). A few hours earlier, half a dozen fascists had come to the house with instructions – so they said – to escort his father to Party headquarters to explain some writings criticizing the new régime. General elections were about to take place, and the fascists were out to win the elections with *manganelli*

21

and *olio di ricino* (bludgeons and castor oil). The boy's father had described this reign of violence in two articles recently published in a well-known English weekly. (Tourists back from Italy, ignorant of the real situation – as tourists almost always are – were full of praise for the splendid new Italian government which made the trains run on time and had got rid of the beggars.) The Marchesa S_____, a staunch admirer of fascism, had seen the articles and had quickly passed them on to her fascist friends.

The boy's father refused to be taken to fascist headquarters by the *squadristi*. He said he would go there later, alone, if they wanted to discuss his criticism of fascism. The leader of the group swore that there was no thought of molestation.

Father and son presently went out together. There were letters to be posted; so, while his father went straight to the appointment, the boy took the letters to the station and then went to wait for his father. The square was basking peacefully in the late sunlight. It was empty except for three dirty, unkempt men. Two of them slouched against a wall while the third seemed to be giving instructions. As the boy was sauntering idly back and forth a few words reached his ears:

"Got to bump him off."

"All right, but who gave the order?"

"The order comes from Rome."

The words remained etched in his memory, though he had no thought then of what they implied. Suddenly the stillness of the square was shattered by yells and curses. The door of the *palazzo* opened. Out hurtled a dozen or more black-shirted *squadristi* carrying clubs and daggers, bloodlust in their eyes. In their midst, silent, his face covered with blood, was his father, walking as though in a daze. Instinctively, with no thought for the absurdity of it, the boy hurled himself at the gang and hit one of them in the face as hard as he could. It was all over in a few seconds; more blackshirts burst shouting out of the doorway; an avalanche of blows descended on him and he fell to the ground. Stunned, he lay still, his eyes closed, but in spite of appearances he was vaguely conscious. One of the *squadristi* started to lift him, but let him fall back again with a thud.

"He's dead."

Silence . . . .

When he opened his eyes nobody was in the square. The daylight was fading. He got up unsteadily and staggered off along the dark, narrow alley flanking the *palazzo* opposite the river. Farther along he caught up with his father, whose clothes were stained with the blood still pouring from his face (he had walked away, only half conscious, while the fascists had their attention diverted by the unexpected fracas with the boy). Together they walked on. At Ponte Santa Trinità they were overtaken by the *squadristi* – about fifteen of them – who had guessed that their victim would make for the hospital, and had taken a shorter route so as to intercept him and carry out the 'order from Rome'. When they did not find him they searched until they came across him with his son on the bridge. This time the bludgeons came into action. Pushed against the parapet, the boy was on the point of jumping into the Arno, his only escape, when a senior officer of the *carabineers* appeared.[14] The blackshirts scattered and, thanks to this lucky intervention, the 'order from Rome' was not carried out.

For ten days they could not leave the house. Loyal friends came to express their sympathy, and all strongly advised going away as soon as possible, as the fascists were sure to renew their attack. At the middle of April both father and son crossed the mountains separating Italy from Switzerland. There was still deep snow on the Alps. Twelve miles by sleigh brought them to the hospice near the top of the pass, where the human atmosphere was as different as the air they breathed. It was a new experience, a start in a new world . . . .

— ⧗ —

There was still tension in Italy, though it was becoming clearer every day that the fascists intended to remain in power at all costs, that despotism had usurped the place of freedom and that the efforts of an unarmed opposition would come to nothing. A year and a half later, the young man, as he was by then, returned for a few days to the city which had been his home for so long. He found friends and acquaintances in a state of great agitation. Faces were drawn with strain and fear: the blackshirts had been on the kill once more. This time they could not even justify their crimes as hot-blooded acts committed in times of upheaval. Active opposition had been destroyed; to prove their absolute control squadristi broke into the

---

14 *Carabineers* are Italy's military police, highly respected for their discipline and stern sense of duty.

homes of people known for thier democratic views; they killed in compliance with 'orders from Rome'.

Descriptions of this reign of terror were vivid: A wife sobbing as she begged for her husband's life. . . The terrified eyes of children too young to grasp what was happening . . . . A local *ras*[15] (later a Cabinet minister) had tied an anti-fascist (there were anti-fascists even though there was little anti-fascist action) to the back of his car and dragged him until there was no longer a man but a mutilated corpse at the end of the rope. . . . A harmless passer-by was killed because of his chance resemblance to a man who was marked out by an 'order from Rome'. Friends described how, in cities and villages alike, houses were broken into and plundered, and thousands of civilians brutally beaten up and forced to flee, abandoning all their possessions. The country was ruled by ruffians, not ignorant ruffians, but people who claimed to be educated and spoke of a new civilization, as if anything civilized could come of methods whose only inspiration was brutality.

Life was 'made difficult',[16] as the fascists themselves put it, for opponents of fascism who used what moral authority and prestige they had to keep up some sort of resistance. For some, life was made so very difficult that it eased althogether; many others were forced into exile; others remained, exiled in their own land, unable to get jobs or make a career, imprisoned in their homes, cut off from the life of their country, though by their very existence the

---

15 A '*Ras*' is an Abyssinian chief In Italy, fascist local bosses or leaders were known as *ras*.

16 Life being 'made difficult' included beatings and arbitrary arrest.

influence of some of them was still felt strongly.

In six years, from September, 1920, when the general strike failed, to the end of 1926, Italy had passed from what – for all its faults – had been a noble attempt at liberty, to a régime of despotism. Very few realized the importance of what was happening. To the superficial observer nothing seemed changed. Sky, sea and land were the same. There was no change to be seen in the houses, factories and fields. People got up as usual in the morning, worked, ate, amused themselves and went to sleep at night. The passing days were filled with the usual domestic and economic problems. Cradles and coffins continued to be regularly occupied.

The change was not a visible one. An irresponsible leader and his small group of advisors, friends and favourites decided among themselves how the life of the nation should be organized, how the courts and schools should function, what books and articles should be published. They decided how to use the country's natural resources, its labour and capital. They decided what foreign policy should be followed. If they wanted war, they could prepare for it and provoke it; if they wanted the people to applaud, they could make them applaud. The people had become sheep. Millions cheered the 'gorilla'. At the end of 1926 there was probably a majority in Italy in favour of the dictator, believing that he was indeed working for the welfare of the nation.

CHAPTER II

First Exile (1924-29)

Five years in Switzerland were spent mostly finishing the *lycée* and studying for a degree at the University of Geneva. As there was little or no money the young exile soon realized how lucky he was to be living among people with a strong sense of the dignity of work, who did not despise those who used their hands and did not long for idleness. He had a variety of jobs. He worked at a bench in factories and with a road-making crew. He was in turn waiter, bookshop assistant, door-to-door salesman. These occupations were not exciting. They helped him to understand the feelings of the so-called 'masses', who of necessity spend their lives monotonously on farms, in factories, shops and offices.

He learned what it means to start work while it is still dark, six mornings out of seven, to work with pick and shovel for long hours under a scorching sun or in bitter wind, to reach the dull torpor which is the aftermath of hard physical exertion. He came to know the difficulties of a worker must overcome to be good at his job. He learned to be patient and accurate. He discovered that after nine hours' work there is little energy left – and less inclination – for any of the 'cultural' activities dear to the more leisured classes. The public house has more appeal than the library, the cinema than the concert hall. The trimmings of romantic love, it was clear, are for those with time and money to spare. The average worker or labourer, even in economically advanced countries like Switzerland, has little energy left after a hard day's work to think about the problems which should be the concern of every citizen. If he is out of work, what can he think about except the rent, the unpaid bills, perhaps his cold and hungry children? He found, moreover, that the world takes on different colours according to the kind of work one does and the size of one's pay-packet. He felt the menace of unemployment like the sword of Damocles over his head, and the utter discouragement of not knowing where to turn, what to do next. He became convinced that historians and philosophers, by ignoring the very existence of the anonymous masses, distort the realities of life every bit as much as do poets and novelists; that one's concern should be with the uneducated millions struggling for their daily bread.

— ⧗ —

On his occasional travels he met numerous fellow-exiles. Most of them had settled in France, but smaller groups lived in Switzerland, Belgium, England and Austria. Very few at that time had gone as far as the Americas or Russia. Their experiences were those of all exiles everywhere at all times. They led hard lives, and almost all faced extreme poverty with courage and resolution. A few fell by the roadside; they took the line of least resistance and were eventually driven by their plight to become fascist agents. (One summer's day he was talking with a grandson of Garibaldi, who spoke of plans to stir up rebellion inside Italy, aided by a legion organized among the exiles abroad. He seemed an out-and-out enemy of the dictatorship. A few months later he and some of his friends were exposed as fascist agents.)

Worse than poverty and the intrigues of the fascist secret service was indifference. To the French, English, German, Swiss and Belgians, what was Italy but a rather backward nation which could not be expected to act responsibly? True, there had been Cavour and Mazzini, the *Risorgimento*, and impressive material and intellectual achievements in the decades before the first world war. But these, it was maintained, had been largely the result of French ideas, British aid and German initiative; the Italy of ancient Rome and of the glorious medieval Communes was dead; at present she might be a little better than a Near Eastern kingdom or a Latin-American republic, but not much; left to her own devices, it was only natural that Italy's free institutions should collapse, that the nation should be ruled by a dictator. Italians were not yet politically mature enough to govern themselves democratically; only by force could law and order be maintained, could people be induced to work, trains made to run on time (the main point of interest for foreign visitors). The exiles, it was said, exaggerated. There was nothing to worry about. Admittedly fascist demagogues and crowds were shouting "Empire! Rome! Colonies!" but they were not to be taken seriously.

The exiles knew better. The whole life of the country was being geared for war. What of it? – replied the knowledgeable foreigners: surely the episode of Corfu[1] had proved that the shouting was meaningless. Responsible leaders in France and Great Britain did not add that they

---

1 As the result of an incident at the Greco-Albanian border involving Italians, Mussolini ordered the occupation of Corfu (September, 1923). The occupying forces were withdrawn when news reached Rome that units of the British Navy had sailed from Malta.

thought it easier – and cheaper too – to bribe a dictator than a free people, and that dictators can be made use of – as the English had found, to their advantage, in the question of Mossul's oil-fields. Not many years passed before they discovered that dictators can also be quite impervious to blandishments and economic considerations.

The exiles, following the lead of the best known among them – Nitti, Salvemini, Don Sturzo, Sforza[2] — insisted that it was a mistake to make light of fascism, for it represented an idea and a force which might well enlist the sympathies of large groups in every country; it was then the most serious threat to the free way of life evolved by North Atlantic nations and, if it spread, would inevitably lead to war. Anti-fascist exiles reiterated, rightly, that freedom had not collapsed in Italy because of political immaturity, but rather because the strain to which the nation had been subjected during World War I had been too much for her material and moral strength: let Germany, France, even Britain watch out, lest what had happened in Italy should happen also to them.

— ⌛ —

In Italy the screw was being tightened. The public knew that Matteotti, Gobetti, Amendola, Don Minzoni, had been killed by the fascists, but they did not hear of the thousands of less well-known anti-fascists eliminated by murder.

2   Francesco Saverio Nitti, Prime Minister 1919-20. Gaetano Salvemini, historian; Professor, University of Florence, until compelled to abandon Italy; Professor, Harvard University, 1934-48. Luigi Sturzo, founder of the Catholic *Partito Popolare* in 1919. Carlo Sforza, Foreign Minister 1920-21 and again in post-Liberation Cabinets.

Thousands more were in prisons or concentration camps; after the special laws of 1926 they became tens of thousands. For many more, life had been 'made difficult'. At least ten thousand had left the country after severe persecution. The police was becoming omnipotent, and the mere thought of opposition had become a crime. By November, 1926, with the aid of the example set by the Soviet Union and the formulation of ideas and programmes by sycophantic intellectuals, the dictatorship had become totalitarian: all overt political opposition had been destroyed. To make sure that it would not revive, freedom of expression was banned, as well as freedom of conscience and of teaching. To eliminate any remaining independence, the country's economy was chained to fascism through the corporate system. A horde of servile intellectuals wrote ponderous volumes justifying the dictatorship in the name of Italy's greatness, of law and order, of tradition and progress, even in the name of freedom and democracy.

A few, but very few, Italians understood what was happening. To all appearance life went on as usual. Inded there was, for most, a welcome absence of party strife, of government crises, of the strikes which, betweeen 1919 and 1922, had disrupted the nation's life. The censorship was doing its work successfully: people don't worry about the things they don't know of. Press and wireless stressed only successes – the battle of the *lira*, the battle of the wheat, Corfu, Transjuba, and the reclamation of waste land.[3] The fascists were always belittling the achievements of liberal

---

3 Reference is made to the stabilization of the *lira* (1927), the increase in wheat production, the occupation of Corfu (1923), the cession of Transjuba by Great Britain (1925), the reclamation of the Pontine Marshes.

Italietta[4] but took the credit for many of its achievements (wider educational opportunities, development of industry, public works almost completed by 1922 – the aqueduct in the Puglie, the new railway between Florence and Bologna, the modern port of Genoa). There seemed to be – perhaps there actually was – more contentment in the country than there had been at any time during the two generations of constitutional government.

Fortunately there were still a few citizens with enough moral fibre to oppose the dictatorship and try to check its corrupting influence. Others, although not concerned with the moral issue of freedom and despotism, were worried about the future; they knew that dictatorship would lead first to intellectual and economic stagnation, and then to the decline of the nation; that war would be inevitable and would cause the ruin of Italy. The dictator was able to hide most of the evidence of opposition. There was a great deal of which the public was not aware. Salvemini's friends and disciples, in Florence and elsewhere, were among the first to engage in clandestine activities.[5] Secret groups were formed and conspirators met, ready to exploit any opportunity of making known the moral and material squalor that was hidden behind the bright facade of dictatorship, and what dangers threatened. They lacked experience for their difficult task, and arrests followed in swift succession. Certainly the régime could not be overthrown by underground resistance, but through their

---

4 Pejorative used by the fascists to describe Italy during the constitutional period, 1860-1922.
5 The publication of *Non Mollare* ('Don't give up') in Florence in 1925 by Salvemini, Rosselli, Calamandrei, Rossi, etc., was probably the first instance of anti-fascist organized clandestine activity.

self-sacrifice these courageous opponents accomplished what mattered most: they kept an idea alive. . . .

— ⌛ —

Switzerland was the land of exile; he learned to love it as a land of liberty, with its virtues and its shortcomings. From the outset he had been struck by the absence of beggars, of slums, of barefoot, ragged children. He was impressed by the cleanliness of the people, by the spacious and well-equipped school buildings; by the honesty which allowed people to leave front doors unlocked. He had heard that the Swiss were tight-fisted, selfish, inhospitable. It was true that not many people said, "I am so glad to see you'" yet there was generous help for the tens of thousands of foreigners who needed it. He met anarchists from Italy, Russian exiles of every political colour, German royalists who could not live under the Weimar Republic, French pacifists who had refused to fight in 1914, Catalan separatists, Jewish refugees from Polish or Rumanian anti-semitism, Arab and Indian nationalists, Hungarian and Yugoslav communists.

Class distinctions had always disgusted him. Here in Switzerland, arrogance among the well-to-do was as hard to find as servility in the so-called lower classes. Instead of peasants there were farmers tilling their own land; outside factory and office, workers and employees were on a level with owners and managers. Here, there was no need to be of the 'upper classes' to take time off for a little rest and recreation.

He had heard that the Swiss lacked the generous

33

impulses of the idealist and the prophetic visions of the reformer, that they were a colourless middle-class nation. Admittedly, he met neither Orlandos nor Don Quixotes. He did, however, meet the qualities without which liberty cannot exist – moderation, patience, tolerance, the triumph of reason over emotion, of the spoken word over the act of violence. He also saw those virtues without which prosperity must remain no more than a pious hope – the will to work, and to lead a sober life. He noticed the comparative lack of religious and intellectual dogmatism, the willingness to adjust the means to the end, to be guided by experience rather than by theories. Before launching out on her imperialist career, republican Rome too must have given an impression of drab stolidity.

He saw in practice – and not merely in the written articles of a Constitution – the liberalism which allowed the coexistence of different and equal groups within the confines of one nation. The government carried out the wishes of Parliament, which in turn carried out the wishes of the majority, a majority ready to curb its own desires so as not to make life unbearable for the minorities. Both large and small questions were settled by means of plebiscites; elections were held without the help of knuckle-dusters; the rights of man were a reality and not a farce. Was that *bourgeois* liberty? Or was it not simply liberty, with no need for any qualifying adjective?

He was told that Switzerland was an exceptional case, that it would be impossible for the experiment which had allowed four million Swiss to govern themselves freely to succeed in larger countries. When he went to England he found not four but forty-five million citizens who managed to govern themselves freely. Dark spots there were of course – sharp class distinctions, the poverty of many people contrasted with the wealth of a small minority. But there was the certainty of progress through the free institutions which made radical changes possible without violence and mass slaughter. The British had a deep-rooted respect for Parliament and Law, a sense of responsibility and discipline, willingness to moderate personal and factional ambitions and to take part in public life; every citizen had the right – his own inner right – to be himself, to express himself as he wished, to act freely, to be the master and not the slave of the state. Many intellectuals scoffed at these things. Searching for a better world, they laughed at British liberties. The young exile, instead, was convinced that there would be no better world if those liberties were lost, or even curtailed.

Apart from some wealthy admirers of fascism, and numerous fringe intellectuals gullibly falling for the Soviet 'new civilization', the citizens of Britain knew what it meant to be free and knew what they must do to remain free. Conservative, Liberal, Labour, they all spoke of democratic procedure; hardly any spoke of revolution. Patience, the essence of political maturity, was in evidence. Every major reform had been preceded by thirty to sixty years of lawful agitation. There were no apocalyptic visions. Nobody promised heaven but everyone tried to make the purgatory of this world more pleasant; instead of planning illegal shortcuts, everyone seemed to understand that respect for the law was the best guarantee of the people's freedom and equality.

Facts memorized at school returned to mind and

acquired meaning. It had taken the Roman *plebs* a hundred and fifty years to achieve equality with the patricians. The conflict had taken place and had been solved within the framework of the law and, perhaps because of this, the structure erected by the Romans had lasted for centuries. There was a certain resemblance between republican Romans and modern Britons. The example of Britain was an encouraging one. Only a few generations earlier the British had alternated not between tyranny and liberty but between one tyrannical group and another. Liberals had been just a small minority; in little more than a century that minority had grown into the whole nation, for many conservatives were in fact liberal, as were most labourites. Perhaps one day something similar might happen in other countries.

Through his readings he had always admired France as the country of Voltaire, Montesquieu and the Encyclopædists, of Lamartine, Thiers and Gambetta, of the liberals who successfully fought against the *ancien régime*, jacobinism and bonapartism; who more than anyone else had been an influence for freedom in the rest of Europe and beyond. The unattractive features of France − arrogance, conceit, abuses of both capitalism and of colonialism − did not obscure the good features − tolerance, broader social freedom than in Britain, widespread equality, absence of servility, of racial and religious prejudice. France had as democratic a state as Switzerland, and institutions which allowed defects to be brought to public notice and corrected. He was constantly hearing that France was on the verge of ruin: how could a country save itself when it was torn by disagreements and conflicts of every kind, when it was inefficiently ruled by a paralysed Parliament, when scandal and corruption were rife?

Yet it seemed to him that disagreements were fewer than they appeared to be, that most of the French lived, thought and acted within the liberal tradition of their great revolution. Conflicting trends were countered by the resolve of the majority of the citizens to keep them within the bounds of the law. The paralysis of the French Parliament was mild compared to that which had led to the fall of the Italian Parliament. If there were scandals and corruption, there were millions of honest, sound citizens. From an economic and military standpoint France was certainly behind other major Continental powers, but in political acumen she was probably ahead of them. If ever Europe (or part of Europe) were to be united in a free organization, the initiative for such a union would certainly come from France; besides being her foremost statesman, Briand was also France's European conscience.

The young exile's knowledge of Germany came mainly from German fellow-students. Through them he got the impression of a nation full of contradictions. On the surface there was more liberty and democracy than in France or Britain; below, the understanding of freedom and the sense of responsibility were lacking. The Pied Piper of Hamelin was more than a legend; he was a symbol of the real Germany. The Social Democrats were the only large group sincerely supporting the parliamentary system, but like their Italian brethren they lacked the qualities needed for successful action within the framework of democratic institutions; they were loyal democrats, but their concept of democracy was a narrow and deterministic one, too passive to withstand the pressure of dynamic times. The Catholic Party paradoxically set itself up as the champion of liberal institutions, which were contrary to the doctrines of the Church. The economy was private, but hardly free, as it was more closely bound to the state than either in France or Britain and highly cartelized. The republican régime, the democratic constitution, the citizens' rights, all seemed reflections of things foreign to the nature of most Germans. German rationalism was so dogmatic that it was a hindrance more than a help to the understanding of reality. Educated Germans showed a trait noticeable among Italian intellectuals: a tendency to defeat reason by applying it wrongly.

Geneva was full of people from the 'successor' states,[6] chiefly students, but also officials of international organizations, delegates of every sort of movement, adventurers, tourists. They seemed to share with the Germans, for the most part, an inability to connect ideas with reality. Nationalism was a general scourge, whether they were Poles or Serbs, Hungarians or Bulgarians, whether they called themselves democrats or socialists, conservatives or agrarians. As nationalists, they were unfit to create in their own countries the badly needed atmosphere of freedom. Blinded by nationalist aspirations, they failed to see that the attainment of their objective – independence – would cause its own failure. It did not take gifts of prophecy to foresee that once the wounds of war were healed, this new Europe of exclusively nationalist states would soon fall prey to stronger neighbours.

The nations of the world were all represented in

6 The European states which had resulted from the disintegration of the Russian, German, Austrian and Ottoman Empires.

Geneva. There were Russians and Latin-Americans, Indians, Persians, Arabs. They differed in colour, stature, the shape of their heads and the texture of their hair. But above all they differed in the ideas and values which determined their actions. Undoubtedly each had his contribution to make. Some, mainly those coming from North Atlantic democracies, were willing to respect those whose ideas and actions differed from theirs. Most could not conceive that there might be a truth other than their own. Locked in this dogmatism – the fountain-head of intolerance – they would consider it their moral duty to eliminate heretics, deviationists, opponents. Observing them all the young exile became convinced that international politics is in the first place the reflection of events inside the various states, that the all-important problem of peace is linked to internal structures more than to power relationships. The conditions making for free government also assured peaceful foreign policy. Liberty and peace were indissolubly interwoven. While liberal institutions, based on moderation and patience, on tolerance and respect for other people, continued to exist within the leading countries, the danger of war would be slight. As more countries fell under the rule of dictators, so the danger of war would come nearer. (It did not seem very important to most people, but he found it disturbing that the number of dictatorships was increasing in those years: Poland, Portugal, Yugoslavia. . . .) He watched the League of Nations' attempts to keep the peace. He doubted whether they could succeed because the League lacked the means – as well as the will – to assert those principles of liberty which must prevail if peace is to be maintained among nations.

— ⧖ —

At the University of Geneva teaching did not aim at moulding the students' minds. The aim, rather, was to teach each individual to use his own reasoning powers so as to reach, independently, conclusions which would guide his actions. Points of view ranging from revolutionary syndicalism to orthodox liberalism, from reform marxism to pro-fascist conservatism were freely expressed. To help in the process of broadening the students' minds there was a library where books of all tendencies were available. Then, too, there were a great many long discussions among the students coming from all countries, who questioned everything – economics and law, history and philosophy, past and present, Man and the Universe. . . .

For the young exile, the process of clarifying and integrating his ideas was tortuous and long. He read; he listened. An early conclusion he reached was that the human mind is a limited instrument, that those who claimed to know the truth were presumptuous, that the most one could hope to achieve was a glimmer of one aspect of the truth – the existence of which he did not doubt. Advances in knowledge during the last two centuries had indeed increased our range of vision, but not to the extent of justifying the arrogance of the claim: "I know". He was fascinated by the intricate systems of philosophers who had tried to interpret and explain reality. Each system seemed logical and coherent. But Spencer's system contradicted that of St. Thomas Aquinas; Hegel contradicted Vico, Freud contradicted Marx. This led him to think that they all were probably very far from a correct and complete understanding of reality. If understanding, as he believed, was a good thing, should the human mind not be given maximum freedom to observe, to think, to revise its thinking continuously?

In the second place, he found that the search for truth is meaningless if a human being is no more than the pale reflection of the will of God, as some believe, or (according to others) the even paler expression of the unconscious and unreasoning forces of the material world. The study of history led him to reject determinism; man possessed sufficient free-will to influence the course of events and to be responsible for his destiny. Certainly, both individuals and society are to a large extent governed by their circumstances. But just as the fact that a locomotive cannot be stopped instantaneously or driven at unlimited speed does not mean that there is no choice between stopping it or driving on, so the existence of determining factors does not mean that there is not a field within which free-will operates. (It may well be that liberty which is free choice has only a small part to play; but a minute divergence in direction now may mean a totally different way of life for future generations.)

Thirdly, he disagreed violently with the importance of economic influences, the new creed which had taken hold of most of his contemporaries. It seemed absurd to talk about a single all-pervading influence. Sometimes there may be only a few determining factors, but often there are a great many, and nobody has yet been able to measure their relative importance. In the twentieth century, people confronted with complex and baffling realities sought refuge in over-simplifying the issures, in reducing everything to a single element, therefore falling into the evils of dogmatism and intolerance.

Fourthly, he took exception to the lack of connection between premises and conclusions in some of the ideologies swaying his contemporaries. Socialists and communists criticized the capitalist organization. Their criticisms were generally sound; from these they leapt to the claim that collectivism was heaven while capitalism was hell. Nobody seemed to notice the lack of logical connection of this converse. Socialists and communists, attracted by a mirage, deluded themselves. They were as illogical as the fascists who praised good harvests, reclamation of the Pontine marshes, progress in road construction; from these limited achievements they inferred that there had been general economic advance, ignoring that gains in some sectors did not offset losses elsewhere, that the standard of living, far from going up, was falling. More dangerous than the ignorance of the masses was the gullibility and self-deception of the educated people, from whose ranks future political and economic leaders would be recruited.

Fifthly, he learnt that the world of action does not necessarily reflect the world of ideas. Studies, discussions and comparisons thought him that ideologies must be judged primarily from practice, that ideas can give rise to institutions whose results are often the opposite of what was aimed at. Free enterprise puts an end to economic liberty; nationalism leads to the downfall of national states; freedom of thought and speech flourished where anti-liberal Calvinist theology had triumphed; heretics were burned at the stake in the very countries where brotherly love was most preached; money-loving Britain had led the costly struggle against slavery; in the name of liberty jacobins and communists introduced a sterner despotism than that of King or Tsar; prisons and concentration camps overflowed in lands which proclaimed national or class solidarity. Facts and ideas do not share the same logic; good government could never come from the efforts of those well-meaning people – whether they were followers of Mill, Marx or Leo XIII – who hoped to force reality to conform with the logic of their principles and ideas.

Uppermost in his mind was the problem of liberty, which had been brought to the fore by the triumph of fascism in Italy and of communism in Russia. Hardly any of the foreign students with whom he mixed in Geneva were interested in liberty. Many claimed that there was no real difference between a dictatorship and a liberal democratic régime, that they came to much the same thing. Others maintained roundly that freedom did more than dictatorship to foster brutality, that peace and order, or prosperity and progress, could be assured only by a strong government which was not swayed by the ever-changing wishes and aspirations of the people. Most were convinced that liberal democratic institutions, because of private ownership of property, were in effect a strait-jacket hampering people's freedom of choice, and that the best way to ensure everyone's freedom was to follow the Soviet example and concentrate power in the hands of the few. Pessimists said that whatever developed, it was not worth worrying about because any change would be for the worse. Optimists were equally insistent that there was no need to worry because everything would work out for the best.

He did not agree with those who opposed fascism because they disapproved of the corporate economy, the reform of local administration, the agreement with the Vatican or changes in the army, in the legal or educational system. If a majority favoured the abolition of the right to strike, the introduction of collective labour contracts and compulsory arbitration; if the majority preferred appointed mayors to elected councils, or wanted to present the Vatican with a few billion *lire* or a few acres of land; if they wanted to gaze at great numbers of glossy riding-boots and tight uniforms; if they wanted greater severity for punishment of crimes, or religious instruction in every school – by all means let them have these things. He objected to dictatorship not because of its policies but because those who disagreed with the way the nation's affairs were being managed were deprived of their right to protest, to criticize, to control the government's actions. It was not the corporate state or collectivism elsewhere, which was the enemy of freedom, but the régimes which had put them in power by force and which would brook no opposition: in view of the many defects of capitalism, people were certainly entitled to try a different economic system if the majority so wished.

He was told that he over-estimated the importance of political institutions, that his was an old-fashioned approach, that he would do better to think instead about the problems of property, of class distinctions, of moral values and tradition. He would reply that of all social institutions the state was by far the most important because it represented power – had not Lenin too, said this? It was through state action that religion, economics and family life could be changed.

44

This passing from a liberal to an authoritarian position, characteristic of the times, was due largely to inability to distinguish between what was fundamental in liberty and what secondary. Italy had known liberty in the form of limited monarchy, secular government, universal education, a united nation, free trade and capitalism. However, it was possible to advocate all these things – and yet be a fascist. Elsewhere liberty signified compulsory insurance, equalized incomes, the abolition of the monarchy, unlimited majority rule, the suppression of élites – and those who want all these things were convinced supporters of Stalinist communism. Both sides failed to see that the essence of liberty is the autonomy of the individual, his right to choose whenever alternatives present themselves. From this he arrived at the conclusion – by no means an original one – that the essence of liberty lies in neither political nor economic institutions, but in the activities of the mind on which the act of choice depends. Man is free because he is endowed with reason, and the fundamental freedom, which allows of no compromise, is that of thought and speech.

He was convinced that to work for freedom was more important now than ever before. Hitherto some liberty had always existed. It had not been, usually, the outcome of conscious efforts.

It existed in the first place because there had been no means of completely dominating people's minds; in the second place because there were a variety of conflicting despotisms (Dante could say things at Verona or Ravenna which he could not have said in Florence; Voltaire at Lunéville or Berlin could write things which he could not write in France); in the third place because of the corruption and quarrels which often paralysed despotic régimes.

He believed that the greatest contribution of Western civilization had been the creation of institutions guaranteeing the liberty of the citizens. This had happened three times. Rejecting, as he did, a deterministic view of man's development, he felt no confidence that it might happen a fourth time. During thousands of years wars and invasions had been the most important factors in destroying tyranny. This was still so in the twentieth century. (It had taken the Great War to overthrow the autocracy of the Tsar, just as it had taken the barbarians to overthrow the Roman autocracy.) If, for any reason whatsoever, external pressure were to disappear, dictatorships would become permanent. It was necessary to preserve what liberty remained in the face of the onslaught of fascist and communist totalitarianism.

The struggle for liberty required the acceptance of some unpalatable facts. The fast-growing dictatorships of the post-war era were not merely the fruits of ignorance or brutality. The freedom Italy had enjoyed for two generations had brought to light the poverty, filth, ignorance and corruption, the physical and moral unhealthiness which filled the lives of far too many Italians. It had been possible to launch movements which aimed at correcting the errors of the past and at removing their ill effects. Most of those who – without bothering about Marx, Bakunin or Sorel – had given their support to movements of the Left, whether they were socialists or anarchists, communists or syndicalists, had been inspired by a desire to do good. Their main aims were to abolish poverty and to prevent human beings from exploiting one another. (Freedom? That was an upper-class luxury, an easy excuse for intellectuals to justify large estates and monopolistic industry.) As for nationalists and fascists, it was absurd to say that they were all violent, murderous and ruthless. Violence, murder and ruthlessness were indeed the backbone of fascism, but it also found support from millions of Italians of all classes who only wanted more energetic state action in building schools and hospitals, in getting rid of pellagra and tuberculosis, in assisting maternity and infant welfare, in bringing water where it was needed and in feeding those who were hungry. Supporters of red and black dictatorships were for the most part well-meaning people who were impatient at parliamentary delays, who wanted to know why they had to wait for years instead of enjoying the prompt and energetic state action of a strong government untrammelled by parliamentary procedure and respect for the opposition. All wanted the same thing – to improve economic conditions. Instead of taking the long, winding road of liberty to the top of the hill, why not choose rather the short-cut of dictatorship and get there, out of breath perhaps, but quickly? The fast-growing support for European dictatorships could not be explained without taking into account the humanitarian impulse which probably had little enough influence on most of the leaders and organizers of totalitarian movements, but was sincerely felt by the millions who marched behind them; or without taking into account the strong desire for a better and fuller life.

The young exile was certain that the traditional view of dictatorship as tyranny by a small clique, acting against the will of the overwhelming majority of the citizens, did not apply to the Europe in which he lived. It was by no means the first time that a majority of the people had turned against liberty. It was also by no means accurate to maintain – as most liberal democrats and social democrats did – that all supporters of the communist dictatorship in Russia, of the fascist dictatorship in Italy and of semi-fascist dictatorships in half a dozen other European states were wicked or foolish.

Of course, one needed to find the true explanation for the wave of authoritarianism sweeping so many continental nations. But an explanation is not a justification. Liberty had to be affirmed and an effort had to be made to explain it to those among the millions who, though not sharing the basic beliefs of communism and fascism, provided, through their support and sympathetic attitude, the solid foundation on which the totalitarian dictatorships rested. Whatever class they belonged to, they were not for violence and brutality; they thought they were helping to build a new and higher civilization. In wanting what progressive people have always wanted, what liberals had aimed at when fighting for liberty (an efficient social order, prosperity, peace and justice). they did not realize that these are incompatible with dictatorship.

It was indeed necessary to remind Europeans, not just Italians and Russians, that the struggle for liberty had been a struggle for law and order; that Europe's progress during the last four or five generations was clear evidence of the superiority of free institutions; that economic rights are meaningless when human rights are suppressed; that nothing but the triumph, throughout the world, of democracy understood as the organization of liberty, can guarantee international peace; that justice divorced from liberty turns into injustice.

The time had come to take up once again the work begun two or three centuries earlier by those who – at first in Holland and in England, later in France and other continental countries – had set themselves up as active critics of despotism, of governments under which the governed are subjects and not citizens, of political systems which set no limits to the rulers' powers. There might be need of a new Great Rebellion or Great Revolution. The road had to be prepared through the clarification of ideas and their diffusion. This work had to be resumed before it grew too late.

CHAPTER III

'Speranza': Conspiracy

Student days were over; five years had gone by since father and son had crossed the snowy passes of the Alps. In 1929 the young man left Switzerland for England, where a job had been offered him. In Paris, between trains he went to see Gaetano Salvemini, the mind and soul of democratic anti-fascism. Ever since he had gone into exile, while others talked his main concern had been action.

Known affectionately as 'Uncle', Salvemini was a source of inspiration to many, in Italy and abroad, who were fighting the fascist dictatorship. 'Uncle' had all the qualities – honesty, integrity and selflessness – which were lacking in most fascists. A distinguished scholar and a natural leader, there was in him no trace of personal ambition, envy or greed. Thirty years or more of political activity had included their share of mistakes, due mostly to impulsiveness and pugnacity. He was endowed with the rare quality of being able to admit his mistakes. Everything he had done had been prompted by generous ideals and eagerness to further the emancipation of the working classes. Although some of his young disciples may not have approved the details of Salvemini's ideas and plans, they were drawn to him by his firm conviction that it is the honest man's duty to fight for justice within a framework of freedom, and by his total dedication to the cause of opposing fascism in Italy.

In the course of their brief meeting, the young visitor told Salvemini that if there was anything he could do against fascism he was ready. Salvemini listened, said: yes, there was. He asked him to go and see some of the exiles who, with his guidance and the collaboration of friends in Italy, were organizing a movement whose main field of action – unlike previous efforts by other exiles – was to be in Italy. So the young man went to see Alberto Tarchiani, who a few months earlier, with Gioacchino Dolci and Oxilia, had helped Carlo Rosselli, Emilio Lussu, and Fausto Nitti to escape from the island of Lipari where they were interned by the fascist régime. On the stairs he met Lussu; together they entered Tarchiani's flat where they were joined by Rosselli and Alberto Cianca.[1] These were the leaders abroad of *Giustizia e Libertà*, or *G. L.*, working in close cooperation with Parri, Rossi, Bauer, Fancello[2] and others engaged in building a democratic underground in Italy. It was decided that the newcomer should go to Rome, where the need of an underground organizer was greatest; as a sign of faith in the future, he was to be known from now on as 'Speranza' (hope).

— ⧗ —

Speranza was twenty-one. Until then he had not had much to do with the exiles. He had felt that their

1 Tarchiani: Italian Ambassador to Washington 1945-55, Dolci: Republican Youth leader; and Oxilia: merchant navy captain, organized anti-fascist *coups*. Rosselli: professor of political economy, murdered by French fascists in 1937. Lussu: member of post-war Cabinets, Senator since 1948. Fausto Nitti: nephew of Italy's Prime Minister, F.S. Nitti. Cianca: member of post-war Cabinets, Senator since 1953.

2 *Giustizia e Libertà* means Justice and Freedom. Ferruccio Parri: Prime Minister in 1945. Ernesto Rossi: one of Italy's foremost economists. Riccardo Bauer: director of *Umanitaria* in Milan since 1945. Francesco Fancello: Sardinian lawyer and writer.

GAETANO SALVEMINI

efforts, restricted as they had been to countries outside Italy, were not of much value. The Italian situation was not altered by speeches, resolutions or articles made or printed abroad, which few people read. It was certainly important that somebody in France, England and America, should refute the eulogies of fascism which came from the Chamberlains, Tardieus and Walkers[3] of the day, that somebody should refute the lies spread by propagandists like Villari, Prezzolini and Foligno.[4] But Speranza felt that all this should be secondary, that the first duty of a liberal – as he defined himself – was to work against fascism inside Italy to band together in an underground movement all those who were willing to risk life and liberty in the struggle against dictatorship, and prepare them for the time when a change might be effected. The underground itself could not hope to overthrow a dictator as firmly entrenched as the Duce, but they must be ready, in case, in the continuous fluctuation of human affairs, a crack should appear in the dictatorial bloc.

Giustizia e Libertà was unlike all other groups that had been formed among the exiles. It was not composed of professional politicians (Lussu was the only one who had been, for a short time, a Member of Parliament), but of people united in the firm conviction that action was essential. Action was to include, if necessary, the use of force (but they did not believe, as communists and others do, that violence, collective or individual, must be the rule

3   Sir Austen Chamberlain was an admirer of Italian fascism; as were also, at least in public utterances, Tardieu, Prime Minister of France in the early 'thirties, and Walker, Mayor of New York.
4   Villari: a historian of repute, Prezzolini: Professor at Columbia University, and Foligno: Professor at Oxford University, were among the best-known fascist propagandists in English-speaking countries.

for all political activity). The members of *G.L.* believed that violence was immoral and criminal in a liberal democratic society, where there is a procedure which makes possible the peaceful transfer of power from one group to another; at the same time they were convinced that violence is a legitimate weapon against a dictatorship. They had not shared the delusions of those who joined the *Aventino* and of the members of *Italia Libera*[5], waiting for the monarchy, the economic situation, international complications, 'the march of time', etc., to restore liberty to the Italian people. Liberty cannot be a gift, it must be won.

The Paris group of *G.L.* seemed to realize the union of various tendencies, inspired by a fresh and lively vision of what a democratic régime in Italy should be. Freedom implies difference of opinion. Conservatives and radicals, individualists and socialists, believers and unbelievers, can all be found within a free society. Liberty embraces them all. What was needed in the fight against fascism was a sincere understanding on the part of all who were determined, however different their aspirations, to respect the fundamental liberties of thought and speech, and the rules of democratic procedure – not because these rules were in their favour but because they were inherently good. It is in this sense that *Giustizia e Libertà* was liberal. It

5 After the murder of the socialist deputy, Giacomo Matteotti (June 10th, 1924), by the fascists, deputies of democratic grops (Liberals, Republicans, Catholics and Socialists) left the Parliament. This gesture was symbolically called *Aventino*, from the secession of the Roman plebs to Mount Aventino in the early days of the Republic. *Italia Libera* had been organized by Italian democrats in 1924 with the aim of bringing together individuals and groups opposed to fascism. Among the leaders was Randolfo Pacciardi, later an exile, commander in 1936-37 of the Garibaldi Brigade composed of Italian volunteers in Spain, and Minister of War for several years after the proclamation of the Republic in Italy.

accepted the concept of democracy as the organization of liberty.

Tarchiani had been on the staff of the *Corriera della Sera*, then the leading Italian liberal newspaper; he was a close friend of Count Carlo Sforza and represented the right-wing or conservative liberalism which had governed Italy honestly and well for many years. Cianca, former editor of Il Mondo, had been a close collaborator of Giovanni Amendola[6] and was an intimate friend of F.S. Nitti. He could be considered a left-wing liberal, acutely aware of the need for economic and social reforms, convinced that Church and State must be separate and a check put on the power of private capital. Lussu represented the radical position, which tried to combine the autonomy of the individual stressed by the liberals with the solidarity of the socialists; a combination of Mazzini's and the early socialists' generous (even if Utopian) aspiration towards a society built on the principle that men are brothers, and should always act as such. Rosselli defined himself a socialist; he was inspired not by the dogmas of Marx and Engels but by a humanitarianism which drove him and many others to sacrifice themselves for the under-privileged – a sacrifice much needed in Italy, where poverty and hardship crush so many, where the selfishness of the well-to-do is perhaps greater than anywhere else in Europe.

In Italy, before 1922, there had been liberal-conservatives, liberal-radicals, liberal-socialists, and liberal-catholics. All except the last-named group were represented in *G.L.*, whose members were agreed that the basic and all-important problem was the struggle between freedom

6 Amendola: Liberal Cabinet Minister in 1922, died in 1926 of wounds inflicted by the fascists.

and tyranny. Unlike other revolutionary movements, did not repudiate the victories won by the liberal revolutions of the eighteenth and nineteenth centuries – parliamentary government, liberty of thought, conscience, speech, education, suffrage and equality of all before the law. To Speranza this was of the first importance: how could there be real progress towards greater liberty if earlier advances were denied, as they were by marxist socialists and by the communists who wanted liberty for the proletariat at the cost of so-called bourgeois liberty? One does not go forward by destroying what has already been gained; reforms were needed, but never at the cost of what liberalism had gained in the course of a century and a half of painful struggle.

It seemed to Speranza in that far-away autumn that *Giustizia e Libertà* was avoiding the basic mistake of revolutionary socialists and communists, who were so exclusively preoccupied with freedom from want that they ignored, or at any rate gave second place to all other freedoms. Economic dogmatism had no part in the thinking of the *giellisti*.[7] Salvemini and Rosselli, as well as Parri and Rossi, examined economic problems pragmatically and – without any bias towards free enterprise, controlled economy, or collectivism – looked for solutions of problems on the basis of what best met the needs of the people. They were convinced that there could be no freedom if the people were economically enslaved, either because they were wretchedly poor or because their masters (whether private employers or the state) could deprive them at will of their daily bread. Though still not clearly formulated, the

7 *Giellisti* was the name given to members of *Giustizia e Libertà;* during the Resistance period 1943-45 members of the partisan bands linked to the Action Party were called *Giellisti.*

new movement's economic programme seemed to accept, to some extent at least, the four fundamental points which Speranza hoped would be the basis of Italy's reformed economy after the downfall of fascism:

(1) Diffusion of property, mainly by means of agrarian reforms which would give several million peasant families a chance of independence and economic security.

(2) Legislation to narrow the gap between capital and labour, without bringing them under state control; favouring, for instance, cooperatives (Speranza knew of the remarkable success of producers' cooperatives in Emilia, Liguria and Venetia before the fascists came to power), part-ownership and cooperation between employers and employees in management of both private and public enterprises.

(3) Socialization of public utilities, large monopolies, and essential industries which could not survive without state aid.

(4) More equitable distribution of income by means of a proportional tax, welfare services and a national insurance scheme.

Speranza wrote that he could not after all accept the job in England. Several days were spent in meetings, exchanges of views, and discussion of the work to be done in Italy. Speranza was given the addresses of six people to be contacted immediately: one in Milan, on his way south, and the others in Rome, whre he was to set up his working headquarters. Foreseeing a long stay (in fact it lasted four years), his first concern was that his return to Italy should comply with existing regulations. Since 1928 the fascist authorities had refused to renew his passport, but when he said that he wanted to return to Italy to continue his studies at the University of Rome he was given a new one, valid only for a one-way trip back to Italy. This limitation did not bother him, for he had already crossed the frontier twice without any passport. He knew that at first he would be watched by the OVRA, the dreaded fascist secret police, but that if he succeeded in allaying their suspicions their vigilance would relax and eventually cease.

— ⧗ —

Speranza had a foretaste of what lay ahead as soon as the train, emerging from the Simplon tunnel, entered Italian territory. Knowing that he would be closely searched (his father's name was marked with three asterisks in the *libro nero* – the black list of people to be arrested as soon as they set foot in Italy), he had taken care to bring with him nothing that could arouse suspicion. But he had overlooked a notebook containing the rough copy of an article written some months earlier, and which was to be published – unsigned, of course – in the *Contemporary Review*. In it he commented on the lowering of intellectual standards in Italy as a result of fascist censorship, monopoly of education and control of all media of communication. The police commissioner found the draft of the article; he began to read the first lines, which contained nothing but general remarks unconnected with politics. Luckily Speranza's handwriting was almost undecipherable, and he was asked to read the rest of it aloud. He managed to keep his voice steady in spite of the pounding of his heart and the throbbing in his temples, and 'read' the first page, altering the sense completely as he spoke. The commissioner seemed satisfied, and dismissed him after asking where he was going. Speranza gave the address of a cousin in Milan and then went back to the train, which had been kept waiting an hour while this was going on. He had been the only passenger to be searched. The minute the train left the station he hurried to the lavatory, lit a match, and burned the manuscript which had so nearly put a premature end to his mission. It was a valuable lesson; he learned that he must be ready for – and expect – the unexpected.

In Milan he left his baggage with the cousin whose address he had given to the police. Then he went to find Bauer who, with Rossi (whom Speranza was to meet a few weeks later), Dino, Calace, Parri (not long earler released from *confino*[8]) and others in Milan, was at the heart of the *G.L.* organization in Italy. On meeting Riccardo Bauer one felt that a nation which could produce such a man could rise from the decadence and corruption into which fascism had plunged it. Riccardo had been notified that a friend was coming from abroad, and he welcomed Speranza like a brother. They had a long talk, arranging way of communication, choosing pseudonyms, passwords, and a code for correspondence. He was given two powders – 'agent' and 'reagent' – and was shown how to dissolve them in water or eau-de-cologne so that one could be used for invisible writing and the other to make it visible.

On returning to the house, he found his cousin

---

8 Fascist internment and concentration camps were known as *confino*. Living conditions there were similar to those prevailing in Russian internment camps under the Tsars, considerably better than those in nazi or soviet concentration camps.

panic-stricken. The police had been there twice. Speranza was asked to leave, to go away at once – his presence jeopardized the safety of the household, the sons' careers, and so forth. They were anxious to avoid any trouble with the police at all cost. On no account was Speranza ever to come back. Speranza supposed (correctly) that nothing new had happened, that the frontier police had passed on the news that the son of a *fuoruscito*[9] had arrived from abroad, and the Milan police were merely making a routine check-up on information received. However, Speranza thought it more prudent to avoid seeing Riccardo again before leaving. He asked his frightened cousin to tell the police, if they returned (as they did), that he was going to his father's house in the country (for the last ten years no one had lived there). He did actually stay there briefly to allay suspicion. After making this detour and having spent two days in trains, he finally arrived in Rome. He knew how essential it was to elude the police: he reckoned that if he circulated sufficiently, the bureaucratic nature of the OVRA.[10] itself would cause his file to be lost somewhere – which in fact happened. This allowed him three years of activity before his presence again came to the notice of the OVRA.

During the long hours in the train he thought about what he had heard in Paris and Milan from the *amici* (friends), as the members of the organization were always called. Action was certainly needed, but what kind of action should it be? As a matter of fact, very few definite suggestions had been made. Rosselli had spoken mainly of clandestine publications, Bauer of underground

9 Political exile.
10 The fascist secret police (Opera Vigilanza e Repressione Antifascismo).

organization, Lussu of preparing armed groups. But all had been somewhat vague, and vagueness leads nowhere. Unlike many *amici* in Italy and abroad, Speranza had not much faith in revolutions, in the form of violent uprisings. He knew enough of recent history to realize that revolutions succeed only where there is no government at all or where the government paves the way for them. It was absurd to think of a revolution against the well-armed, well-organized fascist régime. Anyhow, should revolution really be the object of the activity he was hoping to develop? A few thousand conspirators could not overthrow a dictatorship supported by the police, the *carbinieri*, the militia,[11] the regular armed forces, the enthusiastic backing of many citizens, and the indifference of the rest of the population.

There was, however, another objective to work for, an objective of vital importance which was yet within the bounds of possiblility – to prevent fascism from gaining complete control over the minds of the Italian people. As long as there remained groups of Italians, however small, who were clearly and definitely non-fascist or anti-fascist, as long as a few people cherished ideas which were not fascist ideas, there was still hope for the future. The anti-fascists might not be able to launch a revolution, but if one day the country became ready for a change, they would know how to make the most of their opportunity. It was a question of recruiting consciences rather than weapons, and the work must be planned in terms of years, not months. The individual opponents of fascism, until now isolated,

11 Shortly after the fascist seizure of power in 1922, the Action Squads had been reorganized as a militia, paid with public funds, under the direct command of the Duce; it was about 300,000 strong.

must be welded into groups capable of concerted action.

Seven years had gone by since fascism had come to power. Discouragement and disillusion had achieved even more than bludgeons and the Special Tribunal.[12] The isolation in which the anti-fascists lived had to be overcome. The knowledge that they were no longer alone, that others were at their side, that there was something to be done, would fortify and invigorate them. The organization must have room for all who opposed the dictatorship (in contrast to the communist underground which wanted to replace one dictatorship with another), must be able to act as a united whole, and at the same time be sufficiently decentralized to avoid danger to all its members if a few were arrested.

Organization, however, was not enough: it would soon disintegrate unless held together by well-defined activities. Five fields of action presented themselves – limited, of course, but they included everything that could be attempted at the time: (1) New groups must be formed; (2) Groups in different cities and districts must be linked to each other; (3) Propaganda must be made available, legally (so far as it was possible to publish without arousing the suspicions of the police), and illegally by means of clandestine printing presses; (4) Armed groups must be formed (sceptical though he was about any return to the mood of the 1848 revolutions, the possibility of spontaneous uprisings should not be altogether ruled out); (5) *Attentati* (armed attacks) must be planned, not necessarily against individuals, with the aim of creating tension and disturbing the peace and quiet apparently

12 The Special Tribunal had been created in 1926, mainly to enforce the decree outlawing all opposition against the fascist régime.

63

existing under the dictatorship.

— —

It was a drizzly grey morning when Speranza arrived in Rome. By then he had a fairly clear idea of what he intended to do. He would at once try to contact the five people whose names he had been given by the *amici* in Paris. With their help he would try to get to know other people in Rome and in those parts of central and southern Italy which had not been reached by Bauer and Rossi. Small clandestine groups must be formed in as many places as possible. The first duty of each group would be to distribute every kind of resistance literature, from the little newspaper for *amici*, to the leaflets dropped unseen in letter-boxes in the hope of kindling a new spark, and the stamp-sized emblems of *G.L.* – a red flame flanked by an 'I' (Insurrection) and an 'R' (Resurrection) – stuck on walls and in places where people would notice them (in trams, on mail-boxes, on theatre posters, even in public urinals). From within the groups must be singled out those to whom firearms could be entrusted, and who would be prepared to use them; and either within the groups or (better still) outside them, they must pick those who were willing to organize *attentati* – either against fascist headquarters in cities and towns or against the many fascist leaders (Cabinet Ministers, militia commanders, provincial *rases*) who by their own hands or by their orders had caused the death of the three or four thousand opponents killed by the fascist *squadristi*.

— —

Several years later, in 1935, after Speranza had left Italy for his second and longer exile, he wrote the following account of the people he met when he first arrived:

"The evening I arrived in Rome, I went to see Tullio. Some years before, when he was still a student, he had been left almost dying in a university lecture-room after being attacked by fascists. To all appearances he then retired from active politics and, young though he was, launched himself on a brilliant academic career. I confess I did not feel drawn to him. Later, without actually betraying anyone he abandoned us. Less than two years after our first meeting, when his career made it necessary for him to join the fascist party, he did so. In spite of his inner convictions he professed himself an ardent admirer of the dictator and the whole fascist movement. And so he carried on, until the racial laws of 1938 compelled him to be numbered again among the anti-fascists. After leaving Italy he contributed to the Allied cause during the war in the country he went to as a refugee.

"Fancello, whom I met the following day, was just the opposite – moral integrity personified, highly intelligent, strong, loyal, devoted to the cause to which he gave himself unstintingly, incapable of weakness or compromise. Was he too much of an idealist? Perhaps. But the strength of a nation lies in men like Fancello. We were constantly in touch with each other for a year, and I respected him as only a truly superior person can be respected. It was to him I turned whenever I had doubts or uncertainties, or whenever the burden of loneliness and hopelessness became too heavy. Later, after he was arrested and condemned to ten years'

65

imprisonment, whenever discouragement got the better of me and I wondered whether it would not be better to give up the underground activity which seemed so desperately useless, I had only to think of what Fancello would have done in my place, to recover faith and strength.

My third meeting was with Tommasino Smith,[13] a freemason deeply devoted to the Masons' traditional struggle against despotism and obscurantism. He was a man with plenty of fighting spirit and intelligence, but held down by family responsibilities. His uncompromising position had already cost him his job as a journalist. He had a wife and four children to support. I gave him the password. Instead of accepting me as a friend, he seemed terrified, shaking all over and hardly able to speak, almost tearful. He protested that all he wanted was to work for his children, to live in peace, and that he had absolutely no wish to quarrel with the dictator. I left him, assuring him that nobody wanted him to do anything that he felt to be beyond his strength. When by chance I met him later, he told me that he had taken me for an *agent provocateur*. After that we often met. He, too, was an active *amico*, particularly eager to do all he could to keep alive something of the old masonic organization – now a shadow of its former self, but finally divorced from the intriguers who had used only to further their own careers.

"I became a close friend of Peppino[14] who, though not much older than I, had already spent two years in *confino*. He had been the leader of the young republicans. I admired his intelligence, energy and selflessness. Nothing

13 Tommasino Smith: Italian of distant British origin, Senator since 1948.
14 Giuseppe Bruno: Resistance leader during the war, Member of the Consultative Assembly, 1945-46, and member of post-war governments.

ever seemed to discourage him, and during the three years before my arrest he was certainly one of the most dedicated and active members of the *G.L.* in Rome. It was he who sought out old *amici* and discovered new ones, persuading them to emerge from their isolation and join in our work. His position was not an easy one. A lawyer to whom a licence to practise was refused, he was arrested every time the police took precautionary measures on occasions of political celebrations, like the Duce's public appearances, or some public festivity. Many of his closest friends, who had shared persecution, prison and *confino* with him during the early days of fascism, had left the country (illegally, of course). When Peppino was advised to follow their example, he always replied that his duty was to stay in Italy and carry on the work. . . .

"Morara,[15] whom I also got to know at that time, had only recently returned from *confino*. He was an older man, and did not have much strength left. A printer by trade, through long years of work he had managed to set up an independent business, before fascism came to power. The fascists wrecked his workshop; he was ruined. He had spent years in prison and *confino* while his wife and children went hungry. Though he was now too worn out to play an active part in *G.L.*, he was valuable to us, because he introduced me to several of his friends so that groups were organized among the workers in the capital, particularly among the transport workers.

"It is essential for a conspirator to appear to have a normal life. To justify my presence in Rome and to have adequate occupation to explain, if asked how I spent my

---

15 Luigi Morara: democratic socialist.

days, I registered at the University (where I received my Ph. D.). I also began writing and publishing articles in reviews, mainly on economic problems in distant countries. A conspirator also needs to eat, though he can get along without three meals a day. During my three years of underground activity I was always haunted by the problem of cash, and seldom had enough to eat. I had an average of perhaps three meals in two days. Even the cheapest restaurant was beyond my means, so usually I made do with a few slices of salami and some bread. My lodgings were the cheapest I could find. I learned that a conspirator's life consists partly, of course, in the secrecy and "adventure" (*i.e.* the fear of being caught) which are described so often in novels, but mostly of dull everyday worries and the everlasting need to keep body and soul together. During the first few months I lived on a little money given by my father and by Rosselli. The only period when I had enough to eat was the seven months of military service.[16] Later, I found a small, poorly paid job, doing economic research for a public institute, and supplemented this income by writing articles and proofreading.

"Hard as it was to make ends meet for myself, it was even more difficult – because larger sums were needed – to find funds for underground activities. Printers could always be found (they always can) willing to risk arrest and to work enthusiastically, without pay for the underground press. But paper and printers' ink had to be bought. True, it was only a few hundred *lire* (just a few pounds), but where were they to come from? Then it was necessary to have money for travelling so as to keep in touch with groups

16 Speranza did his military service in the *Bersaglieri* at the Cadet Officers' School in Milan, December, 1930 – June 1931.

68

in the provinces and with the centres of the underground movement in northern Italy and the Islands – particularly Sardinia, where some people thought that an uprising might take place. Arms, ammunition, and explosives were needed in case *attentati* were to become practicable. Then there were fellow-conspirators in hiding because the police were on their tracks; they and their families desperately needed help. People had no idea of the hardship which crippled thousands of families whose only financial support had been a father, a husband or a son now condemned to months or years of prison or *confino*, families now living in utter isolation and destitution. Now and again it was necessary to raise funds to send people abroad. From one source or another some money was collected. By devious means, the main sums – apart from those sent by Rosselli – came from a few liberals, members of wealthy aristocratic families, who did not feel equal to taking an active part in the underground movement, but were anxious to show their solidarity with those who were working in it. From them came the twenty or thirty thousand *lire* which made it possible to print clandestine leaflets, to send people abroad and into the provinces, and to pay an allowance to the families of imprisoned members of the organization."

– ⌛ –

Again, to give some idea of life in Italy at that time, here is what Speranza wrote during the autumn of 1935:

"For five years I had been living in Switzerland, which knew nothing of the feeling of being spied upon, a country where there were no "informers". But at the very first station inside Italy, uniforms – those symbols of state authority – were everywhere; on soldiers and frontier guards, on *carabinieri* and fascist militia; ubiquitous, too, were the easily recognized plain-clothes police. The very air was oppressive. Everywhere grim faces were to be seen, everywhere were signs of fear, insecurity and suspicion. In the train the passengers either said nothing or else they talked of trivialities. Fascist Italy was a country of spies.

"I cannot pretend that I enjoyed the part I had volunteered to play. I disliked conspiracies and secret societies, which accustom people to lives of subterfuge and deceit. The need to conspire was in itself a symptom of the moral decadence caused by the dictatorship, which turned the weak into spies, would-be opponents into hypocrites, while the great majority – those who were neither spies nor conspirators – became indifferent and cynical. In a few years the dictatorship which had brought about the moral corruption of a large part of the nation would soon cause its material ruin as well. Conspiracy was most unattractive but it was the only remaining weapon; it had to be used.

"In a few months I had enlarged my circle of friends and acquaintances – purely political ones, for I had no time or energy for others. After a few weeks in Rome I realized that it would be impossible to form any large homogeneous organization, and that in its place we must have a looser body within which various groups (unknown to each other) would bring together individuals of different opinions, tendencies and ideals, so that each group would have different work to do. I felt bound to explain the risks involved to those I approached with the hope that they might join in our work. At that time an underground leader might hope to get off with a sentence of ten years from the Special Tribunal. A rank and file member of the underground charged with no more than unspecified anti-fascist activities could expect to get three to five year in jail or *confino*. After the new penal code was issued, for anyone involved in an *attentato* there was either the firing squad or thirty years' imprisonment. It had to be made clear to a potential conspirator that it was not easy to evade the police for long. It might be a matter of months, with luck a few years but in the end he would be caught – usually when he least expected it, when all would seem to be running smoothly.

"The first parcel containing clandestine printed matter reached me about three weeks after I arrived in Rome. It was brought to me by Rossi, who did not mind spending two nights in the train in order to deliver a few hundred pamphlets and leaflets. For over a year these were brought regularly to Rome either by him or others from northern Italy. Later, they came through railwaymen and merchant seamen, and supplemented the publications which we managed to put out ourselves in Rome. I attached great importance to the clandestine publlications, not only for what they said but also because they could circulate more freely than people. Wherever they appeared they caused (even if in a small way) an atmosphere of tension and excitement. Many, of course, fell into the hands of people easily scared, and were quickly destroyed, but the rest were passed from hand to hand (nobody wanted to keep them for long). Later I discovered that the publications we distributed in Rome circulated throughout the country. I came across them in the cities of Puglia and Campania, in the villages of Umbria and the Marche, in the resorts of the Abruzzi. Often a leaflet or pamphlet reached some enthusiast who would make copies on a typewriter and so increase the circulation. Even before the Special Tribunal began to direct attention to *Giustizia e Libertà* by the great trials of 1931 and 1932,[17] tens of thousands of Italians had come to know about the movement. The clandestine leaflets and pamphlets had a great moral effect, proving to all who felt discouraged – and there were few anti-fascists in those days who did not – that somebody was actively at work. That was enough to give heart and hope to many people. There were complaints that the clandestine publications did not achieve sufficient results to justify the dangers involved. I took the opposite view. Under a dictatorship there is not much that can be done to rouse peoples' minds and consciences, and every opportunity had to be grasped. It was worth doing even if it did no more than spread the knowledge that an organized opposition existed.

As the years passed, the conspirators fell more or less spontaneously into three groups – the "intellectuals", the "organizers", and the "activists", as those who favoured acts of violence were called. These groups were known as A, B, and C conspirators. The A group agreed with Belloni[18] that there was no advantage in having a regular underground organization. They were willing to devote themselves to propaganda through books and pamphlets which, by not obviously criticizing or attacking fascism,

17 In 1931, for instance, Bauer and Rossi were condemned to twenty years' imprisonment, and a host of others to lesser sentences. During the first five months of 1932 there were death sentences and thirty-year sentences.
18 Giulio Andrea Belloni: a jurist, later deputy to the Italian Parliament, and a leader of the Republican Party.

managed to escape the censorship and the political police, and in this way spread our ideas. Biographies and writings of leaders of the *Risorgimento* were particularly valuable in this field – not so much those of Mazzini and Cavour, whose names at once roused the suspicions of the censors, but of others such as Cattaneo, Bovio, Ferrari and Pisacane. Books and pamphlets were to be sold at the lowest possible price so as to reach the widest possible public. Within the limits of our resources we also made cheap bulk purchases of translations of foreign authors whose works held a clear message. We found the works of Unamuno, Jack London and Gorki especially useful. (later the sale of these books was forbidden.)

"The conspirators of the B category formed the largest and most important group. In Rome they were led by Fancello, Bruno, Giannotti, De Sanctis and many others. They were convinced that intellectual resistance was by itself inadequate. They wanted an organization including different groups, composed of cells or sections. Its main object would be direct propaganda (through personal contact) among those who were not yet corrupted by fascism, particularly the masses of artisans and industrial workers in the towns, and of peasants in the country. Members of the cells were expected to make every effort to approach people, to find those already convinced of the need to overthrow fascism, to convince those who were still doubtful, and to convert passive opponents of the régime into active ones. Each cell would have to keep in constant touch, through one of its members, with others. Members were expected to distribute clandestine publications, to be ready to provide hiding-places in case of need, to keep an eye on the local nerve-centres of the state machine – telephone and telegraph exchanges, power stations, reservoirs, railway junctions and depots, stores of arms and ammunition – and to plan to seize control of these in the event of a riot, a *coup d'etat* or an invasion. . . . It would also be the duty of all to spread rumours and stir up discontent and disorder. In the small towns, particularly in southern Italy, riots broke out from time to time because of taxation or quarrels between rival fascists. In the north there were occasional strikes. The B conspirators had to keep the unrest seething as long as possible and spread the news of disorders in the adjacent areas.

"The conspirators of the C category, whose chief inspirer was Lugli,[19] had no faith either in the activities of the "intellectuals" or of the B group's organizers and propagandists. For my part, only in the most exceptional circumstances could I have participated in an *attentato*, but that was no reason to refuse to help those who believed in the value of damaging fascist headquarters through an explosion, or of an attempt against the life of a criminal *ras*. Unlike most of my fellow-conspirators, I was rather eclectic: I didn't care much what my friends did, as long as they did something. Each of the three groups could work independently and all contribute to the common cause – the weakening of fascism's hold over the nation.

"Ours was certainly an odd sort of movement, without any membership cards, subscriptions, executive committees or secretaries. It was both vague and definite: vague because it lacked all the outward signs of a formal association, and definite because every member felt intimately

19 Bruno Lugli: later went into exile, joined the Republican forces during the civil war in Spain and was killed fighting.

united with the others. We agreed to do without formal distinctions of rank or position, because there is a moral equality among friends who are exposing themselveds to the same risks. Whoever did the most work naturally acted as a leader, and if his activities lessened, someone else took his place. During my last year of conspiracy, four of us knew the approximate size of our membership, the names of the heads of groups or at least how to reach them, where to find and how to distribute our meagre funds. Giannotti, with active support from Ciccotti and De Sanctis, led the groups in Rome (divided according to districts and suburbs) and its vicinity, including the hill towns of the Castelli. The provincial groups, covering the whole peninsula except for northern Tuscany, were directed by myself, who also kept in touch, by means of agents and coded correspondence, with the exiles abroad and with some of the main groups in northern Italy. Belloni was mainly concerned with publications, but he also helped to organize groups in the Lazio outside Rome. The fourth leader, Bruno, was on the police list; he had to be particularly careful. But he knew all that the others were doing and – thanks to his very wide experience – acted as coordinator of all our efforts. It was to him we turned whenever tension arose within the organization.

"Most of our members, naturally enough, were in the B group. As far as I knew – my information could only be partial – there were some 800 of us in Rome just before my arrest. The provincial groups numbered between 2,500 and 3,000 members; there were more of them in the Marche and the Abruzzi than in Umbria and Molise, more in Puglia and Basilicata than in Campania or Calabria.

As for the Islands, we had few contacts with Sicily, but many groups scattered throughout the three provinces of Sardinia were in touch with us in Rome through Fancello until he was arrested, then through Siglienti.[20] However, in spite of all our efforts, we achieved less than in the north."

— ⧗ —

"In Rome I was in touch with several other more and less active groups of anti-fascists who were working independently of *G.L.* Among these were what we called the "Young Liberals" who followed Gobetti's[21] example in their attempt to revive Italian liberalism, purging it of conservatism, trying to establish it as the vital foundation of the whole Italian social structure, replacing the old economic dogmas by a common-sense policy based on the need to remedy the country's worst economic injustices. Gobetti had had a very large following. While I was in Geneva a young visitor from Italy had told me about the "Young Liberals'" endeavors, and of their attempt to form an underground organization. The police had had no difficulty in spotting them, and in 1928 hundreds of them had been arrested. I met Ascoli, to whom Rossi introduced me on one of his earliest visits to Rome, and later La Malfa, Cattani, Fenoaltea, and others;[22] I agreed, of course, with their idological position, but felt that they were not

20 Stefano Siglienti: businessman, later Minister of Finance in the post-fascist Liberation government.
21 Journalist, died of wounds inflicted by the fascists in 1926.
22 Max Ascoli: publisher and editor of *The Reporter* in New York; Ugo La Malfa and Leone Cattani: Resistance leaders during the war; deputies and Cabinet Ministers after the war. Sergio Fenoaltea: post-Liberation ambassador to China, then to Canada.

active enough. Perhaps because they had already had their fingers so badly burned, they refused to take part in our "activism". And yet they did form a group, in so far as they met regularly and were active within the limits they set themselves. Underground conspiracy they considered to be a waste of time, leading only to increasing the population of the prisons. They abhorred any kind of compromise with fascism: not one of them ever stooped to applying for membership of the Fascist Party, though their lives, as those of all non-Party members, were exceedingly hard.

"The "Young Liberals" had friends who, though not actually fascist in their sympathies, were Party members and occupied positions of responsibility in the administration, in business and in intellectual life. These contacts could be useful in a moment of crisis[23] in effecting a transfer of power with a minimum of bloodshed. There was another field in which "Young Liberals"' activities could be useful: many things could be said and written in the form of essays on economics, history, and philosophy without direct mention of fascism and dictatorships. The "Young Liberals" joined forces with older intellectuals – not only the most famous like Croce and Einaudi, but also many others in Rome, Naples, Florence, Milan, Turin and Venice – who in the quiet of their studies stayed faithful to the liberal idea.

"There was another group: we called them the "Excellencies" – the few former political leaders who still opposed fascism. I went several times to see Di Cesarò[24] who had the distinction of being followed wherever he went by a fascist plain-clothes detective, who used to make

23 As happened in July, 1943.
24 Duke Giovanni Colonna di Cesarò: pre-fascist deputy and Cabinet Minister.

77

himself useful in small ways, calling taxis for instance, shopping, or carrying parcels and suitcases. Di Cesarò spoke enthusiastically of the following he still claimed to have in Sicily. His enforced inactivity weighed on him, but in spite of constant surveillance he kept in touch through various trusted and well-known intermediaries with other liberal-democratic ex-ministers, generals, etc., who had recovered from their bewilderment at the triumph of fascism. I also frequently visited De Gasperi,[25] the last Secretary of the catholic Popular Party, in his office in the Vatican Library. In spite of his mild appearance, one could sense the vitality which had made him a leading political figure in the Austrian Empire and in Italy while he was still a very young man, and which at a crucial moment had made of him the successor of Don Sturzo and the spokesman for a semi-liberal Catholicism. It was this vitality which had enabled him to stand imprisonment, and to resign himself without bitterness or humiliation to the humble post which now gave him his living. He patiently and regularly kept in touch with the former Popular Party leaders, from Gonella in Rome to Gronchi in northern Italy and Scelba in Sicily.[26] I had always wondered whether a devout Roman Catholic could recognize the principle of personal liberty for all. It seemed to me that with political catholicism, as with traditional socialism, the stress on the rightness of one group excluded the legitimacy of dissent, which is the core of a free society. Theory notwithstanding, I got the impression that De Gasperi, like Don Sturzo, was

---

25 Alcide De Gasperi: the future Prime Minister.
26 Gonella: sometime secretary of the Christian Democratic Party and Cabinet Minister. Scelba: Prime Minister after De Gasperi. Gronchi: President of the Italian Republic sinc 1955.

sincerely convinced that political action should be based on democratic procedure and the toleration of non-Catholic groups.

"Di Cesarò, the freemason ex-Cabinet Minister, and De Gasperi, the former Popular Party leader, met and exchanged views. I was told that their anti-fascist circle included many ex-ministers and ex-deputies, several generals and a couple of field marshals. They were not really "activists" but, rather, *frondeurs*,[27] whose activities belonged to a higher social and political sphere than those of the "Young Liberals". They were comparatively close to the fascist leaders, they had friends among fascist supporters, who had once been liberal democrats, Popular Party members and socialists, and their movements sometimes caused the police – as well as the small circle of fascist leaders – serious anxiety. Their example, to us as well as to others, was a valuable one. In the first place, they had sacrificed their personal interests for the ideals which had inspired them in the days before fascism, so proving that they had moral qualities which the new leaders lacked. Secondly, by cooperating, in spite of their political differences, they had shown ability to rise above old prejudices and antipathies. For some time our main contact with the "Excellencies" was through Volterra, whose father, a Liberal senator, and brother, a University professor, although not active, were staunch anti-fascists.

"In close contact with the "Excellencies" circle and having nothing to do with us, a small group of "activists" had grown up, thinking in terms, not of revolution, but of

---

27 *Fronde* (from the French political movement of the seventeenth century), indicates intent more than actual opposition. It can also indicate (see Chapter VI) the dissatisfied group within the ranks of the ruling clique.

a *coup d'etat* from above. (We felt that this was a forlorn hope.) They put their trust in the King, not perceiving his scepticism, his apathy, his desire for peace at any price and his contempt for all that is noble and generous in liberty and democracy; he was a weak ineffectual man, burdened by fate with a responsibility beyond his moral strength. The *coup d'etat* enthusiasts (whose main leader was Vinciguerra[28]), relied upon retired high-ranking officers, forgetting that only a general or a colonel in active command could do anything decisive, and unaware that not a single officer at that time could be found willing to attempt a *coup de main.* In the end, Vinciguerra and some of his friends were arrested and given heavy sentence – fifteen years' imprisonment – which they served with great fortitude. It was their arrest which led De Bosis,[29] helped by *G.L.* in Paris, to make his fatal flight over Rome.

"To leave no stone unturned, I tried whenever possible to approach members of the armed forces. The many meetings with a colonel of *carabineers* were of little use: he was interested only in the romantic side of conspiracy – the *noms de guerre*, secret *rendezvous*, coded messages – and had no practical suggestions to offer. He dreamed of a *coup de main*, hundreds of us suddenly invading the Palazzo Venezia,[30] kidnapping the dictator, and proclaiming a provisional government. All dreams! Others were more helpful: one was any army engineer, whose brother, arrested for anti-fascism, had been tortured by the OVRA; he helped me to obtain material from the

---

28 Mario Vinciguerra: journalist and author, one of Italy's most distinguished intellectuals.
29 Lauro De Bosis: poet and patriot, a distant relative of the author.
30 The Duce's headquarters in Rome.

military depots. Another was a naval officer, who for a time acted as liaison between the groups in Rome and those at the military naval base at La Spezia. We were not the only ones to look for the cooperation of members of the armed forces. One evening during my military service in Milan, I was ordered to go on sentry duty at a gate between two barracks. The officer who gave me the order said that subversive publications were believed to be passing between the two buildings. That night when the gate opened, the sentry (myself) appeared to be fast asleep. Who passed through? It was certainly an *amico*, another member of the

Max (L) with other members of his unit during his Italian military service as a Bersagliere, a crack corps in that army.

underground.

"Until I met them at Regina Coeli and Ponza,[31] I did not have much to do with members of the communist movement. We were well acquainted with their activities and with the hatred between opposing Stalinists and Trotskyites and other factions. We deplored the Stalinists' triumph because it meant the victory of extreme intolerance and fanaticism. Italian communists at that time were exclusively conspirators of the B variety; they rejected violent action as doing more harm than good to the underground, and the activities of the "intellectuals" (A group) as futile. Their aim was to win members for the Communist Party. Organization and propaganda were the communist by-words, and their efficacy can be judged by the number of communists who were arrested – an average of 100 a month, I was told at one time. They had the advantage over us in that they had a certain number of "professional" organizers paid, very modestly, with Party funds, and therefore able to devote themselves entirely to clandestine work which, if it is to be done properly, must absorb body and sourl. The professionals certainly did not lead luxurious lives. I was told that they were given 800 lire (about £8) a month, a bare minimum. Most of these organizers had spent some time in the "schools", training centres run by the Communist Party in Russia and France. Whenever I came across communists I could not help admiring their energy and conviction. Their self-abnegation was not less than that of Christian missionaries

---

31 Regina Coeli is the name of the principal jail in Rome. Ponza in the Tyrrhenian Sea, was one of the many islands in which *confini* were located; others were Lipari and Ustica, off the coast of Sicily, Lampedusa near Africa, and Tremiti in the southern Adriatic, also Ventotene near Ponza.

in past centuries. It was painful, to me, to see so much self-sacrifice devoted to a movement whose triumph could lead only to the strengthening of the chains which we were trying to break.

"The communists appealed mainly to young intellectuals, and we were always hearing of people who had started working with us and later went over to communism. Most of these new recruits became orthodox communist, obedient members, blind pawns in the hands of their leaders. Others, a minority, adopted a more or less heretical communism, which tried to combine political and intellectual liberalism with economic collectivism; the dictatorship and the totalitarian régime were accepted by them as a provisional step on the road to greater liberty; they were quite unaware of the contradiction between a centralized, bureaucratic economy, strongly rooted in authority and discipline, and the practice of liberty; in the same way they overlooked the fundamental contradiction between the subjection of the citizen to the state and the control of the state by the citizen. Among them were Piperno, whom La Malfa had introduced to me in Rome, and who was afterwards arrested, and Palermo[32] from Naples, whom I met through Rossi. I felt certain that in the end those who were prompted towards communism by their love of liberty would discover how incompatible the two really were, and would return to a position near enough to ours to allow us to work usefully together. . . ."

— ⌛ —

32 Gastone (Pepe) Piperno later returned to the democratic fold and played a role in the Resistance during the war. Mario Palermo: Neapolitan lawyer, under-secretary in post-fascist Cabinets, communist Senator.

"From time to time I came across people who, because they were too old or too closely watched by the police, remained in apparent isolation and yet had a strong influence on all who where searching for daylight beyond the fascist darkness. To us they were oases in the desert. Without any doubt the most influential of these was Croce, whom I visited only twice, because the *palazzo* in which he lived, right in the centre of Naples, was too closely watched. For me (and for many others) his books and articles were what the writings of the poets, philosophers and historians of their day had been to the generation of the *Risorgimento*. What we felt was expressed by Croce in clear, straightforward words: that liberty is the essence of man. Whenever despondency overwhelmed me, all I needed was to think of the words: "*la libertà ha per se l'eternità.*" Besides Croce's *Critica* we read, of course, Einaudi's *Riforma Sociale*, and I tried to time my visits to Turin on the days of Einaudi's lectures. He had only a few students, but those few (apart from a couple of spies) were potential *amici*. From time to time *amici* also visited Casati,[33] whose position in Milan was like that of Croce in Naples and Einaudi in Turin. In Rome I called on De Viti De Marco,[34] whom I had known in the past and now met again through Rossi. He led me to a room on the top floor of his house, and asked me to speak in a whisper as he could not trust his servants or even the members of his own family. We talked of the economic and financial

33 Count Casati: conservative liberal Cabinet Minister in pre- and post-fascist Cabinets.
34 Marchese De Viti De Marco: radical liberal economist, for many years member of Parliament.

crisis which fascism had caused in Italy and which, now that it had become chronic, was accepted as a normal state of affairs. He spoke of liberty, of its meaning for human beings, and of the impossibility for individuals to make progress except by their own free-will, by individual effort.

"I visited Massarenti, the veteran socialist leader – an impressively dignified old man. Time and time again he had been arrested, beaten, and tortured. He had been through so much that his mind sometimes wandered. To him, socialism was not dry marxist dogma, but the will and duty to improve the conditions of the working masses, in an atmosphere of freedom. Massarenti had organized the great Molinella cooperatives, with a pre-war capital of twenty million *lire*, which had assured the well-being of 8,000 families of peasants and workers. Now the cooperatives had been confiscated by the fascists. Massarenti's most active friends were in prison or *confino*; it was a miracle that he himself was still alive. In Milan I met old Maffi, another humanitarian socialist, whose brother was dying in prison. In spite of the apparent hopelessness of the situation, he remained an optimist; his faith in his fellow man was unshaken.

"Buonaiuti[35] lived in Rome. He was, to us, a symbol of how the twin evils of despotism and dogmatism can destroy the finest flowering of man's soul. A priest and a scholar (a great historian) he had been excommunicated, and the fascist state had persecuted him – he was one of those for whom life was "made difficult". He was a liberal, not only in his political and social views (like, to a certain extent, Don Sturzo and De Gasperi) but also, which is

35 Buonaiuti was probably the last great leader of 'modernism' within the Catholic Church.

more important, in his philosophy. One of the best friends of our movement was Zanotti Bianco[36] who gave us moral and financial support, but could not be an "activist" because he was constantly shadowed – not by one plain-clothes man, like Di Cesarò, but by two. A pre-fascist liberal, he had accepted persecution and hardship to remain faithful to the freedom in which he believed.

"We were in touch with "activists" outside Rome. Rossi brought publications, news, and instructions from Milan until his arrest. His good humour, optimism and energy spurred us on, and each time he came he introduced me to new *amici*. From La Spezia came a democratic socialist who had already spent several years in prison, and whose name I never discovered. His field of propaganda (a fruitful one) was among the Ligurian sailors and dockers. Another democratic socialist, from Avezzano, came to get clandestine leaflets and pamphlets which he would mimeograph in his home town and distribute among the labourers and sheperds of the Marsica (the Cafoni, as they are called by Silone). A republican from Teramo paid us regular visits. He had organized several groups in the small coastal towns. Two commercial travellers, one from Jesi and the other from Ancona, kept us in touch with the groups of *G.L.* in the Marche: one of them often went on business to Zara, in Dalmatia, where he met other *giellisti* from the groups organized by Woditzka and his friends in Trieste. We also had regular contacts with Sardinia, though close police supervision prevented Sardinian anti-fascists living in Rome from returning home; there were a good many groups of *G.L.* there, especially in Cagliari and Nuoro.

---

36 Count Zanotti Bianco: social worker, post-war Senator.

To Civitavecchia[37] went Minafò, a seaman, who acted as courier between us in Rome and the exiles in France and Tunisia. His devotion and loyalty were unbounded. He had a wife, four children, a mother and a sister to support, but in spite of these obligations he never wavered in his determination.

"Sometimes I spent whole days and nights in the train (always travelling as cheaply as possible) on my way to see *G.L.* organizers who were unable to come to us. I used to take parcels of clandestine publications with me, relying on the stupidity and laziness of the fascist *polizia ferroviaria*,[38] whose continual patrolling up and down the train was at times quite unnerving. I usually had to be most careful when I went to small towns, where a new face is noticed at once. I would try to time my arrival when there was least chance of being watched, to move on again as soon as possible, and to leave by a different route. I always made a point of finding out how to go in and out of the station without passing through the ticket barrier. The first contact was usually rather difficult. For instance, to meet Morea,[39] on whom we were counting for organizing groups in the Marche, I was introduced at the station in Rome to an unknown *giellista*; we travelled in different carriages and got out of the train at our destination still without seeming to know each other. I followed him until he made a sign directing me to Morea's house.

---

37 Port on the Tyrrhenian coast northwest of Rome.
38 There were many branches of the fascist militia patrolling the frontier area, roads, railways, ports, the wooded areas of Italy (*Milizia Confinaria, Stradale, Ferroviaria, Portuaria, Forestale*, etc.).
39 Alfredo Morea: deputy of the Italian Parliament until deprived of his seat in 1926, Republican Party leader.

"Whenever I visited Pergoli[40] in Falconara, I made my way along lonely paths; I used to take advantage of the siesta hours, when everyone, including the police, was resting. My first meeting with Pane,[41] an active organizer in Naples and the surrounding districts, arranged by a mutual friend, took place on a hill-top near the sea, where the only building was a lighthouse, and the lighthouse keeper was his brother. I trudged for hours to get there, first along a dusty road beside the sea, and afterwards up steep paths from which I could see the island of Ponza in the distance (I didn't think then that one day I would be sent there). Two lawyers, the Pastena brothers, were my contacts in Bari; their district was an interesting one for us because of the frequent riots, like those at Martina Franca and Minervino Murge, caused by the extreme poverty of the workers and peasants. In Naples, besides Palermo and Pane, I often met Bonelli, a true nineteenth-century romantic conspirator, very active but out of step with reality: he dreamed of revolution, barricades, action squads and all the other trappings of the 1821 and 1848 Neapolitan evolutions; but he did organize groups and spread clandestine propaganda, not only in Naples but in Lucania and Calabria.

"On several occasions I went to Terni, where during the early days of the dictatorship revolutionary socialist workers had formed underground groups which remained active for many years. In the province of Grosseto one of our contacts was a miner from Monte Amiata, who managed at times to supply explosives needed by members of the C group. Having spent several years in prison and *confino*, he had moved to Grosseto where he was not known, so had

40 Piero Pergoli: a country doctor.
41 Antonio Pane: philosopher and disciple of Croce.

better chances of carrying on underground organization and propaganda. In Piombino I was always the guest of a steel-worker whose house was a rallying point for other workers and miners. He was wretchedly poor, like Silvetti, on whom we could always count for organization of groups and the diffusion of clandestine leaflets in the province of Ascoli Piceno. Most of the *giellisti* in the Castelli, in Ciociaria and in Sabina were artisans or agricultural workers.

"The most exhausting, because they were the longest, were journeys to northern Italy. (All travelling had to be done in a minimum of time so that no one would notice my absence from Rome.) On one of my early trips I met Umberto Ceva, who soon afterwards took his own life in prison so as to avoid compromising those who had been arrested with him. He gave me a fresh supply of invisible ink, which lasted until I was arrested myself. After the arrest of Bauer and Rossi, the leaders of *G.L.* in northern Italy, trips to Milan and Turin had to be made more often. The Turin *G.L.*, with its relatively large membership drawn from all social classes, its clandestine publications, its frequent contacts abroad, seemed the most efficient in Italy; Garosci, Renzi, and Levi were among the most active members. In Milan, with Bauer and Rossi in jail, the burden of keeping *G.L.* going fell largely on Albasini. One evening I was to meet him in a deserted street. At that time I was doing my military service, and my uniform was a protection. He didn't turn up. This worried me and next day I called on his mother; she did not know me and would only say that her son was away from home and that she did not know when he would be back. I asked for her husband, but she answered that he was ill (as indeed he was, and the shock of his son's arrest killed him soon afterwards). It was old Maffi who told me that his son and Albasini had both been arrested. . . . The news had a bracing effect on me. I had been discouraged and recently come to feel that all our efforts were useless. I was near the frontier. . . . The arrest of my friends made me realize that I must stay and carry on. It made all the difference to those in jail to know that we outside were still active."

— ⧗ —

"There were plenty of plans which aimed at the immediate downfall of the fascist régime. For my part, I was convinced that the only really useful activities were organizing, publishing and circulating underground literature, discussing and keeping ideas alive. That was the "minimum" programme, who failed to distinguish between dreams and realities. My father, in Switzerland, and some of his friends in Italy, complained because we did not start guerrilla warfare in the mountains between the Maiella and the Sibilla; Lussu in Paris was also always dreaming of guerrilla warfare and armed troops. These were all tempting pipe dreams for romantic souls who did not realize that guerrilla action needs majority support throughout a country. Another "maximist" proposed that we should buy enough lorries to carry 200 men, drive up in them at top speed and invade the courtyard of the Palazzo Venezia, where the Duce's offices were. We might have found 200 reliable men, but there was no money to buy the lorries; if we had the lorries it would have been quite impossible to capture the well-defended Palazzo Venezia, even if we had contrived to be reasonably well armed. Various people suggested tht we should make our way through the sewers to the Palazzo Venezia, to lay a charge of high explosives. It was absurd to imagine that we could get enough explosive to do any serious damage to the building; however, we decided to look into this plan, and found that it had been anticipated. Twice daily, police patrolled the malodorous sewers under the centre of the city, and there were iron gates in them in the vicinity of Palazzo Venezia and all the main government buildings. Other optimists proposed driving round the city in an armoured car, until there was an opportunity to fire at the dictator – as if there were the faintest chance of penetrating the swarm of police cars and motorcycles perpetually on guard whenever the *Padrone* (Master) was in the streets. Bruni, a former member of the Popular Party, a young friend of De Gaspari, suggested that some of us should buy tickets for an air flight, overpower the pilot, and take over the aircraft; we would then proceed to a prearranged spot where bombs would be loaded, and, on the return journey over Rome, these would be dropped on Palazzo Venezia. Others hoped to succeed where Zaniboni[42] had failed, or wanted to lie in wait with rifle or machine-gun at Gola del Furlo or along the road to Castel Porziano.[43] All this, of course, seemed unpractical romanticism, and did not appeal to my rational mind; on the other hand I knew how

---

42 Major Zaniboni, democratic socialist and deputy to the Italian Parliament, organized an attempt against the Duce's life in 1926. Caught by the OVRA, he spent seventeen years in prison, until liberated by the 1943 Allied invasion.
43 Twice or more a year the Duce passed Gola del Furlo on his way to his home town of Predappio; he spent an occasional weekend at Castel Porziano.

much this kind of unpractical idealism helped the cause of freedom in the nineteenth century, from Ypsilanti's attack against the Ottoman Empire in 1821 to Garibaldi's One Thousand in 1860.

"A number of individual *attentati* were tried. The public learned of only a few of them. I had several *rendezvous* on the roof of St. Peter's with a specialist in *attentati*, a Macedonian revolutionary who had practiced chiefly in the Balkans. Later, a few active *giellisti* detached themselves from the rest of the movement so as not to compromise the other members. They ruled out attacks against individual fascists, but believed it was worthwhile to sabotage fascist buildings, as it was the kind of action that was bound to become known to a great many people. One young Sardinian arrived, enthusiastic about making an *attentato*, and strongly recommended by the exiles in Paris; he meant well but was careless, and too many people in Paris knew about his journey. The police had their eye on him, he was arrested and received a thirty-year sentence.

"As time went on, we discovered that ours was not the only movement thinking in terms of direct action. The communists were not, although some, against Party orders, were collecting arms and ammunition. Abroad, Pacciardi and Facchinetti,[44] after cooperating briefly with *G.L.*, found themselves out of harmony with its programme and formed a short-lived "activist" group which ended with the shooting of Bovone by the fascists. People with anarchist leanings also made *attentati* on their own initiative; for instance, Schirru and Sbardellotto.[45]

44 Leader, as Pacciardi, of the Italian Republican Party, Minister in post fascist Cabinets.
45 Bovone, Schirru and Sbardellotto, all acting independently, were caught by

"Our determination received new impetus every time we learnt of acts of opposition. Early one October morning I was on my way back from a journey to the provinces. The sun had only just risen, and the streets were empty, or nearly so. When I reached the neighbourhood of Piazza di Spagna I saw policemen picking up pieces of paper from the ground. I picked one up too, and saw that it was an appeal against fascism evidently written by people of liberal sentiments. Later that morning I learned that Lauro De Bosis had flown over Rome the night before, dropping hundreds of thousands of leaflets. He had a small plane and knew that he would never get back alive. He disappeared into the Tyrrhenian Sea on his return flight to Corsica, probably shot down by fascist aircraft based at Ortobello. . . . His example was an inspiration to all of us. Previously, Bassanesi and Dolci had flown over Milan, dropping thousands of leaflets.

' "What was the use of it?" asked the sceptics.

' "A great deal," we replied. "While the least activity remains, while people are still ready to sacrifice themselves – as De Bosis was – there is hope."

"On my way to Genoa one day I took an excursion train from Milan. Sitting near me were several employees of the *Corriere della Sera*, and one of them was delightedly telling the others what had happened two days before; in an advertisement column, under the title of *Vero Recostituente* (a real tonic), had appeared the flame and the initials which were the emblem of our movement! It had been a nice successful little joke, which upset the OVRA. The right to strike had been abolished, but mass strikes had taken place

the OVRA and shot in 1932.

in the industrial north; on the anniversary of June 10th, slogans recalling Matteotti had appeared on factory walls in Turin; every now and then in a cinema the paunch and sulky scowl of the dictator had been greeted with hisses; there were people who went to the opera to hear *André Chénier* simply for the pleasure of cheering the lines which glorify liberty. . . .

"From time to time we learned that groups of peasants in the Puglie, Abruzzi and Marche had set fire to town halls and fascist headquarters, assaulting the local fascist bosses. It wasn't politics, it was hunger – no matter, a tense atmosphere had been created. To end local disturbances, the government was obliged to suspend tax collections for awhile in several provinces. Our hope that these local risings would grow into a nation-wide movement was never fulfilled. It took too long for the spark kindled in one village to spread to the next; by the time the second village had been roused, "law and order" had been restored in the first. It was always several days before news of these events could reach Rome.

"I was in Ciociaria when I heard that in a nearby village there had been a violent demonstration by groups of peasants that very morning. We hurried there to find that troops had arrived before us and had restored "order". (When the rioting first started, local fascists had been called out. But they were accustomed to – and were at their best against – defenseless opponents, and had to be replaced by regular troops.) We are heartened, too, by quarrelling within the ruling clique of fascist leaders, and by occasional dissention between the fascists and two of its three main allies, the Court and the Vatican. [46] (The third ally, big business, never gave any trouble.)

"Of events abroad we knew little. We were too deeply absorbed in our work to be able to follow what was happening beyond our frontiers. We often discussed the economic crisis in the capitalist world, the Russian Five-Year Plan, the failure of the Labour Party in Breat Britain. We were distressed by the evidence of moral and political decadence in France – for us, the land of liberty – and by the growth of fascist movements in Germany and everywhere else in central and southern Europe. This was the sad result of Italy's example. We grew more and more convinced that our struggle against fascism in Italy contributed, however modestly, to the defence of liberty in the countries born from the four great Empires destroyed by the Great War. We were Italians, but gradually we were becoming Europeans. . . . The events which cheered us most were certainly the fall of De Rivera and the proclamation a year later of the Spanish Republic.

"The corrupting influence of fascism was very evident. When I first arrived in Rome, a relative (a high official) warned me: "Don't talk. Even walls have ears." It was fear which led a man I had known in Geneva – though he called himself an anti-fascist and a friend of the young followers of Gobetti who had been arrested in 1928 – to pretend that he did not know me when we happened to meet in a tram. It was fear which made a cousin of mine turn away so as to avoid greeting me when by chance we

---

46 Most members of the Royal family formerly were fascists; a few, including the Crown Prince, supported fascism without liking it much; the Crown Princess was reputed to be against fascism. Relations between fascism and the Vatican deteriorated after 1931.

found ourselves sitting at adjacent tables in a café. It was fear which led uncles and cousins to report my family's movements to the police. Almost every day we met people who felt as we did, but begged us to keep away because our presence meant danger. . . .

"As a student at the University of Rome I was in contact with various professors. I had prepared for Professor Rossi,[47] a Liberal Cabinet Minister in the pre-fascist era who had made his peace with the new régime, a paper on the Constitution of Switzerland: his assistant told me confidentially that the professor burned my manuscript as soon as he had read it. For Professor Gini,[48] a scholar then with a great reputation in English-speaking countries, a former member of the fascist commission entrusted with the reform of the Italian constitution in 1925, I wrote a comparison between Italian economics from 1904-13 and from 1922-31. The statistics showed clearly that there was considerably more economic expansion during the first period than in the second. The paper was not returned to me, and Gini commented drily that certain comparisons were best left alone. One day I attended a lecture on the fiscal aspect of local administration, by the economist De Stefani,[49] the Duce's first Minister of Finance; a month later he came back to the same subject, saying the opposite of what he had said before. (A student had told the police that the ex-Minister and authoritative economist had stepped out of line.)

---

47 Not related to Ernesto Rossi.
48 Professor Gini had considerable reputation as statistician and sociologist in American academic circles.
49 The academic work of Professor De Stefani was partly subsidized by the Carnegie Foundation.

"It was fear (for very few of them were fascists) which led all but eleven of the university professors to swear allegiance to the régime in 1931. For us, those were sad days. How could the younger generation respect people who had betrayed their own beliefs? Those who are held in disesteem for moral weakness – cannot be educators in any real sense. It was fear that had created a desert around the few who had refused to bow to the régime. Doctors often refused to attend them or their families even when critically ill; lawyers refused to defend them in the courts; relatives and acquaintances shunned them like lepers. . . .

"Arrest, an occasional well-publicized trial or execution, the atmosphere of suspicion aroused by the OVRA, were enough to keep fear present in people's minds. Almost at once I had definite evidence of the wide scope of police activities. Two or three days after I had arrived, a university student who was one of the lodgers at my boarding-house announced at supper-time that he had found a good job.

' "Tell us about it, what is it?"

' "I am going to work for the police."

' "What kind of work?"

' "Wonderful! I have to go round the cinemas, and whenever I hear anyone criticizing the régime, I call the police."

"The only decent person there was the landlady. "Aren't you ashamed of telling us?" she said. "Do it if you've got to. But at least don't boast about it."

"Even after violence had been legalized, the old terrorism was revived from time to time. There were the episodes in which Toscanini and Borgese were involved:

attacked by the fascist, Toscanini was compelled to stop giving his concerts and Borgese his lectures. (Both had to leave Italy and went to live in the United States.) Officers of the fascist militia had soldiers of the regular army beaten for failing to salute them. At a seaside resort, the elderly General Bencivenga,[50] just released from five years' *confino*, was beaten up by *squadristi*, whose leader was rewarded by being appointed consul-general in Philadelphia.

"How many anti-fascists have been arrested? Who knows? In five years several thousand appeared before the Special Tribunal. Certainly more than 10,000 were sent to *confino*. Tens of thousands of anti-fascists have spent months and sometimes years in prison without either a hearing by the Special Tribunal or by the commissions appointed for the purpose of condemning to *confino*. An official of the Ministry of Interior, who did not know who I was, once told me that besides the "political prisoners" in prison and *confino*, the police's list included 60,000 names recommended for preventive arrest; these were not people charged with any specific activity against the régime; they were those who might become "active", and who were usually rounded up for safety on the occasion of public celebrations, parades, visits from leading fascists, etc.

"The police are today the mainstay of the régime; they take no interest in politics, but enjoy their unlimited authority. They do not bother about the corporate state or the fascist *mystique*, but simply fulfill the function entrusted to them. The fascist leaders are only a façade, their one concern is to get rich. How do they do it? The technique is simple. They take on several jobs at once, sell their

50 Follower of the Liberal leader Amendola, deputy and in 1944 a leader of the Resistance in Rome.

influence and become middlemen, taking their percentage on transactions between the state and business. Is coal wanted? The Minister of Communications and his friends take a commission from exporters in other countries, who reimburse themselves by exacting a higher price from the Italian consumers. Is steel needed for ship-building? The Minister of Defence and friends pocket the commission on the purchase of steel. The national budget allows so many million *lire* for building roads, ports, aqueducts; the contractors hand over a percentage of this to a swarm of fascist leaders and their underlings. A few dozen big industrialists, making use of fascist middlemen whom they reward by appointing them to the board of directors, have succeeded in creating monopolies in the chemical, electrical, steel and automobile industries. A public administration once known for its integrity has now become (at least on its higher levels) probably the most corrupt in Europe. Capitalism as private business based on free enterprise and competition has disappeared from most of the industrial scene. The corporate economy is an improved version of old-time mercantilism. The control which today is centred in the hands of a few fascist captains of industry could, in the event of a revolution, be transferred to cooperatives and free syndicates.[51]....

"When I agreed to return to Italy, I did not expect to find many young people willing to cooperate with me. To the exiles, the younger generation there seemed

51 The fascist corporate economy was based on the principle of rigid state control over all aspects of economic activities. The passage from capitalism to corporatism took place chiefly between 1927 and 1932. As a result, even today (1957) state ownership of the means of production in Italy represents a larger proportion of the economy than in any other Continental country west of the communist bloc.

to be either pro-fascist or sceptical. A few weeks were enough to show how mistaken I had been. Very few of the *gielllisti* in Italy were over thirty; many of them had reacted spontaneously against the régime. The very young were usually enthusiastic fascists, but when they learned to use their own judgment, many changed their minds. Most of them still called themselves fascists: there was no point in inviting trouble. A badge, a black shirt, attendance at a parade now and again – these were enough to ensure a peaceful life.

"Others refused to swim with the stream. In Osimo young men of twenty or so, who had grown up and been educated entirely in a fascist "climate", with no memories of pre-fascist days and with no stimulus from outside, formed their own underground organization and drafted an anti-fascist programme. The same thing, I was told, had happened among the university students at Pavia and on a still larger scale at Pisa. Both in Rome and Milan I met young men who had once been ardent fascists but (in spite of the consequent difficulties in completing their studies and starting their careers) afterwards refused to renew their Party membership, and instead worked with us. One of those who tried unsuccessfully to free themselves from the fascist grip was Trevisonno, the son of one of the many revolutionary syndicalists who had joined the fascists during the early days. Trevisonno joined the Fascist Party at the age of seventeen, and later resigned. But he was engaged to be married, he wanted to start a family, and he had to find work. Influential friends of his father helped him to rejoin the Party. Last time I saw him was quite by chance. He was wearing a black shirt, and walked with his head bent. His humiliation showed clearly on his face. . . .

"I had a fascist friend, Nino, a colleague in the office where I worked. He was sincere about his politics, so I did not mind his company; besides, without knowing it, he sometimes served as a useful screen for my activities. He made big sacrifices for the fascist cause, and expected no reward or privilege in regurn. He was distressed by the corruption he saw among the fascist leaders. He knew what my opinions were, but had no idea that I was an active member of the underground. When I returned from Ponza I asked him what he would have done if he had known what I was doing:

' "I would have denounced you to the police – but I would have warned you in time to get away."

"From the restaurant where we used to eat he noticed groups of army officers making their way through the door of a nearby house. Nino imagined that they were plotting against the régime, and later he told me that he had reported them to the OVRA. Once, to get rid of a rival in love, he denounced him as an anti-fascist. . . . And this was one of the honest, sincere members of the Fascist Party."

— ⧗ —

"As time went on the risks we ran grew greater. A year after I arrived in Rome, the main organization of *G.L.* in the north was disrupted through arrests. Fancello and Battaglia, from our group, were arrested with them. The police had intercepted a postcard with my pseudonym on it, but they were not able to track me down. Then came

101

the arrest of Cinciguerra and his friends, the group which worked in close contact with the "Excellencies". I heard that in the Castelli a raid on communists led to the arrest of several hundred people. In Naples, Bonelli and his friends were taken, and there were numerous other arrests in Ancona, Terni, in the Marsica and in Maremma. In Milan they arrested Albasini, who had tried to carry on the work initiated by Bauer and Rossi. Arrests followed thick and fast in Turin and Trieste. . . . We seemed to be living on the verge of a landslide. In the winter of 1931-32 not a week passed without bad news. It was a sure sign of our activity and of its success. But nerves were badly frayed: we felt the ground crumbling under us, and we knew that in spite of all precautions we would fall. Every arrest brought desertions and sometimes evidence of weakness on the part of people we trusted. Whenever there had been arrests we had to start all over again, looking for *amici* we could trust and whom the police would not suspect, reorganizing groups, renewing contacts, reorganizing the distribution of clandestine publications.

"Who knows how many times I was close to arrest, and saved by a miracle? There was the incident at the frontier. There was the time when I was on my way to Ancona with clandestine leaflets in my suitcase, and a member of the *milizia ferroviaria* ordered me to open it: while I played for time looking for a key, the conductor came along with a passenger who was travelling without a ticket, and the militiaman happily forgot all about me. One day Bruno and I had an appointment with the lawyer Martini, in a cinema. Peppino had a sixth sense about the police, and he had a hunch that something was wrong.

We did not go in. Martini was being shadowed and was arrested shortly afterwards; I saw him next in Ponza.[52]

"On another occasion Bruno and I met Fancello on the Pincio. The police were waiting to arrest him when he got home. If they had followed him that afternoon, we would have been arrested too. At one time, for no specific reason, I did not go to see Vinciguerra for several days; I did not know that he was already in prison, and that the police were watching for any friends who called at his house. One afternoon I did actually stop at his door, and then decided not to go in. Meloni was arrested and sentenced to thirty years; I had to thank my stars – and the care I had taken to meet him only at night and without showing my face – that I was not there to keep him company. Only an unexpected delay had prevented my joining Albasini and Maffi first in San Vittore[53] and later in Regina Coeli. These were the narrow escapes I knew about . . . how many others had there been?

"The causes of the arrests were nearly always the same: spies and carelessness. Among the leaders of G.L. in northern Italy had been a lawyer whose friends were not aware of his financial troubles: he solved them – temporarily – by selling Rossi, Bauer, and many others, for 100,000 *lire*. The OVRA allowed a few recognized underground members to remain at large as decoys. They were watched, and all their contacts were black-listed and arrested at the first opportunity. Sometimes carelessness was even worse than spies. A conspirator must be careful not to talk; he can never unburden himself to friends. Unfortunately there were always some people who could not resist the

52 Martini was shot by the Germans in 1944.
53 Prison in Milan.

103

temptation to boast about their part in the underground movement. One arrest would lead to others. The OVRA are adept at extracting confessions. First they would try false promises – "Come, tell us everything, and you can go home this evening!" – and many victims, particularly very young ones, would fall for this. If not, they would try bribes, then isolation and withholding food and water. If none of this achieved results they had recourse to bludgeons, steel rods (*bastinados*), the lash, holding heads under water, red-hot steel and the arrest of friends and relatives.

"By the spring of 1932 we knew that the OVRA, though they did not know us individually, were certainly on our tracks. The few demonstrations we had been able to arrange (such as the scattering of nearly 100,000 leaflets by forty of us on the first anniversary of the Spanish Republic), letters which we knew had fallen into the hands of the censor, mention of our activities which went from mouth to mouth until they reached the ears of informers; all these things had led the OVRA to look out for a group whose arrest was demanded by the *Presidenza* (the dictator's own office). Our movement grew weaker as it spread wider. Many groups had been formed in Rome and the provinces, and leakages were occurring. The feeling of insecurity was heightened and was beginning to affect our morale. The OVRA was watching Bruno more closely than ever: we knew it because he was visited by people who were undoubedly *agents provocateurs*. The activities of the "intellectuals" had begun to arouse suspicion. Various books and pamphlets had been printed, and to avoid attracting attention, each publication (after it had received its *imprimatur*) had been given to a different printer. And now the printers were being questioned by the police.

"Even in the provinces the police were very suspicious. One day I was ill in bed when a friend rushed in to tell me that the OVRA had ordered the arrest of our courier between Rome and the Marche. (The news came via some mysterious grapevine.) I got up, and after ten hours in the train I reached him – just in time. When questioned, he had nothing compromising on him and could produce a satisfactory reason for every journey and visit he had made. Another time, Lugli had had to stay abroad longer than had been expected. The janitor of the building where he lived had told the police about the prolonged absence, and his rooms were searched. It was vital to get in touch with him and with contacts in various towns who could provide convincing alibis. Luckily it was a Saturday; before getting back to my office on the Monday morning I spent twenty-eight hours in the train, and all was well. Lugli was arrested, questioned and released five days later. . . .

"After three years of conspiracy – for some it was even more – our energy was flagging. Often we felt that we were revolving in a vacuum. Monotonously and exhaustingly, the days passed in continuous appointments, discussions, correspondence and travelling. Just when we thought that we were getting somewhere, and that we had formed a movement capable of spreading word of our cause, the cause of liberty, and that perhaps, later on, it might be strong enough in a moment of crisis to launch revolutionary action; then someone would be arrested and we would have to begin all over again. There was quarelling, just because our nerves were on edge; the absence of normal life oppressed us.

"Black thoughts took hold of me. What was the use of all this work, all this energy devoted to a cause which sensible people agreed was hopeless? What could one man or a small group do in a population of forty milion, against a dictator supported by 300,000 bayonets and the apathy of the masses? Life had become a rat race – from one appointment to another during the week, from one town to another at weekends – and always, behind one, the fear of sudden arrest. Why not do as so many others had – cross the frontier, leave the country, go where one would be free to speak and act freely – where one could live unafraid, where mind and soul were not stifled by the intangible something in the air which surrounded us? But every time that I and my closest friends were tempted with the thought of going abroad, of leaving the dictatorship to get on with its ugly work, we had a vision of the friends who had died, of those who were existing somehow in the penitentiaries of Civitavecchia, Alessandria, Castelfranco, Nisida. We owed it to them to carry on the work for which they had sacrificed so much.

"During this time of increasing nervous tension, police activity intensified for a number of reasons. There were various attempts on the dictator's life, some of them reported in the newspapers (when too many people knew about them), others passed over in silence. Many arrests by the OVRA meant not only that opposition existed, but that it was raising its head, taking courage, reorganizing, and aiming at the heart of the régime. Severe repression had become necessary to quell opposition. Celebrations for the tenth anniversary of fascism were due, and the Party leaders did not want anyone, inside Italy or abroad, to imagine that there were cracks in the structure. I gathered from the editors of the reviews I wrote for that important decisions had been reached at the Palazzo Venezia. The economic crisis was intensifying abroad, though Italy was unaware of it because within her borders it had been the normal state of affairs since 1927. The fascist leaders were convinced that the last hours of the Western powers, of Great Britain and France, were at hand. Plans were made to replace British and French imperialism with fascist imperialism throughout the Moslem world, and friends told me that funds were being sent to dissatisfied groups in Egypt, Syria, Palestine, Tunisia and Abyssinia. The imperialist dream was about to become a reality, and the realization of the dream must not be hindered by the intrigues of a few revolutionaries.

"The OVRA had orders to get rid of the under--ground groups, particularly those (the most dangerous) which were not communist, and within a few days, in the late spring of 1932, the Special Tribunal hatched a sensational trial. From among the hundreds of "political" arrests made during the recent months, a few people were singled out and, though they had nothing to do with each other, were lumped together as though they formed one group. Intellectuals, middle-class citizens, and workers; *giellisti*, socialists, republicans and anarchists, all were grouped together and branded as communists. After a summary trial all the accused were sentenced, two of them getting off with ten years, the others condemned to thirty years or the firing squad. . . . (The OVRA wanted the public to believe that the only opposition came from the communists, and that this had now been dealt with.)

"For some time the OVRA had been keeping their eye on a group of communists who had set up a press to print a clandestine paper. The first issue came out uneventfully and was distributed. When the second issue was in the press, OVRA agents burst in. It was Monday, July 19th, 1932. About twenty people were arrested. While they were searching the house of the group leader, the OVRA found a copy of one of our pamphlets, given him by Giuliani, one of our members who was a personal friend of the communist leader, and who had disregarded our decision to have no contacts at any time with the communists. He, too, was arrested at once. At first he denied that he had ever had anything to do with *Giustizia e Libertà* or with the communists. He was then stripped, laid on a bench used for such operations, and *bastinadoed* with a leather-covered steel rod; the blows cause excruciating pain, not only in the feet but through the spine and up into the head. He was an elderly man, and he stood it as long as he could; finally, to stop the torture, he gave the name of De Sanctis. De Sanctis was arrested at eleven o'clock in the morning. (It was then Tuesday.) The usual procedure: denials; then, at five in the afternoon, the *bastinado*. The victim had been an officer in the *Arditi*,[54] and stood it for a long time; after every ten blows he was made to get up and soak his feet in a basin of salt water; then the beating started again. Each blow was more agonizing than the last. His mind began to wander, his will-power weakened. . . . He gave the name of

---

54 During World War I Italian *Arditi* filled the role of British Commandos and American Rangers in World War II.

Ciccotti, who was arrested that evening at the café where he worked. They didn't waste time questioning him. He was stripped, laid on the bench, and beaten. He, too, had been an *Ardito*, and it took sixty strokes to make him lose control of himself. Within twenty-four hours more than forty members of our group in Rome had been arrested. . . . During those days I was away from Rome, but by Wednesday the OVRA had my name. . . ."

Max in 1930

109

CHAPTER IV

Prison and *Confino*

The office which employed Speranza had given him a few days' leave at the middle of July, 1932. He went to stay in the country with his mother, whom he had not seen for nearly three years as she had come back to Italy only a few weeks before. Tired and nervously exhausted as he was, he went to bed early each night and fell quickly into a deep sleep. One night he awoke suddenly to hear his mother say:

"The police commissioner is here. He wants to speak to you."

At the bedroom door were the local police commissioner and a plain-clothes sergeant.

The commissioner was smiling, polite:

"The *prefect[1]* wants to see you. I must ask you to come along with me at once."

Silently, unhurriedly, Speranza got up and dressed, while the sergeant made a perfunctory search of the room by the dim light of an oil-lamp. Speranza looked at his watch: eleven o'clock. He thought that, though not altogether impossible, the story about going to see the *prefetto* was an unlikely one. *Prefetti* liked to make themselves important, but they also liked their comfort too much to ask for visitors at midnight. he saw in his mind's eye the many friends who had been arrested in the last three years. He decided not to think of such things; so often friends had been suddenly arrested for no apparent reason and, after being taken to

---

1 Representative of the central government in the province.

111

the police station or even to prison, had been released a few days later. Perhaps some fascist boss was coming on a visit, and the police were having their usual round-up of suspects and potential suspects.

The house was some distance from the nearest village. When they arrived, the commissioner, still smiling, said that it was a little late now to go to see the *prefetto* (forty miles away), so perhaps Speranza had better stay overnight in the carabineers' barracks. The moment the commissioner had left, the carabineer sergeant in charge, a good fellow who had known Speranza's family for years, pronounced slowly and reluctantly, but clearly, the usual words: "I'm sorry to have to tell you that you are under arrest."

Speranza experienced a strange sensation, almost of relief. His mouth stretched into a kind of smile – sad, but still a smile: "This is it. Conspiracy is over. I'm going to join the others in jail." It didn't last more than a second. Then he clenched his teeth: "If only I had gone abroad instead of coming here!" Then a third thought: "What the devil has happened in Rome?"

He was led to a small but spotlessly clean cell. Next morning the door opened, and an orderly told him to take a broom and sweep the floor. At that moment a sergeant came along and whispered a few words in the orderly's ear; the orderly took the broom back, saying, "Sorry, I beg your pardon," and began to sweep. Speranza felt a wry sadness: It was nice to be respected; probably this was the last time he would be treated with such civility. A pale young man arrived and introduced himself as a vice-commissioner from the political section of the OVRA. He gave orders for the prisoner to be handcuffed, and Speranza was then escorted by two carabineers to the railway station, on foot. On the way he met several people he knew. The best thing was to give an appearance of self-confidence, so he walked slowly with his head high, in no way trying to hide the handcuffs. Inside himself, he felt far from confident: the immediate departure for Rome meant that things were serious.

The journey lasted all day. It was stiflingly hot. After a few hours the handcuffs began to hurt, and his head felt as if it would burst.

The two carabineers did their best to be courteous; they knew his family and felt embarrassed. One of them tried to make conversation, but all Speranza remembered was his saying that in the law a prisoner has the right to escape, just as his guards have the right to fire on him if he does. He looked out of the window, remembering Rossi's miraculous escape,[2] wondering whether such an opportunity would ever come his way, whether he would be able to take advantage of it if it did, and whether he would be luckier in avoiding people who would hand him back to the OVRA. A police van met them at the station in Rome and took them to the Piazza del Collegio Romano (OVRA headquarters). Outside the door the carabineers shook hands with him: "*Signor Conte, speriamo di rivederla presto* – we hope to see you again soon.

Inside police headquarters it was dark and silent and there were only a few policemen on night duty. It was nearly midnight. He was asked to give his name. Still handcuffed, he was taken in a taxi, this time by a plain-

2 While being taken from Milan to Rome, Ernesto Rossi had jumped from the train handcuffs and all.

113

clothes policeman. He felt so exhausted, and the pain in his head was so unbearable, that he was quite glad when at last they arrived at Regina Coeli. How often from the Gianicolo[3] he had gazed at those silent walls, at the windows behind which some of his friends were existing. "Third wing, fourth wing, sixth wing, white cells. . .," he had heard about them all. The great door opened and a heavy iron gate appeared beyond. The groaning of the huge keys as they turned in the locks echoed grimly along the empty corridors and back again to the door. At that moment the bells rang twelve times. He shivered. . . .

Once again he had to give his name and address, his father's name, etc., and sign the register. He read the name immediately above his own, Alatri; he did not know the man personally, but he knew that he was one of the most active group leaders in a suburb out in the direction of the Castelli. Speranza handed over his belt, shoe-laces, and tie, and the contents of his pockets; he was given a blanket, a bowl, and a spoon. There was no room in the third wing (reserved for political prisoners), so he was led to the fourth. The cell stank. He was alone. The pain in his head was still there, no longer a succession of throbs, it was now a continuous blow.

Morning came at last. Nobody appeared. At eleven o'clock the warder came along the corridor; he asked for Speranza's bowl through an opening high in the door, and poured some soup in it. At three, the door opened and a warder announced "aria". He expected to be led to a courtyard to join other prisoners, thinking that 'air' would mean a walk in single file. When he reached the yard he

---

3 One of the hills of Rome, on the right bank of the Tiber.

was pushed into a cubicle like his cell except that it had no roof and was triangular instead of rectangular. It was a little bigger, three yards at the base of the triangle. Strange as it may seem, Speranza had never heard of the solitary confinement he was now to endure (none of his friends who had experienced it had yet come back). He walked up and down a little, then sat on the floor. Heard a voice – from the next cubicle a prisoner was speaking to whoever was on the other side.

"Who are you?"

"M——— (the voice was not clear), and you?"

"Delfini."

"What are you here for?"

"*Giustizia e Libertà*. And you?"

"*Giustizia e Libertà*."

He shuddered. Delfini had received a thirty-year sentence a few weeks ago, and M——— (if he had well understood the name) had already been two months in prison. They went on speaking through the wall while the warder was some way off with his back turned. M——— said that 200 people had been arrested with him. Delfini spoke wearily, told how he had been tortured and could no longer stand up, how he felt that he would soon die.

"Courage, my friend," he concluded. "We shall win." Then:

"Who are you, friend?" No answer. Speranza had not yet been questioned, and did not know what he would be accused of: it might be that the two were *agents provocateurs*, although the voices sounded genuine and he thought he recognized one of them. He said nothing.

Once, when he was being taken back to his cell by

a warder who was more talkative than others, Speranza asked how it happened that the warders allowed Delfini to talk in the cubicle.

"Poor fellow!" was the answer. "He has been tortured to death. He won't last long. We let him do."

— 🏳 —

As the hours passed, Speranza's anxiety increased. He had been arrested forty-eight hours earlier, and nobody had come to question him. He did not know then that the OVRA relied at first on delay and uncertainty and isolation to weaken a prisoner's spirit, when they had one who might produce valuable information. When he had left Rome a week before, everything had been in order. But in his room were the little bottles of invisible ink and reagent. It had certainly been unsafe to leave them there, but he had not wanted to involve his friends in greater risks than he himself was prepared to take, by leaving them with anyone else. He was certain that none of his friends would have betrayed him, but if the police had found those little bottles they would have the evidence they wanted. His frantic efforts to think things out sometimes made his mind wander; already there was the feeling of abandonment and total isolation, the despair that comes of losing all contact with the world of living people, the world of men and women who are free to walk and talk freely in the open air.

Next morning the cell door suddenly opened. A warder escorted Speranza to the prison office, where he found two police agents waiting for him; they were not a comforting sight – small, ugly and evil looking (he learned afterwards that these two had the special task of torturing prisoners when other methods to make them speak had failed). His handcuffs were taken off before he entered the office of the OVRA commissioner who was to question him. Pushed into the room, he found himself facing a fat, round little man who might have been a monk except for the malign glint in his eyes. The little man was polite, and asked Speranza to sit down. Without further ceremony, he showed him a copy of a *G.L.* pamphlet, and began in a cheerful voice:

"Look, we know everything now, we have arrested all your friends. You know Giannotti . . . Ciccotti . . . Belloni . . . . We don't take a serious view of what has happened. You are a gentleman, and you will tell us the whole truth, all there is to tell. We will let you and your friends off with an *ammonizione*,[4] and in a week's time you will be free."

His answer was, of course, that given by ninety-nine percent, if not all, of those who were arrested.

"I know nobody."

A vicious look came over the commissioner's face. The two policemen came back, the handcuffs were put on again, and he was led along dark corridors till they arrived at a half-open door. Someone was being interrogated.

"So is it true that you were given the pamphlets by G———?"

"No, I got them from S———."

He recognized the voice, and tried to think. It was a good thing if they were only concerned about the

---

4 *Ammonizione* meant to report once or twice a day to the police, not to travel without police authorization, to be at home from dusk to dawn and never to enter public places (theatres, cafés, etc.). *Ammonizione* could last a maximum of two years.

pamphlets; it would mean *confino*, not prison, so long as they did not find out about the organization, the foreign contacts, and above all about the 'activists'.

He was taken back to the commissioner. There was just time for a brief glance at the desk. On the left, only partly covered by other papers, was a typed list of names. He could read the top one – Abati, also an *amico* and active organizer. Next to the last name was a figure – forty-eight. So forty-eight people had been arrested. To judge from the names he had heard and read, it seemed that the arrests were limited to only a small section of the Roman group; no one from the provinces was involved. The commissioner made no allusion to the conversation Speranza had been taken to overhear.

"So you know nobody?"

"No."

A burst of anger. "Liar! I'll teach you to tell the truth!"

He got up and shook his fist. From behind, one of the policemen struck the prisoner violently on the temple.

"*Mascalzone*," screamed the commissioner. "Take him away."

Two minutes later he was in a ground-floor cell. The stench was terrible. The cell measured six feet by three, most of it taken up by a bare bench. There was no window. A glimmer of light came from a tiny grating over the door into the corridor. He sat down on the bench.... Forty-eight arrests, and evidence of the underground publications. The number of those who had been arrested, and their standing, were evidence enough that an organization existed. It was absurd to try to deny what the police already knew; he would only bring torture on himself, and he could not be sure that he would be able to stand it. (Torture is like death: it can be spoken of calmly so long as it is far off; the nearer it comes the more terrifying it is.) The essential thing was to admit as little as possible, so that nobody would be compromised, to give a satisfactory explanation of what the police already knew, so as to limit the arrests to those already made, to prevent their catching members of other groups in Rome and the provinces. Those were his thoughts as he sat on the bench, while his brain seemed about to burst, his head throbbed with pain, his mouth ached atrociously. He felt sick from the stink of the walls, the floor, the ceiling, and faint from lack of air, space and light.

After a few hours his eyes grew accustomed to the darkness. The walls were covered in scribblings, scratched with fingernails or with splinters of wood torn from the bench. 'Holy Mother, help me!' had been written by someone who was probably not at all religious in his ordinary life, though at that moment he had called upon the only support available to him. 'The assassins have murdered me,' '——— has been a spy,' others had scratched. And there were several messages of encouragement: 'The future is ours,' 'Courage, friends.' Evidently none but political prisoners had passed through this cell since the walls had been whitewashed.

Night fell. He was so exhausted that in spite of the pain and anxiety he fell asleep. When he awoke it was dead of night, and eleven was striking. He felt as if his skin were covered with little burns; legs, arms and neck were red with small blotches. The bench was swarming with filthy insects – infernal bed-bugs. He tried to rub them off his back, but there were too many. He remembered how once he had listened admiringly to the story of a traveller from India, and he decided to make a supreme effort to lie still, trying to minimize the sensitivity of his skin. It was a new torment. All was quiet. Suddenly there were screams, which seemed to come from the prison office . . . . another poor wretch under torture.

When dawn came he could breathe again, the bugs disappeared, and the air became less stifling. His mind went on working as he planned what he would say when he was next questioned. Then the feeling of oppression returned again, and with it the headache and discouragement. It was almost the end of July, and after ten o'clock the heat was unbearable. The morning dragged to an end. It was four days since he had last had anything to eat, except for the soup (which he had scarcely touched) of sixty hours before. But he was not hungry. It was thirst which really began to trouble him, as he had not had a drop to drink for two days. Suddenly he thought: "What if they go on refusing me water? What if I become delirious?" He was terrified, not yet of what might happen to him, but of letting out names, of compromising friends, of being the cause of other arrests. When evening came a warder opened the door of the cell and took him to drink at the fountain in the courtyard.

"Isn't there anything to eat?"

"We haven't had any orders."

Later he was again escorted to the commissioner. This time he had decided, for better or for worse, what he would do. He did not feel able to stand up to hours of cross-examination without contradicting himself. He would assume responsibility for receiving and distributing the clandestine leaflets. This would destroy the possibility of being released, but it might put an end to the interrogation and prevent others from being arrested. He said that (as the OVRA already knew) he had never had any liking for the régime; but, he said, he had never taken part in any underground movement, as he considered such activity completely futile. Years ago, he said, when he was abroad, he had known some exiles from Italy, and one of them had sent him a parcel of clandestine leaflets, through someone he did not know by name; he had met the man only once, he could only describe his appearance. (Here followed a carefully thought out description that could not possibly fit any of his friends.) Some of the leaflets and pamphlets he had thrown away, the rest he had passed on to acquaintances, who didn't think much of them.

The main difficulty was in giving the names of those who had received the leaflets. It was clear that the police thought he knew only four of the forty-eight people who had been arrested. Speranza was convinced that Peppino and Giulio would never have given his name, so he denied having handed on pamphlets to them. He knew that Aristide had given his name, and the only thing to do was to confirm what the police already knew. As for the fourth, Dante, he made a statement that did not tally with what Dante had said, which caused him bitter remorse.

Speranza had the impression that the commissioner did not believe what he said, but that was the commissioner's problem: at a moment like this he could be pleased at having rounded up forty-eight Roman *giellisti*, with having under his thumb (or thinking he had) the group he had been trying to catch for months. From what he knew now he could turn in a fine report for Bocchini, the head of the police. It was in his interest to prove that, with these forty-eight out of the way, there was no longer a single member of *G.L.* at large in Rome. All was in order again, the conspirators' final attempt had been thwarted. The Duce would be satisfied, and the commissioner would get a promotion, or at least a decoration.

After another three days in the same cell, the commissioner sent for him again.

"I know perfectly well that you all knew each other, because you all agreed about selling the books. But I want to know what else there was beside these books."

Of course, the books![5] Speranza had forgotten them. Even if their publication was evidence of opposition to the régime, they had been authorized by the police, who could hardly send people to the Special Tribunal for having done something which, whatever its aim, was not illegal. He made the most of this relatively innocuous activity, and told the commissioner about the books, about his intention of criticizing some aspect of the dictatorship to the public without in any way going outside the law. (This, of course, meant *confino*, but not long-term imprisonment.)

Luckily his account matched that of his best friend, Peppino, who was released a few weeks later. Another time, while a vice-commissioner was questioning him, he noticed a screen that he had not seen in the office before. He guessed, accurately, that Giulio was behind it, and alluded to him as a person who not only had never had anything to do with the leaflets or anything else, but

---

5 The reprinting of books was a less compromising activity than the formation of groups of *G.L.* Speranza and his friends explained their mutual connection on the basis of being interested in the circulation of these books.

who was incapable of any kind of action. Giulio, too, was released a few days later. Altogether, Speranza spent twenty days in the interrogation cell at police headquarters. His only contact with the outside world during that time was when, after ten or twelve days, he was allowed to see his mother and the girl who was later to become his wife, for a few minutes. (The girl had been on her way from England to visit his family when he was arrested.) All efforts to find out where he had been taken had at first been unavailing. As usual with political prisoners, the police pretended not to know anything. If it had not been for the girl's foreign nationality the family would not have known for months what had befallen Speranza.

After two months those who had been arrested were divided into two groups – nine were detained, the rest were released, but under *ammonizione*. Back in Regina Coeli, he was crossing a corridor one day when in the distance he saw Aristide; his feet were bandaged. In the van which had taken them back were two other friends, neither of whom could walk yet, though it was a month since they had been arrested and *bastinadoed*. "I still pass blood instead of water," said the one who had received sixty strokes of the rod.

– ⌛ –

A new chapter began. He was in the third wing now, the 'tomb'. For months on end he was left alone in his cell, without saying a word, without seeing anyone except the warder, who never spoke to him. He got up with the six o'clock bell, and went to bed in the evening with the eight o'clock bell. Fourteen hours of absolute inactivity. Nothing to do, nothing to read. Afterwards he learned that all the others in his group who were in solitary confinement had been allowed books; who wouldn't be able to hold out if, like one of them, he had the *Summa* of St. Thomas Aquinas to read? No books were given to him because he came of a Protestant family.

With nothing to do, his mind began to whirl confusedly in spite of efforts to occupy his thoughts. Sometimes, when he first woke in the morning, he felt almost relieved: it was over now, the work he had come to Italy for, three years ago; there were no more meetings, appointments, discussions, there was no longer any need to worry about a friend's arrest, about being shadowed, or the interception of a letter written in secret ink. He had done what he could. The results had been small, but at least he had joined hands for three years with hundreds, perhaps thousands, of people whose main object was to keep the idea of freedom alive in Italy. Now he could rest.

Then suddenly all these thoughts would vanish. There was only the desperate question: "How long shall I be in here?" Those who were older and had a calmer sense of the value of time might be able to endure the prospect of several years in prison. But when one has only just started to live? When complete inactivity follows frantically busy days? When there is not a line, not a message, not even a tap on the wall to establish the slightest contact with other human beings? He was sure he would be sentenced to at least ten years' imprisonment, and when one is twenty-four ten years seem an eternity. Ten years ago he had been at school; in ten years he had grown up, the world had opened out before him; he had experienced more, felt more, probably in his own way achieved more, than most young men of his age. And now? Life was over, his ambitions and hopes crushed and lost in the emptiness.

It was not ambition or spirit of adventure which had led him to conspire against the régime; he had only done it because it seemed to him to be a duty. Life meant having a family, working, travelling, learning, having fresh experiences. He had always loved open-air life, the sun, the stars, the wind and the clouds; he remembered the long-ago joy of running along the shore in stormy weather, when his lungs were filled with air, and his ears with the thunder of waves on the stony beach. He loved the earth and all that it produced – grass, flowers and trees; and now he knew that he would not see them again for years, that his existence would drag on within the four walls of a cell, where a few faint streaks were all he could see of the sky. He thought of the work he had done, of his friends, of the intense activity of the last three years; the emotions, the disappointments of those days now seemed small indeed. The only thing that mattered was to get away from these suffocating walls, to run, to breathe freely, to be free. From his cell he could hear the far-away noises of trams and cars, the hum of a city at work. There were no more than a dozen yards between life and death, between heaven and hell, between the outside world and this prison where nothing was heard except the daily tapping to test the bars, and the cries which came every now and then from the infirmary where a prisoner who was slowly dying called out, 'Mother! Mother!'

Growing doubts were undermining him. He had lost all contact with reality and was succumbing to weakness.

125

(His was to be the bitter and humiliating experience shared by many enemies of totalitarianism when finally arrested, imprisoned and entirely cut off from the human contact which is indispensable for keeping a sense of values – the experience not shared by political prisoners in democracies who are always able to keep in touch with their friends.) Was it really worthwhile to struggle against the inevitable? What was the liberty of the individual on which he had based his opposition to fascism? Isn't the individual free even if there is a dictator, even if he is a slave? He is free so long as he can set his feet on the earth and look at the sky. What had been the use of all those meetings, of the clandestine leaflets, the days of hunger and strain, the renunciation of normal life, of carefree pleasures? Perhaps those who had gone abroad were right to refuse to return to Italy, preferring to carry on their resistance under the protection of a French or Swiss or some other flag? Perhaps the others were right, too, those who were still opposed to the régime but wouldn't run any personal risks on that score? What had come of all his fervent hopes and all his exhausting efforts? A cell in Regina Coeli! Outside, except for his mother, there was probably hardly a soul who remembered his existence, hardly a soul who remembered his existence, hardly anybody who thought of him at all. (The girl he had loved for a long time would, he felt sure, forget about him sooner or later, and someone else, with less hopeless prospects, would share his life with her.) If life meant having some part in the feelings and thoughts and actions of human beings, he was certainly not alive. . . .

The early morning hours passed fairly calmly. As the day wore on Speranza's nerves would grow more and more on edge. When the bell rang in the evening he would lie on his cot, but it would take hours before he could fall into a troubled sleep; nightmares woke him with a start again and again. In spite of his efforts at self-control, he was falling prey to the same fear he had had when he was being held at OVRA headquarters: fear that the nervous strain would make him ill, that he would be feverish, delirious, and in his delirium would mention names. If only he had some idea of the fate awaiting him . . . if at least there had been further interrogations, or one living soul with whom to exchange one word, instead of the silence of this tomb of living corpses – anything, anything to anchor his drifting mind to reality.

Inaction, despair, confusion, painful conflicting emotions; the inability, through isolation, to evaluate actions and situations clearly – these were the causes of an act which lay heavily on his conscience for years. In his moments of deepest despair, when he was terrified at the thought of remaining immured within those four bare walls, of being forever deprived of the joys which are the birthright of all living beings, the idea came to Speranza that anything that would get him out was justifiable, anything that would get him out of these walls that were crushing him, shutting him off in the dark from the world of the living. Escape? Hopeless. Only one person had ever managed to escape from Regina Coeli; nobody escaped from penitentiaries. Only a miracle and plenty of financial support (which certainly would not be available to him) had enabled Rosselli to escape from Lipari and to take two friends with him. But there was a simple expedient that many had had recourse to; the police had hinted at it during the interrogations. A political offence is not a true crime; what matters in the eyes of a dictator is the character of the offender, not the offence. If he gives the impression of being a broken man, of being morally bankrupt, so that he can no longer have sufficient energy and prestige to lead and to inspire others, he may even be released. In this way, by debasing themselves, political prisoners have managed to get off lightly from time immemorials, under all tyrannies.

La letterina: a short note, a few words of self-abasement, would make the difference between death and life, between living death in dark prison cells and the bountiful life outside. Speranza was under no obligation to anybody: he had done his best. After years of exile he had come back and had renounced his youth to devote himself to fighting the dictatorship. Caught by the OVRA, he had taken full responsibility for what had happened, and so a disaster which could have involved hundred, perhaps thousands of people, in fact, affected less than fifty. He had stopped the landslide. Now there was nothing more he could do, so what did an abject gesture matter if in return he could leave these four walls? He knew that the humiliation would stay with him, but nothing mattered except getting out. He recalled those who had deserted the ranks of the conspirators; those who had gone abroad; those who were against the régime but refused to run risks. Why should he care if any of them criticized his actions? What right had they to criticize, anyway? They had taken good care not to end up in this kind of a nightmare. . . .

It was done. He had done what he could to get out. He was calm again. But with the calm, a sense of proportion returned. The prisoners were allowed to write one letter a week. The following week he wrote to the director of the institute at which he had been employed (the banker, Jung, shortly to become Minister of Finance in the Duce's Cabinet), reaffirming his opposition to the dictatorship, his conviction that fascism was a cancer which having corrupted the nation morally would proceed to destroy it physically. . . . Now he would not be released, he would not owe his freedom to what, whatever its justification, was an act of cowardice. Nevertheless, his conscience was not at rest until, eleven years later, he felt that he had paid the price for his weakness, which, though unknown to others, weighed heavily on him.

One day, sometime later, a warder escorted Speranza to the director's office. Walking along the prison corridors was like liberty, after so many weeks of seeing nothing but his cell and the cubicle in the yard. An OVRA vice-commissioner told him that his sentence was five years' *confino*. Speranza heaved a sigh of relief. It was not release, which would have horrified him (it might have been due to the *letterina*); nor was it the Special Tribunal and the ten years in the penitentiary he had expected. At that moment there were 600 political prisoners in Regina Coeli; none of them were sent before the Special Tribunal, not even groups of anarchists who had been organizing *attentati* against the Duce himself. Since the trials of June, 1932, the régime wanted to give the impression that all opposition had vanished, so preferred to avoid the publicity attendant on the Special Tribunal trials. The maximum penalty for all those lucky enough to have been arrested in those summer months was the five years' deportation to *confino* which the

OVRA could give without benefit of trial, and which could be renewed time after time. Four of Speranza's group were also sent to *confino* for five years. Three were given four years and one had a three-year sentence.

— ⧗ —

Solitary confinement was at an end. Speranza was now put in a cell with De Sanctis, still suffering from his recent torture, and Baldazzi. A few days later they were taken to a larger cell which they shared with Ciccotti, who was just beginning to recover from the *bastinado*. Giannotti was there too, as calm as ever, and Giuliani, whom Speranza now met for the first time. They went for 'air' with other prisoners, among them the leaders of young communists arrested several months before in the villages of the Castelli. Some had got off with ordinary beatings; the stubborn ones – there were plenty – had been subjected to the *bastinado*. Others had had to endure worse. A young girl arrested with the Castelli communists had had her breast and genitals slashed with razor blades. Enzo, a communist, had had to endure the same tortures as Delfini: cheeks burned with an oil-lamp, testicles crushed, needles driven under his fingernails; his heart had been damaged through repeated poundings of a sandbag on his chest. Mario, also a communist, had had his arm dislocated and could no longer use it. Marco, a socialist, had gone quite out of his mind during solitary confinement – he never completely recovered.

Weeks went by. There was no sign of departure for *confino*. They hadn't the slightest idea which of the islands they would be sent to: Tremiti? Lampedusa? Ustica? The temporary permission to have books from the prison library was withdrawn, but a few illustrated papers were allowed. With wry amusement they read an article about what were considered sensational barbarities in Persia where, it was said, prisoners were still tortured with the *bastinado* . . . the public did not know that it was widely used at home by the OVRA! In another magazine was a photograph of the dictator surrounded by cheering workers: the prison inmates at once recognized the happy 'workers' as OVRA agents they had seen at police headquarters.

It was a relief to have human company once again; nevertheless, there was great distress in the cell. Two of the prisoners were unmarried. The other four had families; they knew that there was nothing to eat at home, that their wives and children might be turned into the streets at any moment for inability to pay the rent. Sometimes news came that a wife or a child was ill, and the man would sit there helplessly weeping.

Sometimes the warders were friendly and allowed them the little privileges which transform prison life: to stay in their cots a little longer on cold winter mornings, to spend a few more minutes at 'air', to have an extra ration of bread or soup, a page of a newspaper; sometimes the warders would even take a message to the families. On the whole, the warders had tried to be helpful: soon after Speranza had been interrogated a young guard asked him how things were going.

"Badly."

"Have you confessed?"

"I had to admit a few things."

"Don't ever confess a thing" – in a whisper – "keep on denying everything. The OVRA will keep you here for a few months and then they will have to let you go."

Another day while he was taking 'air' a warder called out in surprise: "What! You here again?"

"I'm still being questioned."

"Lucky you to be questioned so long without having to go to the infirmary."

Another said to him: "Prison is just as bad for me as it is for you. I can't stand it, but what can I do? I can't get any other job."

On New Year's Day, the warder in charge came to the cell and made a little speech, wishing them all an early release. Another warder, who had to tell a prisoner that his mother had died, did so with much tact and genuine kindness. One warder used to come whenever he was on night duty and have a long chat, telling the prisoners what was happening outside. All this took place in the sixth wing, where they occupied what had been General Capello's cell.[6]

After six months the prisoners left Regina Coeli. It was a cold winter morning and still dark when they arrived, handcuffed and chained together, at the station. It was a slow unpleasant journey in the small cells of the prison truck. At Naples they spent several hours in the guard-room of Poggioreale (the main jail). While they waited, a group of prisoners from the penitentiary of Nisida[7] arrived – ordinary criminals, to all appearances. One of them spoke

6 General Capello, a distinguished military leader in World War I, had tried to organize an *attentato* against the Duce in 1926. He had been sentenced to thirty years' imprisonment.
7 Nisida is a small island in the Gulf of Naples.

to Speranza:

"Are you a 'political'?"

"Yes."

"We've got a 'political' with us. Come and have a word with him. It will cheer him up."

Speranza was taken to a corner of the room where a tall emaciated ghost of a man was leaning against the wall as though he couldn't stand without support. He talked, as in a trance, of events of long ago. On one of the dictator's visits to Bologna, in 1926, a group of anti-fascists had decided to try to rid Italy of him. Several of them, armed with revolvers, scattered among the crowds; one of them fired at the dictator, but missed. A young man called Zamboni, who had been standing near the man who fired, was killed on the spot by the fascists. Afterwards his relatives were arrested and sentenced to thirty years' imprisonment. The Special Tribunal which sentenced them knew that it was not Zamboni who had fired the shot. Some time later, without any publicity, the OVRA released Zamboni's relations from the penitentiary, but to make sure they would not talk sent them to *confino*. This much was known by the underground. What was not known was what the prisoner told Speranza. Zamboni was the son of a friend of one of the conspirators; this friend, his conscience tormented, told his wife that he himself and his friend, not Zamboni, were implicated in the *attentato*. From person to person, this reached the OVRA. The Special Tribunal held a special session in Bologna. Twenty people were arrested, one was condemned to eighteen years' imprisonment and the others to thirty. Orders were given to the prison governors to treat all members of this group with extra severity; that morning for the first time the prisoner from Nisida had left the underground cell in which he had been immured for eleven months. His hands had become quite transparent and his body was shrunken; but his eyes still shone with the inner determination which had enable him to keep sane. He ended by saying: "Courage, friend. We will win."

At Poggioreale Speranza was put in a cell with two members of *G.L.*, three communists and an anarchist who had been arrested for placing flowers on Malatesta's grave.[8] Poggioreale was a paradise compared to Regina Coeli. Speranza wanted to send a telegram, so he asked the prisoner who was acting as clerk:

"Can I send a telegram to my mother?"

"No. You have to have the governor's permission."

"But I must send one. . . . Where are you from?"

"Sardinia."

"Do you know Lussu?"

"Oh! Are you a friend of his?"

"Yes. . . ."

Two hours later the telegram had been sent.

At 'air' periods there were forty of them, all bound for *confino*. There were *giellisti*, socialists, communists, anarchists; all social classes were represented, though most of the prisoners were artisans. One day on returning to his cell Speranza heard his name being called, and saw hands waving behind bars. It was good to see a friend, though it was sad to know that Nino Woditzka had been caught. An incorrigible optimist, Nino had been one of the most active and energetic organizers of *Giustizia e Libertà* in Trieste.

---

8 Malatesta had been a prominent figure among humanitarian anarchists.

Formerly an Austrian subject and an Italian patriot, he had been condemned to death by the Austrians at the end of the first world war. Arrested by the fascists a few year later, he had spent months with sixty other political prisoners in a prison cell hewn out of solid rock. He emerged with tuberculosis. After his release from his first fascist imprisonment he organized various groups of *giellisti*; in the autumn of 1932 one man's carelessness led to the arrest of fifty. Nino and four other organizers were sentenced to from three to five years' *confino*.

After three or four days at Poggioreale, Speranza noticed a newcomer, a sailor, at 'air' each day. Speranza asked him where he came from. Sicily. Where had he been arrested? On his ship, and from there he was taken to Tripoli. Had they found anything on him? Yes. . . . He turned out to be the courier Minafò, who for months had been bringing from abroad the clandestine pamphlets and leaflets Speranza used to collect from Civitavecchia. Minafò had stood torture without giving away a single name. First the OVRA had tried to break him down with drugs which, he explained, had the effect of weakening his muscular control, so that, as he put it, he was 'disjointed', each part of his body acting independently from the rest. As this failed he was *bastinadoed* regularly every day for three weeks. That achieved no results either, so they applied burrowing insects under a glass to his navel. Still not a word. And he had the added torture of thinking of his family, who had no means of support.

"What makes you do it?" a police sergeant asked him one day. "You are against fascism, but this isn't fascism. It is we police who rule the country. Why don't you think of your families and your work, and mind your own business?"

Like Woditzka and Minafò, another who had refused to mind his own business was Giuseppe Germani, a doctor, whom Speranza met on his last day at Poggioreale. His offence? He had tried to take some money to the needy widow and children of Giacomo Matteotti, who had been his friend.

— ⧖ —

It took six hours to reach the island. De Sanctis, who had arrived a few days earlier, described the local arrangements. The prisoners were allowed to walk about in one section of the village that was included in the twenty-five acre camp. Their quarters were in the old Bourbon penitentiary.[9] At the camp boundary stood a double row of sentries, and the points where prisoners might be tempted to escape were reinforced with barbed wire. A force of over 600 armed men (400 were fascist militia, sixty were police and carabineers, and the rest soldiers and sailors of the regular forces) were employed to guard 350 prisoners. The atmosphere of the camp varied with each successive commander; the last two had been dismissed, one because of financial irregularities, and the other, a regular army officer, for leniency towards the prisoners and for trying to enforce discipline on the fascist militia, who were given a free hand by the commander in charge when Speranza arrived.

The prisoners could leave their quarters at seven in the morning, and at 7 p.m. they had to be back. They spent

9 The Romans had used Ponza as an internment island. The Bourbons, who reigned in Naples from 1735 to 1806 and again from 1815 to 1860, had a penitentiary for political and common criminals in Ponza.

their days in various ways according to their temperaments. Most of them walked about doing nothing. Some did manual work, while others studied. Two small libraries, each of a few hundred volumes, had been assembled, one by the communists, the other by the non-communists. The prisoners received five *lire* (1*S*.) a day for all necessities, including food; some ate alone, others organized messes according to their political views. The *giellisti* mess served two meals a day, one usually consisting of beans or *pasta*, the other of vegetables, sometimes with a small piece of fish or meat. Prisoners had organized a cooperative store and a

137

'café' the proceeds of which went to the non-communist library. Compared with prison it was a return to normal life – or so it seemed at first.

There were prisoners of all shades of anti-fascist opinion. Highly respected by his fellow-prisoners was Fabbri, an old humanitarian and democratic socialist, once an active cooperative organizer in Romagna. He was the fourth man who was to have escaped from Lipari with Rosselli. When on his way to the shore on the night of the escape, he heard a patrol approaching. He stopped on the pathway leading to the beach, and by letting himself be arrested he enabled the others to get away. For punishment he had been sent to a penitentiary for three years. After the 1943 armistice he was an active Resistance organizer; caught by the fascists, he was tortured and killed. . . .

No less respected was Cencio Baldazzi, who had come to Ponza after having spent five years in a penitentiary in Sardinia. Marco Riccardi, whose voice Speranza had once heard at Regina Coeli, was there too. An enthusiastic and loyal young socialist, he had returned to Italy bringing clandestine leaflets. The companion with whom he had crossed the frontier on foot turned out to be a spy who denounced him as soon as they were in Italy. After being severely *bastinadoed* by OVRA agents in Lombardy, he was brought to Rome. During six months' solitary confinement at Regina Coeli he had, for a while, gone out of his mind. As he became violent, he was first beaten by the warders, then sent to the infirmary. A few years later he was killed by the fascists. . . .

Rinaldi, a prisoner from Romagna, never got over the effects of the beatings he had had. One night at Ponza he saw through his cell window the swaying branches of a tree, imagined they were the police coming to fetch him for another beating, and began howling like a madman. (He had been arrested in the early days of fascism. After his arrest an officer of the fascist militia beat his wife to death; when their schoolboy son heard the news he went home and shot at the officer who had killed his mother; the boy was sent to a reformatory while his father was in prison.) Mazzei's family also had been destroyed by the fascists. To celebrate the victory of the new régime, a gang of fascists had been amusing themselves riotously in the Quartiere Trionfale, a working-class district in Rome; that evening Mazzei went to look for his father, an old socialist organizer, as he had not come home; the fascists saw him and beat him until he lost consciousness. He came to in a hospital three days later. There had been so many people brutally attacked by the fascists that the hospital was over-crowded, with men and women in the same wards. Mazzei saw his sister in a bed not far from his. She, alarmed when her father and brother did not come home, had also gone out in search. She found her father, who had been stabbed to death after being lashed to a door. The shock was too much; the girl died in hospital. Mazzei's life dragged on, between prison and *confino*. . . .

Many prisoners developed tuberculosis after the tortures and the long months spent in damp cells. One communist, Pratolongo[10] from Venezia, had been made deaf by blows on his ears. Giovetti, also a communist, had had his skull fractured. Each *questura* seemed to develop its own particular system of torture; only the *bastinado* was

10   Later a Resistance leader and a member of Parliament after the establishment of the Italian Republic.

universally applied. The most elaborate methods appeared to be those of the *questura* in Romagna. One of these involved lowering the prisoner by a rope onto a sheet of red-hot metal until he made up his mind to talk. Elsewhere the police used the rack. One police station counted on getting good results by holding the prisoner's head in a bucket of water. Many prisoners had died from torture, and others had taken their own lives because they could stand no more of it.

The *confino* at Ponza was a portrait in miniature of underground Italy. About half of the prisoners were communists; the orthodox ones, the Stalinists, lived apart, and only a few of them had anything to do with non-communists. One could not help admiring their spirit of self-sacrifice and their discipline and the deep faith they had in their cause. It was sometimes hard to resist being attracted by what was good and fine in the communist, and to make a distinction between their ideals, their humanitarian zeal, their desire to create a better world, on one hand, and on the other the institutions they wanted to introduce, the means they used, the brutality and indifference to human values which are always brought by a régime based on force and intolerance (one had to keep reminding oneself that many people had been misled by the sincerity and selflessness that had existed among some fascists).

Even here, Communist Party discipline was not relaxed. A member of *G.L.*, on his arrival at Ponza, had met a former communist deputy from his home town. They greeted each other delightedly, spent an hour or two in friendly talk, and agreed to meet again the following day.

But the communist didn't turn up, on that or any other day. When they eventually met by chance, the *giellista* asked: "Why didn't you come?" "I was told to have nothing to do with you."

Speranza met Giorgio Amendola[11] at Ponza. They agreed – both of them intellectuals – to start a series of debates on social problems, Speranza to take the liberal line, Amendola the communist. But the debates never took place. Giovetti, the 'Red Pope', as the non-communists called the leader of the Ponza communists, a man of iron will, had forbidden them: there was no need, he said, to hear other points of view in order to understand marxist truth.

The anarchists, the second largest group at Ponza, had nothing in common with the classical bomb-throwing type. Utopian idealists, almost all working men, they were always ready to help anyone who needed it, and they respected those who disagreed with them – except for the orthodox communists, whom they could not forgive for having destroyed, in 1918, the attempt which all anarchists had hoped would transform the whole Russian nation into a free union of self-governing communities of peasants and workers. They came from all parts of Italy; some called themselves individualists, but most of them had read Kropotkin and called themselves collectivists.

The third largest group consisted of democrats, the *giellisti* and a few democratic socialists, republicans and freemasons. In spite of dissensions one could feel what

---

11   Son of the Liberal leader Giovanni Amendola, Giorgio joined the Communist Party in his youth. A Resistance leader and Member of the post-war Parliament, he later became one of the three or four top men in the hierarchy of the Italian Communist Party.

the democratic followers of Cavour, Marx and Mazzini had in common: the conviction that government must spring from the freely expressed wishes of the people, that under no circumstances may the people be deprived of their control over the government; that citizens have no right to relinquish liberty of their own will; that greater liberty cannot be won by denying what liberties previous generations have achieved.

If the *confino* was the Italian underground on a small scale, Ponza was Italy in microcosm. Four hundred insolent blackshirts represented fascism; two hundred police, soldiers and sailors represented the *fiancheggiatori*, the monarchy and the reactionary groups which supported fascism and gave it respectability. The three hundred and fifty prisoners represented the anti-fascist movement with its various tendencies. In the little town and villages lived six thousand people who took no interest in fascism or anti-fascism, who cheered the blackshirts as their grandfathers had cheered King Victor Emanuel, and their great-grandfathers the Bourbon Re Bomba.[12] They wanted to live in peace, undisturbed, minding their own business; hard-working people with many fine qualities, who, when a problem arose and they needed advice, asked (and followed) the counsel of the priest whom they had been taught to respect, fear, and even love; for he belonged to the Church, which represented wisdom, moderation and stability in a restless world. The only lay inhabitant of the village who had anything to do with the prisoners was the chemist, and the only other person who saw them and invited them to his house was the *arciprete*, the head of the local clergy. An

---

12 Ferdinand II, King of the Two Sicilies, 1830-59.

intelligent man with a quiet manner, he did what he could
– usually successful – to restrain the fascist militia in their
wildest moments. He was really the chief authority on the
island. Fascism? Anti-fascism? Were they perhaps only
superficial phenomena, small ripples scarcely ruffling the
country's surface? During the last one hundred years there
had certainly been great changes in Italy: the *Risorgimento*;
the unification; the modest efforts of the liberals, first
corrupted and then crushed by nationalism and monopoly
capitalism; now fascism. Maybe these were only skin-deep
things. Underneath, immovable and immutable, was the
Italian nation, still, as for sixteen hundred years, a Catholic
nation guided and dominated by the Church.

As time went on restrictions at the *confino*
increased. When Speranza first arrived the prisoners were
free to move about as they liked inside the building which
housed all except those who, either because they had been
joined by their families or because of ill-health, had been
given permission to rent a room in the section of the
village included in the camp. A few days after his arrival
orders came to lock the gates between corridors and floors
in the evening; many of the prisoners carried their cots
into the courtyards in protest. Then the prisoners living
in the village were forbidden to invite any others to their
rooms. At this order, each politial group sent delegates
to the commander, asking him to relax the rule; three of
them were detained, and that night at about two o'clock
seventy policemen arrived from the mainland and took one
hundred and fifty prisoners (most of them communists)
to Naples, where they received fresh sentences to further
imprisonment. Later came the order forbidding prisoners

to move about in groups of more than three at a time, and another forbidding letter-writing to any but near relations.

Life at *confino* was, of course, infinitely better than prison, but at times it could be very oppressive. Some who had been there five, six, or seven years showed signs of mental unbalance, developing persecution mania and morbid depression. There were plenty of elaborate escape plans, but no one ever succeeded in escaping from Ponza. The prisoners gazed out at the sea, the smaller islands, Palmarola, Zannone, and Gavi, whose rocky cliffs rose from the water not far off. Sometimes on clear days they could see Mount Circeo on the mainland . . . but how to get there? Speranza knew that prisoners had escaped from Lampedusa and from Lipari. But here it seemed impossible.

The feeling of oppression did not stop the prisoners from thinking about the problems which passionately interested them all. News reached them, it was possible to keep in touch with outside events. Ever since he had come back to Italy four years before, Speranza had thought of nothing but his all-absorbing work; he was well-informed about the fascist régime, but his knowledge about what was happening abroad was sketchy. During the long months in prison there had been no contact at all with the outside world. Once he had heard that the next cell at Regina Coeli was occupied by four young Austrian nazis, who had fled to Italy after taking part in an unsuccessful *coup d'etat*. This was all he had known of the nazi seizure of power in Germany. A few papers and periodicals reached them in Ponza. It was clear that an already serious situation was rapidly deteriorating. The clouds were gathering, and it was easy to foresee – all the prisoners were convinced of it – that in a few years a major catastrophe, no one knew exactly what, would hit Europe. Hitler had come to power; another fascist movement had destroyed the attempt made by the better part of the German people, unfortunately a minority, to govern themselves freely. Ponza was lost in the Mediterranean waters, but even from Ponza one could see the relentless advance, in close order, of thousands and hundreds of thousands of Germans of all ages and classes, impassioned and ardent and at the same time cold and cruel, ready to die for their beliefs.

The Führer of German fascism was a man who, though certainly mad, was no charlatan. Unlike the intellectually mediocre and morally corrupt Duce, he was no ordinary power-crazy tyrant. He was the prophet of Evil, but some of the qualities of a prophet he did have. The Duce's was a bravura performance with a supporting cast of hooligans, cynics, and opportunists who would sell themselves to the highest bidder. Behind the Führer were millions of Germans, some mad like him, but most them sane. There were stupid and lazy and corrupt citizens among them, but most were intelligent, honest and vigorous. The Italian operetta had become Wagnerian opera in Germany, the farce had become tragedy. Italian fascism was flatulent with parades, bombast and gold braid; but the heavy tramp of hundreds of thousands of boots marching through the streets of Nuremberg, Munich and Berlin was no hollow threat; they would one day march beyond thir own frontiers. In Germany words were implemented by deeds; beneath the uniforms, instead of blusterers daring to do battle only with unarmed enemies, marched dedicated fanatical men ready, if need be, to sacrifice their lives.

If Italian fascism could do so much damage in spite of its intellectual and moral turpitude, the potentialities of the German nazis was appalling to contemplate. They would not stop at setting fire to the homes and factories of their opponents, they would set the whole continent on fire, the corpses would be numbered in millions, not thousands. Those who had been combating Italian fascism had a truer insight into German fascism than had the spokesmen of the Western nations; than the English, for instance, who thought they had one more petty tyrant to deal with. Misled by their theories, even the Russian leaders mistook a dynamic movement based on passionate faith for just another decadent product of capitalism.

The democratic states which the fortunes of war had raised a few years before from the ruins of four empires were all falling to pieces. Dictatorship had taken hold in Hungary as in Poland, in Bulgaria as in Lithuania and other nations. It was only fifteen years since the time when it had seemed that liberty was permanently secure throughout the civilized world. In so short a time had eight generations of effort to free man's spirit from the fetters of tyranny and dogmatism been annihilated. The liberty so painfully gained on both sides of the Atlantic was retreating in face of the tremendous economic crisis spreading through the western world; perhaps liberty would survive only in those countries which had created it in modern times, liberal England and democratic France and their offspring in other continents. In Europe as in Asia and the Americas *coup d'etat* followed *coup d'etat*. One day the mounting tension would develop into a war. A war might destroy the destroyers of liberty – or it might complete the

146

destruction of liberty, not just for this generation but for all time. Not for centuries had humanity experienced such a crisis. Nobody could tell how it would end, whether slaves or free men would emerge from the cataclysm.

These were Speranza's thoughts as day after day he walked back and forth from one end of the *confino* to the other.

A bearded Max during the years
of prison and confinement.

147

CHAPTER V

Second Exile (1933 – 43)

British cousin with considerable influence succeeded in obtaining his release from *confino*. Speranza went back to his parents' home in the country, to the house where he had been arrested a year earlier. The police had ordered him to stay there; any attempt to get in touch with friends would have meant immediate arrest; he was completely isolated. Acquaintances met by chance shunned him; so did all but his nearest relations. Except for the few who had previously cooperated in clandestine activities, the peasants and workers made clear their disapproval of the ex-political prisoner. Theirs was the traditional respect for authority, right or wrong. He felt more cut off at home than he had at Ponza.

He decided to leave the country. He had believed it to be his duty to oppose fascism and he had done all he could in Italy. Now that he was so closely watched by the police and their informers he could go nowhere and do nothing. It seemed clear, at the time, that whatever anti-fascists did in Italy, their efforts alone could not bring about the overthrow of the dictatorship; that this could be accomplished only with the help of strong pressure from outside. It was essential that there should be in the country a group capable of forming a democratic government in the event of the dictatorship falling, but until such time they should lie low and avoid arrest. The main field of anti-fascist action was bound to be outside Italy. Moreover, fascism was no longer an exclusively Italian phenomenon;

it was spreading like wildfire to other countries and other continents. Beyond the Alps he could – and should – carry on the work interrupted by his arrest in Italy.

While he was in prison, friends had found and destroyed a passport he had used several times and of which the police knew nothing. The first thing he had done on leaving Ponza was to get another without the police hearing of it. It would take twenty-four hours to reach the frontier, and the police had to be kept informed of his movements. If he were to disappear the police everywhere would be alerted at once. So (a couple of months after his return home) he sent a peasant with a note, saying that he was going to Switzerland, to the police commissioner, who took it for granted that the Home Secretary had given permission for the journey and did not notify the frontier aurthorities. (The unfortunate man was later severely punished for his negligence.) For Speranza it was a relief beyond description to emerge from the Simplon tunnel and see the broad Rhône Valley open out before his eyes. The nightmare he had lived in for years was over. Now he could breathe freely, walk without furtive glances over his shoulder, say what he liked, go where he pleased.

— ⧗ —

Switzerland, then France. The train sped across the hills, fields and vineyards of Burgundy. The one other passenger in the compartment, a Frenchman, broke the silence first and talked pessimistically:

"We are trying to have a good time so as not to have to think. Do you suppose we don't know what's happening?

150

Germany is getting prepared – Hitler is a madman who wants war, and the German people are with him. Weimar was a hoax – they pretended to be democratic just to get off more lightly. They never disarmed. Their munitions factories are working day and night. Here in France corruption is rife. The press is corrupt, the politicians are corrupt, so are the intellectuals, the businessmen, the bankers and labour leaders. We are afraid of the future, we don't want to think about it. I was in the last war, one of my brothers was killed at Soissons, another died in a German prison camp. Today we couldn't make the effort we made in 1916. We don't say so, we even deny it, but we can't fight again. We haven't any friends. The English prefer Germany's friendship to ours, and blame us because Europe has not settled down. The Russians want us all to cut each other's throats. The Americans are fools who understand nothing but dollars. You Italians are just waiting for the right moment to pounce on us and take Nice, Corsica and Tunisia."

– ⌛ –

Rosselli had been trying to obtain the cooperation of British political leaders, especially those who were then in opposition. A few years earlier there had been hope that France might be able to stem the tide of dictatorship. Now every day it was becoming clearer that she would not be able to hold the front line for democracy. It was doubtful whether the Third Republic could survive the combined attacks of the reorganized extreme Right and of the extreme Left – enemies who, without any formal alliance, worked along parallel lines against democracy, as they had done in

151

Germany during the tragic two years before Hitler came to power. Perhaps there was more tenacity in Britain, where some were seriously concerned at what was happening on the Continent.

Speranza went to England. As he neared the high cliffs of Dover he gazed at them and wondered whether the island could once again produce the will and power to fight back the destructive forces of despotism. The first impression he had was not encouraging. A few people were beginning to wake up, but they were the exceptions; most Britishers – the non-politically minded and also most of the politicians, whether conservative, socialist or liberal – took little interest in what was happening abroad. They had their own urgent problems at home – unemployment, economic stagnation, trade going from bad to worse, and declining income which the nation tried to hide by living on capital.

In various lectures he was invited to give, he spoke about the growing threat of dictatorships, which seemed to appeal to most central and eastern Europeans, of their barbarizing influence, and of the war which fascism was bound to launch. Audiences listened politely, but it was clear from their expressions and from their comments that they found the speaker a likeable young man, but something of a fanatic who exaggerated, doubtless because of his unpleasant personal experiences. Who would be thinking of another war after the horrors and tragedies of the last? With all their ranting, the Italian dictator and his German counterpart only wanted the acclaim of their countrymen; they shouted to let off steam, and did not represent a serious danger. Britain was governed by the older generation, who still lived in a world that had come to an end in August, 1914. Those who had fought and survived would not listen to any talk about war, and were convinced that their contemporaries in other countries shared their horror of further bloodshed. As for the younger generation, they seemed ready to be interested in anything provided it was not serious.

— ⧖ —

For the first time he met exiles and refugees from nazi Germany. He seemed to be re-living his meetings with the Italian exiles some eight or nine years earlier.

"In a few months Hitler will be got rid of."

"The economy is getting worse and worse."

"People are getting more and more discontented."

"Nazi leaders are quarrelling among themselves."

"The generals . . . big business . . . the workng classes . . . Hindenburg . . . the Church . . . ."

Still the same stupid illusions. What did popular discontent matter to a despotic government, when a few machine-guns could silence a whole city? The censorship had done its work efficiently; now that discussion was not allowed, things appeared as the Führer and his colleagues wanted them to, and the people instinctively put all dangerous ideas out of their minds. Disagreements among the party leaders were settled without reference to public opinion. A liberal government can be weakened by economic difficulties; in an authoritarian state economics are controlled by the government instead of the other way round. With a few reforms, today's economy and finance could be changed to suit the dictator's wishes; what did inflation, an unbalanced budget and a growing national debt matter if the government could produce an illusion of stability by controlling prices, wages and profits? There were liberals, social democrats and catholics among the refugees, but none of them seemed to have any idea of the revolution nazism was bringing about in Germany, of the nationalistic and racial fanaticism which had inflamed tens of millions of Germans.

— ⧗ —

In Italy he had seen a few instances of anti-semitism, but he had never paid much attention to them. Now he saw in the German refugees the tragic result of the most senseless of passions and ideologies. Left to themselves, German Jews would have behaved exactly as Italian Jews had – that is to say as Germans and not as Jews. As middle-class Germans, most them would have become nazis just as most Italian Jews became fascist, or were at least well-disposed towards fascism; others would have behaved differently, some supporting the opposition not because they were Jews, but because they were liberals, socialists or communists. But since nazism was anti-semitic, all the Jews were of necessity anti-nazi. This helped the cause of freedom – at the cost, of course, of untold suffering. Twenty million Jews all over the world were concerned with what was happening in Germany. The persecution of the Jews moved public opinion in Britain and in the United States more than had the destruction of German parliamentary institutions, the murder of several thousand political

154

opponents, or the arrest of tens of thousands of liberals, socialists and communists. In the name of freedom, liberal Europeans had emancipated the Jews; their sufferings were to be a determining element in re-establishing freedom in much of Europe.

— ⧗ —

February, 1934. Speranza was in Paris for a few grey days in winter. Greyness was in the hearts of the people as well as in the leaden sky; it seemed that what had happened in Italy and Germany was bound to happen in France too.[1] History was repeating itself – parliamentary government was on the decline because many of the people's representatives lacked dignity, integrity and sense of responsibility. The people were indifferent to liberty, the reality of which was so meagre compared with the dreams that had accompanied its birth. Groups of violent agitators were prepared to do anything to get power and keep it. They had large followings. Rioting began and the spark soon became a blaze. At first it seemed that the communists would repeat what they had done in Germany, joining forces with the fascists in order to destroy democratic institutions. But the German example had perhaps taught something. The tradition of the French Revolution regained the upper hand; government and people acting together were strong enough then to save the Republic. But the danger had been grave, more serious perhaps than most Frenchmen realized.

— ⧗ —

1 The February, 1934, riots in Paris were the culmination of rightist agitation against the Third Republic.

A few days later Austrian democracy fell, fighting. The clerical majority was afraid both of nazism and German nationalism, and of socialism. Italian fascism, it was said, had provided the Heimwehr for years with arms and money, Hitler's triumph had inflamed Austrian Germaniscism. The socialists resisted Dolfuss' order outlawing them, and defended themselves in the Matteotti Hof. It was a severe blow for democracy, and both in France and in Britain politicians comforted themselves with the illusion that it was helpful to have in Austria a dictatorship unlike (and therefore, they thought, antagonistic to) the ones in Italy and Germany. Instead of taking sides in the struggle between liberty and dictatorship, they were taking sides in the struggle between one dictatorship and another.

— ⧗ —

To solve the endless problem of keeping body and soul together, Speranza lectured and taught, wrote articles and did translations. It was hard going and ends would not meet. It was clear that some other way of solving the problem must be tried. He scraped together a loan and sailed for East Africa, a part of the world he was familiar with from travel books, and which had always held a certain fascination for him. He settled in the Rift Valley east of the Mau range, a few miles from the equator, on a large farm which he tried – not very successfully – to cultivate. For the next three years there were new problems, new interests. There was the farmer's concern about the weather, about the rain that never comes – and when it does, comes much too heavily –about falling prices and about diseases of crops and animals; there was also the soothing contact with nature, the getting to know people whose colour is no excuse for denying them equality and human dignity, the conviction that his work was useful both to himself and to others and the restful sight of wide plains, high mountains, flamingo-ringed lakes and countless wild animals still living freely in the valley.

— 🏛 —

Close contact with Bantu and Nilotic tribes[2] proved, as he had always believed, that there was no question of their being inferior to white people. They were intelligent, energetic and enterprising, and it was certainly not the colour of their skins that had kept them back. Their backwardness was probably due to circumstances which had not provided a stimulus, and to the kind of work they did. There was little difference between the peasants of southern Italy, Greece, or Spain and these African peasants who only a generation ago had emerged from the forests where they had sheltered from predatory nomadic tribes. Give the peasant of southern Europe a chance and he will soon be as advanced as anyone (as has happened to those who migrated to the United States). Give the negro a chance, and he will soon be on an equal footing with his white brothers.

— 🏛 —

---

2 Most of the farm workers wre Kikuyus; there were also Ja-luos, Kavirondos, Lumbwas, etc.

157

Occasionally he was able to see something of neighbouring territories. In Uganda he saw the good results of a colonial administration which (unwittingly, perhaps) had encouraged progress by entrusting the natives with responsibilities. There, the white man had limited his intervention to the abolition of slavery, of inter-tribal warfare and of barbaric customs – no more barbaric of course, than European customs of five centuries earlier, and less barbaric than those of totalitarian states in the twentieth century. For the rest they had let things be. To enable the natives to pay the taxes needed for law-courts, schools and hospitals, for roads, railways and harbours, the white man had taught them how to grow cotton and coffee, and already these crops had brought about a flourishing trade with other countries. Authority was vested in the native parliament, education spread rapidly (he was much impressed by Makerere College), good roads were built, the administration of justice was largely in native hands. Uganda had achieved in little more than a generation what had taken several European countries centuries of unceasing effort. Barbarians? No. Human beings with virtues and defects like everybody else.

— ⧗ —

Somalis arrived after crossing the wide desert which lies between their country and the Kenya highlands. They were probably no less civilized than the people of many parts of Europe three hundred years before. They were remarkable for their scrupulous observance of the Koran, which they tried to follow in the spirit as well as the

Above: Max and his wife at Equator Farm in Kenya.

Below: Maxh on an outing with locals
at a lake near the farm.

letter. They represented another world, the world of Islam, already in a ferment, which retained virtues that have vanished (or almost) from the so-called Christian world. The Koran says that all the Prophet's followers are equal, and so the Somalis, the Arabs and the Moslem Indians who were living in East Africa all acted as equals. The Koran says that interest must not be asked on loans, and therefore money was lent without interest. The black man who finds the Moslem example more inspiring than that of many so-called Christians may have better judgment than the white man gives him credit for.

— ⧗ —

"Bwana, why am I paid less than the white man or the half-caste?"

"Because there is no justice, Mochiri."

"Do I work less well?"

"No, on the contrary, you work better."

"How can we put an end to injustice?"

"Join together, and down tools. See that no one goes on working."

"They will send the soldiers."

"If they send the soldiers, you have the right to use force too."

They went on strike. The soldiers did not come. An official came to settle labour problems. He listened to what the natives had to say, and their wages were increased."

"Bwana, Wainana has committed a crime."

"What crime, Ngunu?"

"He has raped a young girl."

"You must tell the police and have him arrested."

"The police do not understand the crimes of natives."

"Then call the elders, and act as though there were no white people."

The punishment was decided in accordance with the law inherited from generations of ancestors.

"Bwana, we want a school."

"What for, Ngodia?"

"We want to learn to read and write."

"Why?"

"The white people are stronger because they know more."

"Are they also better?"

"Not towards us."

"Do as you like. If I can help you, I will."

"Bwana, the new house-boy was educated by the missionaries."

"What of it, Kairu?"

"Those who have been in the Mission wear a shirt and trousers. They learn to lie and steal."

"They can't possibly learn that at the Mission."

"The Spirit punishes the ones who betray him by making them wicked."

"What Spirit?"

"The Spirit that is everything and causes everything, the Spirit that made the world and made us, that makes the plants grow and makes us think."

"Yes, the Christians call that Spirit God. . . ."

— ⧗ —

On the way out, the ship had called at Suez. In the late afternoon Speranza was sitting in a café, next to an Arab who was reading a French newspaper.

"You speak French?"

"Yes, I was a student at Geneva in 1923."

"So was I. What are you doing now?"

"I am a lawyer and a journalist, but my main interest is politics."

"Ah! What is going to happen?"

"There are going to be big changes before long. The Italian government is spending a good deal of money; they have given scholarships to those who want to go and study at Bari, Naples and Rome. Bari radio is inciting revolt. They are setting up centres at Cairo, Beirut and Baghdad, and from these they will launch the Arab revolt which, with their help, will eliminate British and French influence in the Near East."

"But why are the fascists so keen to create disorders?"

"They told us why from Bari. There is to be a great Empire. The Western powers are on the verge of collapse. North Africa and Western Asia were Roman once before, they will be Roman again."

"Do you approve of this?"

"We? Of course we do! We need Italy in order to get rid of France and Britain. Then we will get rid of the Italians by ourselves. The Senussi have already shown us how to do it. The east was enslaved by the west because it was divided. Now the west is divided – fascism is killing democracy, Italy will kill France. Islam is regaining its unity, and one day in Rome, in the very heart of the West, we shall do what we failed to do at Poitiers and Vienna. . . ."

– 🏺 –

A number of people had come on board at Djibuti. Evening brought some respite from the heat, and the passengers would foregather and talk. (It was several months before Walwal and no one in Europe had yet mentioned the possibility of war in Abyssinia. . . .)

"We shall soon have war," said one passenger of unguessable nationality.

"Impossible."

"It's a certainty. More troops have arrived at Mogadishu and Asmara; they can't be replacements, because the others are still there. War supplies have been landed – rifles, ammunition, field artillery, lorries and armoured cars. The King's visit was arranged to deceive everyone, including the Abyssinians. Roads are being built, the ports are working at capacity, barracks are going up, and the authorities are buying quantities of beef cattle."

"So you are quite sure of it?"

"Quite certain. The Abyssinians won't surrender. They never do. When they are beaten, they take to the mountains and start all over again. For my part, I'm glad of it. We've no reason to be pleased with the Abyssinians, and if Italy is tied up in Ethiopia – as she will be for years – France will be all right. . . ."

163

That was how an article in *Giustizia e Libertà*, the weekly that his friends published in Paris, was the first in the European press to predict the war that the fascists were to start in a few months' time, initiating a chain reaction which through the remilitarization of the Rhineland, the Spanish civil war, the invasions of Austria, Czechoslovakia, Albania and Poland, culminated in World War II and finally in the destruction of fascism.

— ⧗ —

Three years had passed, three sowings and three harvests. He had left fascism thousands of miles away, and now here it was again close at hand, as menacing after its victory in Abyssinia in 1936 as after its victory in Italy in 1922. Its success had encouraged imitation. The weariness born of the Great War, of the tension which followed it, and of the economic crisis, was reaching its nadir. Democrats were losing ground nearly everywhere on the Continent and were quickly replaced by fascists or fascist sympathizers.

It was time to go back to Europe. . . .

— ⧗ —

In Geneva shocking news reached him. Carlo and Nello Rosselli had been murdered. There had been three Rosselli brothers; the eldest had been killed in his twentieth year in the Great War; now only their mother was left, with the two widows and their children.

Carlo had been the life and soul of *Giustizia*

e Libertà. Broad-minded, undogmatic, and generous without a trace of romanticism or sentimentality, he was outstanding among his fellow-exiles and all active anti-fascists. He translated his thoughts into action. To him the ideal of a society of free citizens, each responsible for his own actions, was not a dream but a reality, as was the sense of brotherhood – he called it socialism – which would unite the citizens as firmly as force united the totalitarians. Carlo's socialism strengthened the liberalism from which it derived instead of rejecting it as did communists, *massimalisti*, even those who called themselves social democrats or liberal socialists. He was one of the very few anti-fascists who had managed to free themselves from past prejudices and biases. If he had ever been able to set foot in Italy again, he would have been one of the country's outstanding leaders. Nello Rosselli, author of valuable historical works, whom Speranza had known in Rome, was not an 'activist', though he, too, had been in prison and at the *confino*. He was murdered chiefly because he happened to be with Carlo.

The fascists at once started rumours that the Rosellis had been murdered by communists; and if not by communists, by anarchists; if by neither communists nor anarchists, then by trotskyites, or perhaps some other group of Italian anti-fascists. Actually the murders had been committed by French fascists acting on behalf of the Italian fascists who financed them. It was well known at the Palazzo Venezia that the easiest and most effective way of destroying a movement was to strike at its head. (There are usually only a few people who inspire others to action.) The socialist opposition to fascism died in Italy with Matteotti, the liberal opposition with Amendola, that

165

of the younger generation with Gobetti. The democratic underground opposition – much more dangerous for the régime than the communists – would, the fascists hoped, die with Carlo Rosselli.

— ⧗ —

Back in Paris, he renewed his acquaintance with Cianca, perhaps the most active and devoted of Rosselli's friends. Two problems had to be solved: it was essential that the movement Rosselli had founded and died for should go on; secondly, there must be some action to avenge the murders. Speranza managed to collect funds enabling the movement and its newspaper to carry on for another eighteen months. To explore the possibilities of retaliation against Rosselli's murderers, he went to Spain.

Valencia was then the Republican capital. Speranza had decided to go to see Prieto, one of the most influential members of the republican government, to try to enlist his support. He knew by experience the difficulties which were met with every time a plan of action was proposed – technical difficulties not mentioned in romanticized versions of clandestine activities. They could be overcome only with the help of people having financial means and material at their disposal. The plan – an old idea that had often been discussed among the conspirators in Rome – was simple: two or three exiles, or perhaps Speranza alone, would be given a pilot's training in Spain; the Spanish military authorities would turn a blind eye when a plane disappeared; the pilot would repeat, on a larger scale, the atttempts made by Dolci, Bassanesi and De Bosis. . . .

166

Prieto listened to Speranza and rejected his proposal. Yes, it was true that the fascist government had collaborated with Sanjurjo[3] and the other generals in their plot against the Spanish Republic, that Italian aircraft had been placed at the rebels' disposal from the very first, that a hundred thousand mercenaries had been sent to Franco's aid, that Italian submarines had sunk the ships that were bringing scanty and sorely-needed help to the Republic. But if Speranza's plan was carried out it would, whether it failed or succeeded, bring increased pressure on Republican Spain. The appeasers who were then governing France and England would make it a pretext for abandoning the Spanish Republic altogether. It might even lead to a European war. . . .

Speranza stayed some time in Madrid before returning to France. Fighting between the republicans and the fascists went on uninterruptedly in the University City. Standing behind the remains of a wall, a few yards from Franco's soldiers, he had time to think. He tried to envisage the future – or at least some of it. There in Madrid the curtain had lifted on the prelude to the second world war. In spite of the bravery of its defenders, the Spanish Republic was bound to fall: because of the help which Italian and German fascism sent to Franco; because, also, of communist pressure destroying the will to fight of the non-communists. The victory of the nationalists would be hailed in Rome and Berlin as a fascist victory, it would be taken as evidence of the superiority of fascist states over the Western democracies; this would spur them on to other

3 The real organizer of the generals' conspiracy against the Spanish republic. His sudden death left Mola as the most influential nationalist leader. Mola's death put Franco in command of the rebels.

aggressions, other wars. The devastation in the university city would soon be a familiar sight all over Europe. For years Speranza had felt convinced that fascism was bound to lead to another European war, if not a world war. Now he knew when that war would start: as soon as the Spanish Republic was defeated. It was impossible to say who would win, whether the forces now gathered in Berlin (no longer in Rome), or those which later gathered around Britain. In any case, it would be war. The fascists preached *la bella guerra*, the beauty of war. Well, they would have their war. Those who had welcomed the attack on the Italian liberal state in 1922 and, even more, those who had eulogized the war against Abyssinia and now applauded Axis intervention in Spain, would have plenty of opportunity to find out the intimate relationship between death and dictatorship.

— ⌛ —

His journey took him through the arid highlands of Castile and the fertile hills and valleys of Catalonia. Somewhere were the graves of Angeloni, Lugli, Battistelli, De Rosa. Hundreds of others, some known to him, some unknown, had died or were yet to die there. He met volunteers from Germany, France, Britain, Scandinavia and the United States. Some had come partly in a spirit of adventure; most were there because of their devotion to political and social ideals. It was the anarchists' last battle, and it seemed that they knew it; for the communists, more numerous among the foreigners in the International Brigades than among the Spaniards, it was one of many battles; for the few who upheld the liberal tradition, it was

– who knew? Perhaps the end of an epoch, perhaps the beginning of another. Spain was no more than the backdrop for the struggling forces and movements colouring and inspiring Europe. Whichever way things went, liberalism would be the loser. Instead of forging ahead and gaining strength, the attempt to replace authoritarian states by free ones was losing ground. The French and the British were blind. A little help to Azaña and Prieto would have been enough to give victory to the cause of liberty (in Spain, unlike Germany, the majority wanted liberty). But no help came, and Franco was winning. The price paid for the little help sent by the Soviet Union was high: communists had to be put in key positions. Also it proved to weaken rather than strengthen the Spanish Republic: democrats, socialists and syndicalists who formed the bulk of the Republicans had as little love for the communists as for the fascists.

– ⌛ –

Speranza's former professors at the University of Geneva remembered him. He was accepted as *privat-docent* and gave lectures in economics. Salvemini (now at Harvard) proposed a lecture tour in the United States (lectures to academic audiences would pay for the journey, those to Italian or Italo-American ones would provide some badly needed financial help for *Giustizia e Libertà*). He had read widely about the United States and was interested in the development of the American nation. Nevertheless, he had all the usual commonplace prejudices of educated Europeans about American cultural inferiority, materialism, the corruption of their political life and so forth.

His lectures took him to a number of States. He met Americans of all sorts, and through them discovered an America very different from the picture he had had in mind. He found that on the whole Americans were less materialistic than Europeans. There was less selfishness: he had never known a country where so much was done to create and foster a spirit of solidarity, where so many people were ready to help their fellow-man, for no better reason than that he needed help. (What could have been more generous than American help to the victims of the Russian famine and of the Japanese earthquake?) Under pressure from the labour movement and farmers' associations, the country's economy was being transformed. Roosevelt's administration had introduced reforms correcting some of the worst evils of the capitalistic system, while preserving economic liberty and avoiding the deceptive lure of socialism with its stultifying influence. A vast social security scheme already guaranteed a minimum of economic security to millions of wage-earners. The country's wealth, already fairly widely distributed, now spread even more instead of accumulating in the hands of the few. There was certainly less corruption in American public life than, for instance, in France, not to mention any of the totalitarian countries of Europe. Contact with American universities and publications showed the falsity of the commonplace about American cultural inferiority: the European intellectuals' air of superiority was the result of crass ignorance of things American.

An ugly side of American life showed in prejudice against the Negroes and, to a lesser extent, the Jews. But improvement there was. Lynchings were now very rare indeed. The coloured people were – laboriously, of course – winning for themselves a place in the country's economic and intellectual life. The Deep South was no more the United States than backward Southern Ireland had been the United Kingdom before 1921. As for the Jews, nothing prevented them rising to the top in any field, as many were doing. Jewish culture destroyed in Russia and in Germany, lived on in the Jewish American communities.

Without doubt more Americans were aware of their country's shortcomings than were most foreign nations of theirs. The United States made a bad impression on superficial observers because facts were not disguised and matters were discussed openly. One had only to read books by a mass of contemporary American authors to be aware of the plight of the under-privileged. But educated Italians (except for a very few) had no feelings for the Lucanian peasants, nor did educated Germans feel pity for the hundreds of thousands in concentration camps, nor the educated Russians for the millions of victims of communism. Unawareness was a comfortable screen behind which to hide indifference. America had great, indeed huge, shortcomings; she also had the institutions which made possible the correction of faults, and efforts were constantly and effectively made to put things right.

— ⧗ —

Besides, as in Switzerland, the respect for work, what impressed Speranza most during this first visit to America was the comparative lack – as in Switzerland – of class distinctions, the non-existence of the barriers

171

which nearly everywhere in the Old World prevent two people who live next door from considering themselves equal. He met many Europeans who disliked this feature of American life because in their opinion the existence of an *élite* was a sign of superiority and greater culture. Distinctions there certainly were, but they were nothing compared with European distinctions. Americans lacked pompousness, arrogance, conceit – the qualities which, often unconsciously, characterize the so-called upper classes in Europe, even among those who profess democracy and proletarianism. There was none of the servility of the so-called lower classes in Europe. Americans did not talk about their ancestors; instead they talked of what so-and-so had done or wanted to do. The past weighed less heavily, and different backgrounds made for fellowship rather than distance.

— ⌛ —

The Italian in America was a changed man. Speranza met immigrants from his own province, fishermen, peasants and artisans whose families he knew well. In America they had become energetic, sure of themselves, with a sense of responsibility and an awareness of their right to shape their own lives. For nine out of ten Italian immigrants – the failures made up the remainder – America was the country where they were freed from the two chains which had weighed so heavily upon them in Italy: *il padrone* (the master) and the government. In America there were no *padroni*, and not much was heard of the government.

The Italian American had advanced economically

and even intellectually, but not politically. He admired the United States and President Roosevelt, he voted regularly and conscientiously for the Democratic Party. With this went a blind faith in fascism. The years had passed: what the Italian American remembered of Italy were her good points, especially those that are missing in America – the blue sky, the solidarity of a large family and a village community, a life that was peaceful in comparison to the hurry and bustle of American life. For a variety of reasons Italian immigrants had felt inferior. What they thought to be the achievements of fascism had given them a new pride in their national origin. They felt proud because Italy had occupied Corfu, annexed Fiume, made other countries cede territories in Africa to her. Italy had threatened France, Great Britain in Abyssinia, was making a stand against all-powerful and rich nations. What did six million Italian Americans know about fascism or anti-fascism? They knew that now people talked a great deal about Italy, that the Pontine marshes had been reclaimed, that the new *Via dell'Impero* had been opened. In Italy they had never felt that they belonged to the Italian nation; in America they had become Italian nationalists and, as such, fascists. Anti-fascist among them were one in a thousand. American democracy could not count on them, as it could not count on millions of other recent immigrants, easy tools in the hands of authoritarian demagogues.

– ⧖ –

Friends wrote to Speranza in the United States to say that they were counting on him to help carry out a new undertaking. Returning to Europe, he had meetings with several German exiles. One had been a leader of the Catholic Party, and had opposed the policies of von Papen and his friends. Another had been a leading social democrat, and a third one of the main organizers of the *Reichsbänner.* The danger of war was drawing nearer. Italian fascism was no longer the problem. The menace was the infinitely more powerful and dynamic German fascism. A group formed of democrats, catholics and socialists among the exiles wanted, somewhat belatedly (it was 1938), to inform Germans in Germany, to make them understand that the war being prepared by the nazis would bring misery and destruction, not glory and prosperity.

The project was to take a small boat close enough to the German coast for the voice of Free Germany to be heard on the air. It was, as all these things are, a modest enterprise, but it was nevertheless worth trying; it was a symbol of the new international phase of the struggle against fascism. The initiative had come from German exiles; it was financed by some American liberals, it was supported by a British group who did not share the unwarranted optimism of their government and fellow citizens; the execution of it was entrusted to exiles from five different countries. Speranza hired a converted trawler in England and a wireless transmitter was put on board. While in port after a few days at sea, an explosion put an untimely end to the enterprise. Speranza was in his cabin when he felt a gust of hot air and saw a burst of flame. In a second flames were everywhere. Nearly blinded by smoke, he rushed on deck, grabbed a sailor who had been hurt, and abandoned ship. The boat sank in a few minutes. Was it an accident? Sabotage? No one could say. The secret had been well kept, or so at least they thought. But the Gestapo, and perhaps also the OVRA had long arms and a sharp eye. (Speranza later had evidence of the OVRA's efficiency. During the war he got hold of a police file about himself. Among other things he found an accurate summary of a conversation he had had with three trusted friends in New York. One of them had been an informer. Which? Better probably not to try to find out.)

— ⧗ —

From time to time Speranza was able to send non-Italian friends to Italy. They brought back news, some of which appeared in *Giustizia e Libertà*: when facts pointing to preparations for future aggressions were communicated to responsible leaders in France and Great Britain, no notice was taken. War was being prepared for feverishly – as predicted by Salvemini. Airports were being built, air-strips prepared, new military units formed. Military expenditure was rising sharply. The whole of Sardinia was being transformed into a military base – evidently for an attack on Corsica or southern France. Pantelleria had become a fortress and one of the Egadi was a secret submarine base – for attacks on Tunisia or Malta. The troops sent to Libya, harbour works in Cyrenaica, the building of roads with no economic usefulness, all indicated that an attack on Egypt was being prepared. Speranza felt despairing: here were the facts and there was no way to make people believe them. All that was needed was to face realities, adopt a firm attitude, and war might well have been avoided.

175

— ⧗ —

The day the Munich agreement was signed Speranza was in London. Excepting two friends, he saw only contented faces. The menace of war had been really serious this time and the relief was correspondingly great. Majority and opposition alike congratulated the Prime Minister, and people had only kind words (the last he was to hear) for the Italian dictator. Speranza had not felt so depressed since the days of his arrest. Those who knew the spirit of fascism were certain that war was only postponed; futhermore, they felt that it would come when conditions were less favourable than they had been in September 1938. Then the fear of fascism had brought about a coalition (albeit a strange one) between the liberal Anglo-Saxon nations, French lay democracy, nationalist states of central Europe, the Roman Catholic community, and the communist movement. Others maintained that the time gained strengthened the Western powers more than the Axis. This was nonsense: the prevailing mood of France, Britain and the United States made any serious rearmament out of the question. Munich gave further military advantage to the Axis besides being a moral victory for fascism, which had got what it wanted without firing a shot.

— ⧗ —

Feeling that there was nothing useful he could do in Europe, Speranza returned to the United States on the strength of an invitation to give one lecture at a university in Virginia. Other lectures followed and led to the offer of an assistant professorship, teaching economics and sociology at a university in New York State; there his wife and child joined him.

Doubts were tormenting him. He would ask himself if he should not revise his position *vis-à-vis* Italian fascism. The future of liberty would be decided in Germany, not Italy. Since Italy was now playing a very minor part, would it not be wiser to consider how she might be spared the sufferings of a second world war? The exiles' task seemed as Sisyphean as that of the underground inside Italy. Quarrels were endless. It was pleasant to dream of working together towards a common goal: but, in fact, the ten or twelve thousand exiles were hopelessly divided and from divisions came a sense of impotence and futility. Speranza was particularly concerned about the movement of which he had been a member for the last ten years. *Giustizia e Libertà* had changed; it had lost the liberal spirit that pervaded it while Carlo Rosselli had been the main inspiration. Speranza had no difficulty in cooperating with people of widely divergent opinions so long as they accepted basic principles of democratic procedure. He agreed that against force, force must be used. But he did not want the struggle against the fascist dictatorship to aim at installing another dictatorship, so that the Special Tribunal, the internment camp, the OVRA, should give place to another Special Tribunal, another internment camp, another OVRA. Since Rosselli's death, the most influential leaders had been Lussu, Schiavetti and their friends, for whom liberty meant chiefly the enforcement of their point of view; they were socialist, not even social democrats, and lacked the tolerance and respect for others which are basic in the liberal position. Their autocratic attitude had been particularly noticeable at the last meeting Speranza had attended. He remained in the movement for a few months more. Finally he felt he must resign. It was a painful decision because it meant the end of what had been nearest to his heart for ten long years.

— ⧖ —

Constant pressure from the police, both in Italy and abroad, added to Speranza's anxieties. One day in 1937 he learned that his mother had been summoned to the *capoluogo di provincia* (country town). She was brought before the members of the internment committee – the *prefetto*, the county attorney, the chief of police, the commanding officer of the carabineers, and a senior officer of the fascist militia. The charge was active hostility to the fascist regime. The sentence a mild one, was two years' *ammonizione*.

"We know quite well that you haven't done anything," the local police commissioner told her. "But just the fact that you live in the district means that there is a centre of resistance here."

She could not help smiling. If to live was an act of resistance, well, *evviva* life! There were not many visitors at the house in the country, but from time to time fishermen, peasants, workers and commercial travellers from the neighbouring towns dropped in for a chat. Some called themselves socialists, others republicans, communists or anarchists. Except maybe for the communists, certainly they had no clear idea of what those terms meant, but at least they knew that they stood for anti-fascism. His mother was always ready to help those who, for political reasons, could not find work, or who – like three communist bricklayers – were forced to leave the country. People came from far and near to hear a word of encouragement and comfort, they carried away news which had not appeared in the papers, and went on their way with renewed strength and serenity. For someone living a quiet country life, the *ammonizione* wasn't much more than a nuisance. Worse was to come later. At the end of August, 1941, Speranza's mother was arrested. After spending several weeks in the jail in the county town, in the company of common criminals (for the most part prostitutes and women who had killed their babies, who did all they could to make things comfortable for the old lady whose white hair they respected), she was sentenced by the usual commission to two years' *confino*. She was taken to a village high in the Abruzzi mountains.

Informers were legion. (During the war Speranza found a list of people who, either to curry favour or to earn a few *lire*, acted as regular informers: uncles, aunts, cousins, the local schoolteacher, the gardener, etc.) *Ammonizione* and *confino*, continual police supervision, the thousand and one small vexations were certainly not the consequence of what Speranza was doing abroad. But his activities might add to his mother's difficulties. Had he any right to make her suffer?

The Italian police kept track of Speranza abroad. The United States forbade the immigration of anarchists – a precaution surviving from the terrorism of two generations earlier – so he was reported as an anarchist to the American authorities. Switzerland did not recognize the USSR then, and there were restrictions on communists entering the country. He was accordingly reported to the Swiss Government as a communist. When the Geneva police sent for him the superintendent said: "We get so many false reports about Italians abroad from the Italian police that we don't take much notice of them any more. But when one comes along, we have to investigate it so as to send our report to the Swiss Government, which writes to thank the Italian police for their trouble."

— ⌛ —

In moments of discouragement Speranza thought of giving up and going back to Italy. In those moments he was saved from what would have been another grievous mistake by the thought of the friends in jail in Italy, of those who had died.

Suddenly all doubts left him. He was spending a few days in a Canadian village with his wife and child. The days were hot and heavy, and besides walking and bathing there was not much to do except listen to the wireless. The crisis in Europe was coming to a head. On the evening of August 23rd he heard the news of the agreement between Germany and Russia. This meant war. This meant the punishment for those who had committed crimes, the Germans and the Russians who had abandoned themselves to a fanatical and cruel passion and had betrayed civilization. It meant expiation for those who had erred, the British who had run away from reality, the Americans who had rejected responsibilities.

On August 28th came a telegram from the British friend who had helped him find the trawler for the anti-nazi operation in the North Sea. The telegram summoned him to London. He had no misgivings: he did not care whether there was a conservative or a labour government in Great Britain, whether some people had sympathized with the Italian fascists, whether grave mistakes had been made by MacDonald, Chamberlain and Hoare. What mattered was what Britain stood for through her spirit and traditions. As a geographical expression, Britain was no more important than Germany, but just as Germany had come to stand for fascism, so Britain stood for liberty. If she won the war, one would feel assured that the countries which now had fascist dictatorships would be allowed to choose their own governments. British conservatives would not force a monarchy on Italy, nor would British socialists force collectivism on the Italian people if the majority were against it.

Once war was declared, one had to enlist on the side that was right. Since wearing a uniform meant submitting to strict discipline and renouncing one's freedom of action, it was essential to have faith in Britain. This he had, and events did not prove him wrong. Friends and acquaintances asked him: "Didn't you mind wearing a British uniform?" Why should he mind? Fascism had become international, it was necessary to rise above nationalistic considerations to fight it.

As soon as the telegram arrived, he took his family back to the States. In a few hours he left the hysterical atmosphere of peacetime America for the calm atmosphere of wartime Britain. 'David', who had sent for him, introduced Speranza to the heads of a group hurriedly organized to work with and strengthen underground movements in Axis-controlled countries. Italy was not yet at war, so everything possible must be done to keep her out of it. Both in London and Paris (where he went a few days later), official circles had confidence that Italian businessmen would exert anti-war pressure on their government. It was an illusion: it was absurd to think that those who had served the régime for nearly twenty years could or would influence their masters. Speranza insisted, instead, that one should first of all look for the cooperation of the groups which for years had resisted fascism. These groups could not be expected to overthrow the government, but they could undermine it, loosening its hold on the people. Secondly, one had to see what could be done by dissatisfied groups within the fascist ranks: ex-nationalists, former trade unionists, monarchists, clericals – all those who had joined the party without being real fascists. Working on such people as Federzoni, Rossoni, Grandi, Bottai, Badoglio, De Bono[4] (those who did in fact constitute a *fronde* and revolt against Mussolini three and a half years later, when it was too late), it might be possible to neutralize the pro-nazi wing of the party leadership.

---

4 Before joining the fascist party, Federzoni had been a leader of the Nationalist Party; Rossoni, Grandi and Bottai had been revolutionary syndicalists. General De Bono and Marshal Badoglio belonged to the regular army and were more monarchist than fascist. All, except Badoglio, were members of the Fascist Grand Council, all voted against Mussolini at the meeting which led to the monarchist *coup d'etat* of July 25th, 1943. De Bono was caught by the Germans and shot with Ciano and a few others by order of Mussolini. After the Armistice of September 8th, 1943, Badoglio fled to Brindisi, the others saved themselves by hiding.

His impression was that British and French leaders assessed the Italian situation differently. They put their faith in the capitalists, forgetting that under a totalitarian régime economics are ruled by politics and not the converse; in the Vatican, which could hardly be expected to support French secular republicanism and Protestant Britain; in the King of Italy who could not be expected to become suddenly the man of energy and decision he had never been. Projects were presented, plans were made, but unfortunately nothing was done for months. In Switzerland at the end of March Speranza heard that Mussolini had already decided when and where to attack. Any cracks in the fascist party were insignificant, the *fronde* had no intention of acting when nazism seemed to be winning. There was nothing to be done: Italy would come into the war, and it would be largely in Italy that this war, like almost all the great wars of Europe for centuries past, would be fought.

— ⧗ —

Crossing the Channel one day in March he met a group of Italians – professional men, businessmen and students on their way home. They were educated, informed people, moderate in their opinions. None had a fascist outlook. But all, separately, said the same thing.

"France is finished, Britain is finished, Germany will win. We must remain on good terms with the Germans or they will suppress us. If we stay friendly, we will get Nice, Corsica, Malta, more colonies, and we will be strong enough to resist any German attempt to rule us."

Evidently that was what people thought in Italy and

elsewhere on the Continent. How right were they? Would France fall? Very likely. Would Britain fall? Unlikely. If Britain did not fall, the war would go on for years. After a year in America, Speranza was amazed at the change in Britain. A nation which had been profoundly pacifist was now determined to fight and go on fighting. Appeasement was a thing of the past. Decadence had vanished, and the younger generation's superficiality and love of pleasure had given place to determination and a spirit of sacrifice. Far from the government preparing the people for war, it was the people who spurred on Chamberlain, who worked overtime voluntarily, who kept the factories going day and night to increase the country's war production. There were not enough arms or uniforms for the volunteers. One thing was certain – if Britain did go under, she would go down fighting, and it would take years to sink her.

— ⧗ —

Poland had fallen, Finland had been defeated; Denmark was invaded; German troops had landed in Norway; the invasion of Belgium and Holland followed, the destruction of Rotterdam, the Battle of France. In London and Paris, Speranza met those exiles most determined not to give up in the face of what seemed a hopeless situation. It was no longer a question of trying to widen the breach inside Italy between pro-nazi fascists and the *fronde*. The only possible action was that of the anti-fascists. It was necessary to increase contacts with clandestine groups, to provide them with the material means required for their activities. It was a difficult undertaking because German

184

victories and arrests had disrupted both the underground in Italy and the exiles' organizations in France.

The London group entrusted with keeping in touch with resistance movements in Axis-occupied countries and supporting their activities, was formed of excellent people intent on doing their best. Unfortunately they lacked experience of underground movements and comprehension of the situation in fascist countries. They had never lived under a dictatorship, and they believed that the romantic initiatives of small groups who had been able to start revolts and revolutions in the nineteenth century could be repeated in the twentieth. In a conversation with the head of the organization, Speranza was told that all was now ready, that at a signal to be given on the Nth day of that month, thousands of rebels would emerge from their hiding-places, would seize power and put an end to the dictatorship in Germany and to the war. This conversation, following on other similar ones, convinced Speranza that nothing useful could possibly be achieved. His request to be allowed to join the regular forces having been turned down, he returned to the United States.

— ⧖ —

In June, 1940, he was less discouraged than he had been the previous September. There had been Dunkirk, a defeat, but a defeat which proved that victory was possible. On the morning of May 28th, a cousin at the Foreign Office had said: "We may be able to save 40,000 men". Instead of 40,000 they saved over 300,000 – enough for twenty divisions. The British people had acted with the discipline, speed and courage of a well-organized army. When the owners of a thousand boats from Lowestoft to Poole had been told to proceed with all speed to a given place, nobody asked questions, nobody refused to go, nobody grumbled. Without benefit of admirals or captains, the fleet of fishing boats and pleasure craft gave Britain, in defeat, a badly needed success against Hitler.

Before returning to America he was sent on a last visit to Paris. He came back convinced that the heavy losses suffered by the French troops proved that the spirit of 1914 and 1916 had not vanished. In spite of the defeat the situation was not desperate. The French overseas empire was still there, intact; also part of the army and navy. It was still possible to hold on, to reorganize, to start afresh. This was clear to the best Frenchmen, but not to Pétain, Laval, the generals, businessmen and politicians, who in their heart of hearts were on Germany's side – not because she was Germany but because Germany was fascism. A few days before, Leopold III of Belgium had set an example of the surrender that was longed for by all who loathed democracy and the tradition of the French Revolution. Things threatened to be just as bad for Britain; yet in those June days, as in the September days, there was no despondency, no hysteria, no panic. If the Germans invaded, the island might well be occupied, but Britain would carry on from Canada the campaign that France had refused to carry on from North Africa.

– ⧗ –

After June 10th, many of the Italians then living in Britain were arrested. Most were deported to Canada and of these a large number perished when the *Arandora Star* was sunk by the Germans – among them one of Speranza's best and oldest friends, who had helped him generously on various occasions and who, though an anarchist, had a deep admiration for the British way of life. There were plenty of sincere anti-fascists among those who reached Canada safely. Speranza was able to get some of them, whose integrity and courage he could vouch for, set free and given a chance to take part in the war against fascism.

A few months after the fall of France, New York saw the arrival of the first of the exiles whom the British Navy had helped to escape from France, or who had managed to reach the unoccupied zone. Like other exiles who had been living in the United States for years and who did not, like the communists and a few non-communists, put hatred of Britain above everything else, they were anxious to do all they could for the war effort. They began to organize Free Italy groups all the way from Canada to the Argentine, and to counteract fascist propaganda among the Italian Americans in the western hemisphere. They also sent representatives to Italian prisoners-of-war, numerous since the first successful British offensive in Africa and the unexpected Greek resistance in Albania. Other plans included the formation of an Italian Legion (to be responsible to a committee representing democratic Italy), and initiatives in Italy which sounded romantic, were certainly courageous, and some of which were actually carried out.

Speranza went to New York to see what help he could give. Unable for the time being to join the army, this – little though it was – was better than nothing. He could help exiles who had not left Europe in time in June, and who were stranded in Lisbon, southern France, and North Africa. Many were able to get to America, among them members of *Giustizia e Libertà* as well as socialists, republicans and anarchists. After June, 1941, Speranza helped some communists and ex-communists to reach Mexico.

– ⊠ –

In a few months, with the support of pro-Allied Italian Americans, the exiles succeeded in making the Allies and others realize that there was an alternative to fascism, that Mussolini's fall would not leave a vacuum, that there were enough democrats to bring Italy back into the fold of free nations. This rendered futile the attempt made in Italy to change the fascist war into a national war and to bring about a 'sacred union' based on patriotism.

The Free Italies formed in Commonwealth countries before the end of 1941, were joined by the Mazzini Association of the United States and Mexico and by the Free Italies of Argentine, Uruguay, Central America and other countries. The Mazzini Associations had refused to admit communists, who after the invasion of Russia had suddenly become enthusiastic supporters of the Allied war effort: they organized Garibaldi Associations which also had intervention as their main objective. The exiles' initiatives had considerable importance in the Western Hemisphere. Most of the six million Italian Americans in the United States passed from a pro-Axis to a pro-Allied position. The same happened, on a smaller scale, in the Argentine where a third of the population is of Italian origin, and in Brazil where one-sixth is of Italian origin.

There was no central committee to coordinate these organizations, but public opinion recognized in Count Sforza their main spokesman. (The British government had arranged for Sforza and Tarchiani to leave France at the moment of the collapse and had helped them to reach the United States.) Some would have liked the Free Italies and Mazzini societies to become the basis for a government-in-exile, like those in London and Cairo. But common sense prevailed: a government-in-exile would have meant mortgaging Italy's future, anticipating events, and affirming what nobody could be sure of – that when fascism fell, the Italian nation would support the semi-socialist secularism which was the main characteristic of non-communist anti-fascism.

With the attack on Pearl Harbour and the United States' participation in the war, the activities of Italian exiles among their fellow countrymen in the Western Hemisphere lost much of their importance. Efforts now turned once again to Italy where the clandestine movements were being reorganized and contacts maintained through Vichy France. During 1941 and the beginning of 1942, a number of Italian exiles had been helped to reach America. Now it was Speranza's job to help those who were willing to go back clandestinely to Italy. Britain's cooperation with the resistance movements in France, Belgium, Holland, Norway, Czechoslovakia and Poland had borne fruit. Sometimes even a little help from outside was enough to create serious difficulties for the nazis and their puppets.

The net which already covered occupied Europe had to be stretched to include the Axis countries. It was no simple matter to select from those who volunteered for the hardest of all wars, the underground war. The returning exile needed many qualities – a strong character, steady nerves and the gift of leadership; unable to rely on anyone else, he had to have strong convictions. The British and Americans could provide the means – boat, submarine or plane – of reaching German-occupied Europe; once there, he was entirely on his own with no other guide than his own conscience.

The return of exiles, few though they were, had an important bearing on future developments in Italy. The alternative to fascism could not be represented by people who were outside the country. By the end of 1942, the *fronde*, maybe anti-German but still fascist, seemed the most likely group to take over in case Mussolini were to fall. (The many fascists who tried to get in touch with the Allies at Lisbon, Berne, Ankara and Stockholm were all *frondeurs*.) The *fronde's* attempt to salvage fascism by replacing the pro-Hitler policy with one similar to that of Vichy France was weakened when the anti-fascists returned to Italy during the war. Their presence not only reinforced the resistance as the Allies – especially the British – had hoped; it also increased the chances of putting an end to fascism in all its forms.

— ⧗ —

After trips to Canada for meetings with exiles volunteering to return to Italy, Speranza went to Central America. He already knew that, in Mexico as in Venezuela, in El Salvador as in Colombia, the pro-nazi authoritarian groups were in the ascendant, that dislike of the British and of the *gringos* (North Americans) often created situations favourable to Germany and Japan. Those who wanted to maintain the superiority of the whites, who dreamed of a mystical *hispanidad*, or were determined to prevent the emancipation of the peasants, were a hundred percent in favour of European fascism and its Far Eastern partner. If the war in the Eastern Hemisphere were to be won by the Axis, Germany and Japan would have found in some Latin American countries excellent bases for a final attack on the United States.

In Central America there was a wireless station of some strategic importance, since local groups helped the nazis to use it to keep in touch with German submarines attacking Allied shipping in the Caribbean. The station might also be very useful to the Japanese. Speranza was asked to put it out of action. He had to solve the problem of crossing the border unnoticed, and without leaving any traces, so no passport could be used. The river forming the boundary was wide and turbulent, and for most of the year had a good many alligators in it. He decided to try swimming across, and managed to reach the opposite bank. As he dried himself off among the reeds during the still hours of a hot night, he thought how strange it was, here in the Western Hemisphere which was still at peace, to be doing what so many others were doing in Europe where the war was going on. (It was before Pearl Harbor.) Nominally the Americas were still at peace, but this was only an illusion; things had gone so far that there could no longer be any neutrality, and even those who professed to be neutral had to be on one side or the other.

When the sun was high, Speranza started off towards a village that was indicated on his rather inaccurate map. He soon found that he had crossed the wrong river; or rather, the river had changed its course and he had crossed the old river bed, also filled with water, and was still on the same side of the border – and too exhausted to try again. He had to go back on his tracks; after hiding from the patrols for several hours in the long grass, he got back to his starting point. Next day he made another attempt, which also failed. The third succeeded. When he reached his destination two other exiles helped him to carry out the mission. The wireless station did not collapse, but the bang was enough to frighten off the nazis and their sympathizers and it was no longer used for communicating with German submarines.

— ⧖ —

Mexico City had become what London must have been after the revolutions of 1848 and 1849 on the Continent, when Metternich, Louis Philippe, Mazzini, Kossuth and Marx, as exiles, shared British hospitality. From Austrian legitimists to Spanish anarchists, through all the gradations of the political rainbow, exiles of all creeds and of all countries could be found there. Thousands of Spanish Republicans forced to leave Spain after the fall of Barcelona and Madrid had come to Mexico in 1939. They were soon followed by thousands of refugees from the countries taken over by the fascists. All these added to the usual exiles from other Latin American countries.

192

The vicissitudes of the war were followed with a passion that was more than political; for most, victory of one side or the other meant the difference between being able to go home and life-long exile. If some Mexicans favoured the Axis, there were only two groups among the exiles and refugees – those who preferred the Western powers to the USSR, and those who preferred the USSR. Here was a repetition of what Speranza had experienced during the previous twenty years. What divided those who wanted progress and change was liberty, the same old problem of liberty, of whether people could live peaceably together or not, no matter what opinions they held. On one side there in Mexico were communists and left-wing socialists who wanted government by force. Liberals and radicals, Christian democrats and democratic socialists, were able to work together because in spite of the the great difference which separated them, they shared the vision of a state which embodied the freely expressed wishes of its citizens; and because they all agreed on the motto adopted by an association of Spanish, Catalan, Italian, German, Belgian, Austrian and other exiles all alike convinced that their own liberty involved respect for the liberty of the others: *No hay Libertad sin Libertad.*

CHAPTER VI

Two Years of War[1]

M*exico City, January 20th, 1943*: Yesterday I had a phone call from the British Consulate. My old application to enlist in the British Army has finally been accepted. I am asked to go to London as soon as possible. I feel much relieved. For years I have been convinced that fascism would lead to war, and that when it came it was one's duty to fight; I preached intervention yet stayed out. . . . Now I can be at peace with myself.

Mexico City, January 30th, 1943: I have settled my affairs as best I could. Joyce and the children will go back to the States in April and stay there for the duration. It is hard, extremely hard, to leave the family. I can scarcely believe my luck that Joyce has put up with me; she didn't leave me when I was in prison; she married me when I had no money, no career and no prospects of either; she has put up with this continuous moving about and my frequent absences – she knew about some of my enterprises, and worried, but never tried to hold me back. She has never even hinted that I should forget that I am a political exile, that I should settle down and make a home for the children and think of a career. Cynthia is six, Clement is three and they haven't yet had a home. Maybe I am cruel to them.

---

1 This chapter and the following have been compiled from letters, an intermittent diary, and reports written between January, 1943, and May, 1945.

I have said goodbye to Goltz[2] who does not understand my eagerness to leave: war is a very ugly thing; one fights if one must; why not stay out of it as long as one can?

I have seen the Pierleoni brothers, Valiani, and other friends.[3] They want me to help them to get back to Europe to carry on the work interrupted by the German invasion. They are tired of the increasing quarrels and arguments among the small group of Italian anti-fascist exiles here. I have done what was possible, but without much success; only four or five of them will be helped to reach England, from where they will make their way to occupied Europe. Our Spanish fiends are rather disheartened: their position is somewhat like ours was three years ago – if Franco comes into the war on either side, sooner or later he will fall and the republicans will again get the upper hand in Spain. If he keeps out of it, he will stay in power. With the Allies in Africa he will not dare to side with the Germans; with the Germans at the Pyrenees, he will not dare join the Allies. So the dictatorship is likely to continue.

Los Angeles, February 2nd, 1943: I have seen Korda, and thanked him for what he has done – through the job he gave me I have been able to earn a living for the family

2 The author was employed by Sir Alexander Korda as literary agent for United Artists. J. Goltz was the head of the United Artists office in Mexico City.

3 Bruno and Renato Pierleoni: two skilled workers who were members of G.L. had lived in exile and worked in Lyons. After the surrender of France in June, 1940, they had escaped to North Africa and then made their way to Mexico. Leo Valiani had spent seven years in a fascist jail for his underground activities. He later became a member of the supreme organ of the Resistance in German-occupied Italy. He is now a bank official and a leader of the Radical Party.

196

while doing some useful political work in Mexico. As his sympathies have been with the Allies ever since war broke out, I decided to tell him what I had done: that I had made use of my stay in Mexico City to obstruct the activities of nazis and their friends, to help Italian and German refugees to get back to Europe, and to organize among the large foreign community a pro-Allied group to neutralize nazi and franquist propaganda.

New York, February 6th, 1943: I shall have to stay here two or three days, until my visa, passport, etc., are ready. I had hoped to fly the Atlantic, but I have to go by sea from Halifax. German submarines are not an attractive prospect.

I have used this unexpected delay to see Tarchiani and Cianca, and to get some idea of how things are going for Italian exiles. The situation is very different from what it was two years ago when most Italian-Americans were sympathetic to fascism, and isolationist. Some of the Italian fascists have gone back to Italy; others asked to stay here, claiming that they had always admired American democracy, that they hated the Axis, that they wanted to work for the Allies. Apparently one of them, before leaving the fascist office where he was employed, made off with $14,000. Another conveniently remembered that he had a brother who was an Italian admiral, and put himself at the disposal of the American Intelligence. One big industrialist and former fascist official asked asylum on the pretext that he had been fighting the dictatorship for years. The American propaganda offices are full of such people, and of refugees whose democratic convictions date only from the racial laws of 1938. This set-up is rather unedifying: it is all very well for older people to work on propaganda, but there are too many young people fighting the war comfortably on the air waves from New York.

The only reliable people, of course, are those who have always opposed fascism. For them war does not mean staying safely in America, they are longing to get to North Africa, from where it should be possible to make contact with Italy again. The two men I sent to South America have done excellent work among Argentinians and Brazilians of Italian origin, especially those belonging to workers' organization. It hasn't taken much of an effort to make the 'Free Italies' grow everywhere in the Western Hemisphere; the initiative of a few exiles has snow-balled. When Sforza speaks, he is no longer just an isolated individual, but the representative of hundreds of thousands of Italian-Americans and Italians in both Americas. Pacciardi still dreams of legions but very few are willing to become legionaries; those who want to fight prefer to join the American forces which guarantee greater economic security to the families. As in Mexico, the Italian communists, after the failure of their approaches a year and a half ago, try to sabotage where they cannot lead. Their 'party line', now that the danger of a Soviet collapse has passed and they are surer of themselves, seems to be based on the desire to divide the world between the Soviet Union and the United States. They consider Great Britain their chief enemy and the main obstacle (if the Axis falls)to Soviet expansion throughout Europe and Asia.

Halifax, February 16th, 1943: I have been here a week. The security officer says that he will let me know as soon as the ship is ready to sail. It is filthy weather – cold, fog, ice, snow and wind. I knew that Canada had bad winters but I didn't know they were quite as bad as this. I spend most of the day in the library. Today I finished a book by Anna Seghers, whom I knew in Mexico. . . she has a sincere and unshakeable faith in the miraculous powers of collectivism; it would make one laugh if it weren't a tragic example of the evil one can do, intending to do good. I have met a number of Canadians, who all seem to take the war philosophically. They are convinced that the Allies will win and that the Commonwealth will continue to be a pillar of the world. Losses in the Atlantic have been enormous, but things are better now, and German submarines considerably less of a menace.

On board ship, February 18th, 1943: We sail at high tide. We are going alone, without a convoy. The ship is Norwegian. In peacetime she carried bananas, now she is loaded with salt pork. Two of the six passengers are businessmen from Toronto, going 'home' for the first time in their lives. Fine fellows – they have never been to England, yet now they are proud to be risking their lives to see the old country. Then there is an English major who got a DSO in the first world war and drinks whiskey by the gallon. With him is a Yorkshireman, with a broad accent and clumsy hands and a talent for absorbing unlimited quantities of beer. They say they have been in Chile on business; certainly they know all about Chile and everyone who lives there. The sixth passenger is a boy of eighteen, full of enthusiasm at the prospect of joining the R.A.F.

199

On board ship, February 27ᵗʰ, 1943: For some hours now we have been hugging the coast of Ireland. It is a relief to be too near shore for submarines. There was one yesterday evening, but the captain – who has not left the bridge for nine days – sailed right ahead into the fog, and then it grew dark. Today, the danger past, he told us that because of some of the damage or other to the screw the ship had lost several knots. And we were deluding ourselves that we were fairly safe because we were faster than the submarines!

Ireland . . . Everybody sympathizes with the poor Irish, martyrs for liberty under British oppression. For independence perhaps, but not for liberty. If the Irish really had liberty at heart, they would not have given their support to the Germans. It is their doing that so many ships have gone to the bottom and so many lives have been lost, starting with the seventy children on their way to the United States whose ship was sunk in Irish waters. Nationalists are all equally stupid. Italian nationalists have sold their country to Germany; the Irish have turned against Great Britain, who alone can save Ireland from becoming a German province.

— ⧖ —

London, March 1ˢᵗ, 1943: It was already dark when we went ashore at Liverpool. There wasn't a light to be seen, it was cold, and raining hard. On the way from the harbour to the station, we sensed rather than saw the bomb-damage . . . there were black voids where houses had been, and the pavements were covered with bricks in neat rows, as though the builders would be using them in the morning. All was silent, except for the sound of the rain. By the half-light inside the station faces looked weirdly pale, like ghosts. I was told that if ever men and women had been near to utter exhaustion, it was the people of Liverpool a few months ago. But there, as in London in 1940, the Luftwaffe called off its attacks only a few days – perhaps a few hours – before the breaking point was reached.

We got to London late at night. The two Canadians have gone to the Savoy, and I have put up at a hotel near the station. This morning I phoned the War Office, and soon afterwards received a visit from a young captain – he did not look very British, he has spent most of his life in Italy – who took me to see his commanding officer, Major Alp. Alp explained that it is up to me to decide which branch of the army to join. He himself is in charge of the Italian section of Special Operations, whose job it is to carry the war into enemy and enemy-occupied territory by getting in touch with Resistance groups, forming others where they are needed and providing whatever help the British Armed Forces are able to give. He told me that both he and his colleagues are aware of the political issues of the Resistance, that their orders are to help all groups indiscriminately, with reference not to their political colour but only to their military efficiency. He said that none of his officers knows much about the Italian situation. Did I feel like joining Special Operations? I said: "Yes, on condition that I am allowed to enlist in the British Army." Once in uniform, I will obey orders to the best of my ability.

Alp assured me that I could enlist at once as a private, and after the necessary training period I would

201

receive a commission. Alp talked, without mentioning names, of help that had already been given by Special Operations to Resistance groups, mainly in France but also in the Netherlands, Scandinavia, the Balkans, Poland and Czechoslovakia. Sometimes Special Operations have cooperated with the information and propaganda services of the Armed Forces, but more often they have been on their own. Their efforts have helped to create effective guerrilla armies in most occupied countries which immobilize a number of nazi divisions, terrify all quislings and make the consolidation of German rule impossible.

My anti-fascist friends are horrified at the idea of wearing an Allied uniform. (Scratch a socialist, Mazzinian or *giellista*, and you still find a nationalist.) I see things differently. It is obviously a question of values. If one is convinced that the war is right and necessary, one should take part in it as a combatant, not as an arm-chair critic or radio orator. There can be no victory without military discipline: better to obey some wrong orders than to evade orders. What I aim at is the collapse of fascism, so that the Italians can once again be free to choose their own government. Many of my friends think an Allied victory will mean that the Allies will just substitute their government for fascism. As I see it, the war will end not in substitution but in liberation. Once they are free, it is the Italians themselves who will have to decide whether they want a republic or a monarchy, unitarian or federal government, private or collective enterprise, the crucifix in the schools or secular education. Rightly or wrongly, I have faith in the British. Whatever the views of the leaders (certainly I could never agree with the conservatives' support of archaic undemocratic foreign monarchies) the British will make it possible for the Italian people to express their wishes freely, to establish representative institutions and to choose their own government. What more can one or should one ask of them? But first we must win the war.

London, March 6ᵗʰ, 1943: Tomorrow I go to camp. For three months I am to train as a Commando, partly in the Scottish Highlands. Then I hope to be sent to Africa, to join either the First or the Eighth Army. Meanwhile I have been reading documents about what little is known by Special Operations in Italy. Alp told me that he had managed to get in touch with active Resistance groups, and that he had doubts whether these were genuine contacts. It looks to me as if they have been bogus, so far. In Switzerland, at Lisbon and elsewhere all sorts of people have presented themselves to the British authorities, professing to represent groups – political, trade union or other – belonging to the underground movement. Some Italians who are now naturalized British subjects have reached Italy clandestinely, to make contacts. My impression is that the foreign contacts they have made are either with agents of OVRA or of the fascist information services (political or military); that the 'agents' who have gone to Italy have been caught and are speaking and writing under duress. It is hard to be certain, but the underground activities in which these people say that they are engaged are the kind one reads about in thrillers; they bear no resemblance to the reality of conspiracy under dictatorship, as I knew it. They speak of groups and organizations that cannot possibly exist, of activities which sound quite implausible.

I have told Alp that I cannot recognize in any of these reports the activities of either anti-fascists or *frondeurs*; on the other hand it would be absurd to suppose that there are not several groups of *giellisti*, communists and other anti-fascists actively at work, as well as the usual *fronde* (monarchist, military, clerical or business as may be) . . . . The attitude of the fascist government and the declarations of a great many prisoners of war are proof enough that the country is in a considerable ferment. The contact in Lugano, through a member of the Italian consular service, is probably the only reliable one. It is certainly difficult to size up the situation. . . . A year ago a book was published in the United States which gave detailed descriptions of two Italian underground organizations – one with 100,000 and the other with 300,000 members – and this fraud quite took in the Italian refugees who were working with the American information services. My suggestion is to take no notice of the information collected to date, to write off the contacts in Italy, and report to the Cabinet that so far nothing has been accomplished. We must get in touch with the Italian exiles hiding in France (fortunately this project is already under way), and with their help contact the bona fide underground groups in Italy. At the War Office nothing is said about future operations, but it is clear that once North Africa is occupied, the Allies will invade the Italian islands and then the mainland, either in Italy or – which would be preferable – the Balkans.

Contacts through France (now entirely occupied by the Germans), the only ones that are any use, are slow to give results as it takes at least six weeks for a courier to get there and back. Alp is counting on some Italian exiles and ex-prisoners of war who have come to England, to establish direct contact with Italy. But these exiles are mostly recent refugees whose good intentions do not go beyond visiting prisoner of war camps, speaking on the radio or publishing news-sheets. They are not willing to take risks. It is enough to read their *curricula vitae* to feel certain that – except for a few – they will never do anything useful. At no small trouble and expense, Alp sent for Lussu and his wife[4] and helped them to come from southern France to England. He had great hopes of them. Lussu submitted plans which could not be carried out as they presupposed popular uprisings which I am sure are now out of the question. In an invasion attempt taking no account of fortifications, the number of Italian and German divisions and the population's indifference (if not hostility) to the Allies, the Allies were to provide submarines, aircraft and troops; if the plans had been practicable the Allies would have acted on their own. The arm-chair critics who complain of the Allies' lack of comprehension, of their failure to send help to the Resistance, ought to come here and see for themselves the difficulties involved in translating hopes and plans into action. As I see it, the Allies would join forces with the Devil himself to end the war, let alone any individual or group which really means business in fighting the Germans and their satellites.

London, April 23rd, 1943: I have been called to London for the day to see two prisoners of war. One of them is a close connection (brother-in-law, I believe) of the Speaker of the fascist Senate, and offers to return to

4 The author's sister, Joyce Lussu — not to be confused with the author's wife Joyce.

Italy as a liaison between the Allied High Command and the fascist *frondeurs* who, according to him, want to save Italy (and themselves) by getting rid of the dictator and getting the country out of the war. I told Alp, to pass on to whom it may concern, that in my opinion Federzoni, Suardo, De Bono, Grandi and Bottai – the same names always crop up – are not people one can count on. There probably are more *frondeurs* than there are anti-fascists, but they are unreliable and might betray us just as they betrayed the other side before. Let them send this man to Italy and see what he does – but without having excessively high hopes of him.

The other prisoner is quite a different case. This is the second time since I have been here that there has been an opporturnity of making contact with the genuine underground movement in Italy. He is a young pilot who, during a reconnaissance flight over the coast of Tunisia, landed on the island of Galite. A few days earlier he had been in Naples, his home town. He was, he said, the spokesman of a group in Naples which was led by active opponents of the fascist dictatorship. Among the names he gave me were those of Bonelli and Palermo, who had worked with *Giustizia e Libertà* years ago, and this as well as other details convinced me that his story was genuine. Both Alp and the General seemed unconvinced. They have had so many disappointments where Italy is concerned – not knowing how to separate the chaff from the grain – that their scepticism is understandable. Their chief preoccupation is that the Germans might use the Italians as decoys to trap the Allies. It is up to them to decide. My feeling is that this prisoner can be trusted.

London, June 10th, 1943: The situation in the British camps where Italian prisoners of war are held tallies with Lussu's reports from Malta, Vittorelli's from Egypt and young Lucio Tarchiani's from India. The men are for the most part apathetic. They don't care whether Germany or the Allies win the war. Either way Italy loses, they say. All that matters to them is the fact that they are now out of it. The officers are preponderantly nationalists full of the usual *clichés* – the King, the flag, honour, the fatherland. (Hardly anyone mentions fascism.) In each camp the nationalists try to make things difficult for those who are considered anti-nationalist because they are against the fascist government. I suppose this corresponds roughly to the situation in Italy – the mass of the people tired of the war, a few fascists, a larger number of short-sighted narrow-minded nationalists who do not understand that Italy can only save herself by getting rid of fascism, that instead of identifying the government with the country, the country should be considered quite separately from the government. As they are incapable of thinking for themselves, these people will not modify their attitude until there is a change of government and of policy. Among both men and officers there are just a few who say, probably without exactly understanding the terms, that they are republicans, socialists, or communists. Their anti-fascism makes life hellish for them in the camps, but it is hard to get them out: to the military authorities a p.o.w. is a p.o.w. and that is that.

Glasgow, June 20th, 1943: After the Commando course I was to have gone on a parachutists' course, but orders came from London to go to Glasgow to meet Tarchiani and Cianca on their arrival from New York. I was pleased to see Garosci with them. Zevi was there too, he seems to have something against the British. Tarchiani and Cianca are glad to have got away from the *imbroglio* of Italian and Italian-American politics in New York. They have done everything that was possible. Thanks to their efforts the Allies have got over their mistrust of democratic anti-fascists, whom they took to be a small group of dreamers without any following. If things in Italy are anything like they are among Italians abroad, fascism might be replaced by democratic forces instead of by the conservative and reactionary *fronde*. In London and Washington people are talking less of Grandi[5] and more of Sforza, less of changes inside the government and more of revolution against it, less of the King and more of what Italian democrats can achieve. This is a satisfactory result of two and a half years' work. There is hope that when the Allies deal with Italy they will be able to avoid the errors they made in relation to Vichy and Franco.

— ⧗ —

Gibraltar, July 6ᵗʰ, 1943: I left England unexpectedly this morning. At nine I arrived at the War Office, where Alp's secretary told me that a plane was leaving shortly. Just time to go back and pack my bags (seven minutes) and make some last-minute arrangements (you know when you leave, but not when you'll come back) and I was ready.

---

5 Grandi, better known than other fascist leaders because he had been Minister of Foreign Affairs and Ambassador to London, was usually considered the leader of the anti-German faction among fascists.

I had known that I would be going soon. The opportunity came as a result of the incident in which Sikorski[6] lost his life at Gibraltar: a special plane was to take some members of the Polish Government-in-exile to Gibraltar. There were two seats to spare, one of them for me. Poor Poland! Italy is unfortunate but Poland is even more so. At least we have the sea; they are hopelessly caught between the Russians and the Germans. Two or three milllion Poles are reported to be in German forced-labour camps, two million in Russian ones – Poland is disintegrating before our eyes.

Algiers, July 9th, 1943: The heat is stifling. I am waiting for my orders. I am to accompany Munthe[7] if and when there is a landing in Sicily. Meanwhile he is in Malta. There are several parachutists at the camp, a few miles west of Algiers. I have seen young men leaving for Corsica and Provence: they are all Gaullists. I would like to talk with the Arabs; they are polite but will say nothing. The French too are mostly reticent. Lavergne,[8] a convinced democrat, teaches at the University. He is a good chap and the only one who is willing to talk freely. I get the impression that most Algerian Frenchmen have been pro-Pétain in varying degrees, supporting Darlan after the arrival of the Allies. At all events I have met very few who have a good word for de Gaulle or Giraud. Of course this is more or

6 General Sikorski was Prime Minister of the Polish Government-in-exile when he was killed in a plane crash.
7 Major Malcolm Munthe, M.C., is the author of *Sweet is War* . . . ., in which he describes his exploits as an S.O.E. officer in Norway and in Italy.
8 Bernard Lavergne, political scientist, had been a professor at the University of Lille until the German invasion. Now he was teaching at the University of Algiers.

less a colony, and I dare say the French people here do not have the same feelings as the French in France, but it is likely that the majority in France are for Pétain too. It is sad. I prefer Giraud to de Gaulle, though his entourage is not to be relied on – ex-Pétainists who have changed too quickly. It is difficult to have any confidence in de Gaulle as a leader. I am sure he dreams of an authoritarian government, something like that of the Valois with a semi-absolute ruler and States General.

Tunis, July 11ᵗʰ, 1943: So, the invasion of the Fortress of Europe is beginning! The news of the landing in Sicily, though long expected and necessary, has distressed me. It probably means war not only on the Italian islands but also on the mainland. War will be terrible for the Italians. It will be a war of expiation. My father always spoke of nemesis in history; I don't believe in it but there may be some kind of historical justice; the British are paying for their short-sightedness, insularity and appeasement; Italians will pay for fascism. A crime being worse than an error, the punishment will be greater. Tragically, those who suffer most won't be the fascists but the masses who were little interested in fascism. But perhaps there is still hope that the war won't spread to the mainland. Control of Sicily and Sardinia is essential for security of the Mediterranean. To attack Germany, there will have to be a landing on the Continent; Churchill insists – rightly, I think – on the Balkans, Roosevelt and his advisers insist short-sightedly on France. Italy would represent a compromise between divergent theories and plans. We must have an air base for attacking Central Europe, but Thessaly in Greece would do as well as the Capitanata around Foggia. I have seen some officers who have returned from Greece: Zervas[9] controls the Epirus, and the ELAS parts of the Peloponnesus and central Greece. As the defence of Crete showed two years ago, Allied troops can count on more help from the population in Greece than in Italy.

Colonel Dodds-Parker,[10] our commanding officer in North Africa, has sent me to Tunis to get in touch with the officers who are in charge of getting us to Sicily, where we will be under Montgomery. The situation in Tunis isn't pleasant. The French are more Pétainist than in Algeria, the Arabs more nationalist. They both detest the large Italian, or rather Sicilian, colony. Certainly the local Italians have done some idiotic things; they have been playing at fascist imperialism for years; at the invitation of the commanders of the Italian forces stationed here, ten thousand young Italian Tunisians enlisted under Messe, I am told. They were taken prisoner before they had fired a single shot. The French want to drive all the Italians out, and the Arabs are of the same mind.

In Algiers there has never been a real group of militant anti-fascists, but in Tunis there were organizations, clubs and newspapers. I would have gone to see Spano, the Sardinian communist, but apparently he already works for Allied Intelligence, and either doesn't want to go back to Italy or, more likely, has lost touch with people there. A group pretending to be connected with the *Mafia* has turned up, busily selling false information. They purposely exaggerate the efficiency of the Sicilian *mafiosi*, just as exiles

9   General Zervas led the nationalist guerrilla bands; ELAS was the organization of communist guerrilla bands.
10 Conservative M.P. since 1945.

from Sardinia, in good faith, exaggerate the efficiency of the underground and the anti-fascism of the Sardinians. All exaggerations discredit the opponents of fascism.

Susa, July 18ᵗʰ, 1943: I have come to see Munthe who is in command of our detachment. He has an inspiring personality and is incredibly brave, but he only has a very vague idea of what he will do in Sicily and knows little or nothing of the situation in Italy. Montgomery, as a regular soldier, is said to have little or no confidence in guerrilla warfare and less sympathy for underground activities in occupied territory, so he can't be expected to give us much support. We ought to enlist the cooperation of the anti-fascists of long standing in Syracuse, now securely in British hands. (I have given Munthe the name of Failla who was at Ponza with me; if he isn't there, there will be some relative or friend of his.) One should find out from them who the active anti-fascists are in Palermo, Catania and other German-occupied centres. Some of us should land on the northern coast of Sicily to organize clandestine groups in the towns and guerrilla bands in the mountains. Apparently none of the Italians are taking up arms against the Allies and there are not very many Germans. A few hundred guerrillas could make a lot of trouble for the Germans; if they could occupy the chief towns before the Allies get there, they would be in a position to keep the administration in their hands; otherwise A.M.G. will have to rely on priests and ex-fascists.

I passed in front of the cemetery where Arturino is buried.[11] He was my age, and we looked like brothers.

---

11   Major Arthur Galletti di Cadilhac, M.C., a cousin of the author.

(Years ago I used his passport to cross the frontier between Italy and Switzerland.) He was killed by a German shell during the last days of the Tunisian campaign. He has left a wife and two children. . . .

— ⧗ —

Somewhere in Sicily, July 26th, 1943: On my return to the airport, I heard on the wireless that the Duce had been arrested. So it is ended. I didn't close my eyes all night except for a few minutes when I had nightmares, seeing flames everywhere. It had been called the comedy of October 28th: well-fed fascist party leaders and retired generals had conquered Rome in *wagons-lits* in 1922. The comedy became tragedy. We had been saying for years that it would become tragedy. How many hadn't applauded it? "Empire!" "Glory" "Rather one day as a lion. . .!" "Kill me if I retreat!" "Eight million bayonets!"

Bravo! On with the applause! Sicily has been invaded, Palermo bombed; and after Palermo will come Naples, Rome, Florence and Milan. The fascist leaders will escape to safety, the generals will run away; it is the ordinary people who will die. Those who said they had no use for liberty will see now whether dictatorship is so wonderful. Ruins and blood will end twenty years of drunken dreaming. The reactionaries who were not fascists but who in their hatred for democracy helped to establish fascism in Italy, are perhaps even more culpable than the fascists themselves, and I hope they get their deserts.

I don't know where I am, but it must be somewhere

near Girgenti.[12] I have never been here before. What a dismal part of the world! Yesterday morning Cooper[13] and I were ordered to go to Syracuse. We left Tunis by plane at about three in the afternoon. I saw Pantelleria, the Gibraltar of the Axis. Towards five the pilot landed on a deserted airfield; he didn't know where he was. I jumped down. . . . I hadn't set foot on Italian soil for ten years, I felt my heart racing. The sun was scorching. The hills were bare. Nothing but ruins were to be seen. I walked over to a few shacks on the other side of the airfield. An old man was there. He told me that this was Palermo airport, that the Germans had only just left, and the runway was mined. The pilot decided to take off again. Luckily we missed the mines, and for an hour or more we flew over the parched hills and grey countryside of eastern Sicily. The pilot wanted to get to Syracuse, but couldn't find his way. We landed once more, on a strip where there were some Allied aircraft. Cooper and I decided to stretch our legs a bit. There was a farmhouse on the hill, but its doors and windows were barred and there was no sign of life. About a hundred yards away there was a small tower, with one room on the ground floor and another above it. A peasant there told us that there were people in the farmhouse. The fascists had said that the Allies were barbarians who would rape the women, murder the children and loot and set fire to the houses. And they believed this? Of course. They had been shown photographs of atrocities committed by them. (How wise the Allies had been not to count on the cooperation of the population when they planned to invade Sicily!)

12 In southwestern Sicily.
13 Captain Richard Cooper, author of *Adventures of a Secret Agent.*

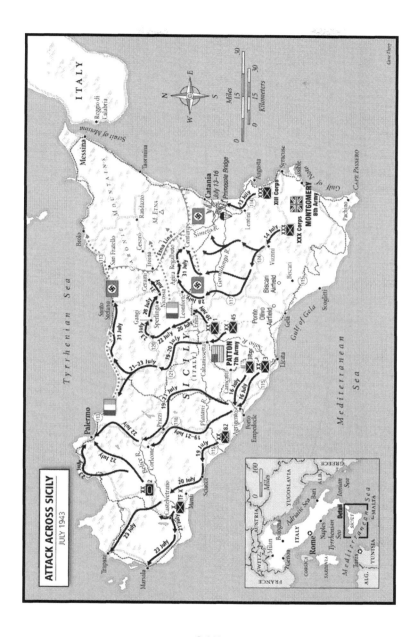

The old man offered us food and we accepted, on condition that he would let us bring him some of our rations in the morning. There was no furniture in his home, just some straw in one corner. The stove consisted of four stones outside the door, the cooking and eating equipment of a large earthenware pot and a few spoons. He set about cooking some spaghetti with tomato sauce. The pot was taken off the fire and placed on a larger stone: our dish and our table. We ate with relish, talking of this and that. The gentry, he said, were fat, the peasants were starving, the workers in the towns – mostly miners in the local sulphur mines – were dying of disease, and the land was yielding little or nothing. What about the fascists? They were like the gentry; they belonged to a different world with which the peasants had nothing in common. This is how I find Italy again. Years have gone by, but the problems are still the same – the rich few and the many poor; not classes but castes; poverty, frustration, bitterness.

Syracuse, July 27th, 1943: If it were not for Cooper, who has ten years in the Foreign Legion behind him, I would still be on my way here. He threw his weight about and got people to take us from one place to another until we found our unit, on the top floor of a building in old Syracuse. German aircraft were passing overhead, machine-gunning. (The whistle of the bullets is a most unpleasant sound.) Two women were hit as we were crossing the market-place. I saw dozens of abandoned Italian light armoured cars on the hills – their white-painted domes looked like upturned wash-basins and reminded me of Don Quixote. A *carabineer* NCO [non-commissioned officer] of whom

216

I asked the way was eager to talk. He described how the Allied parachutists had dropped from the sky, the chaos in the Italian armed forces, the bewilderment of the officers who had no idea what to do, the welter of orders and counter-orders.

"I have never seen such well ordered disorder," he ended by saying.

Syracuse, August 2nd, 1943: The Germans have shot 'Newton'. He is our first casualty on Italian soil. At Syracuse and Lentini we had met some former internees and political prisoners. (I have had the latest news from Ponza and Ventotene, many of my old friends are still there.) We had been told that there were many active anti-fascists in Catania, still in German hands. It seems there had been a meeting of democrats of various tendencies in Florence, with the aim of establishing a dynamic party of democratic republicans. Two young men from Syracuse had offered to go to Catania with 'Newton', who started off with a wireless set hidden in hollowed-out marrows, through No Man's Land. They met a German patrol, and that was the end. 'Newton' was shot under a bridge, and the other two were handed over to the Italian authorities. At least, that is what a prisoner has told us. Poor Newton. It is saddening news. I do not know what his real name was. He sometimes spoke of his mother and the village where he was born, up in the hills. Who knows which hills? He had no one but his mother, who will wait for him for years because there will be nobody to tell her that her son is dead. Perhaps she will delude herself that he is still alive and well, that he has settled in some other country and

217

has forgotten his old mother and no longer wants to come home. . . .

Catania, August 5ᵗʰ, 1943: After weeks of strenuous German resistance, the Eighth Army has entered Catania. There wasn't a living soul to be seen between the river and the city, only corpses along the road. There was a stench of decomposing corpses by the cemetery. At the airport not a single building was left standing. The city itself seemed to have been abandoned. I have been told that only 15,000 of its 250,000 inhabitants are still here; the rest are scattered through the villages on the slopes of Etna, except for those who are buried under the ruins. I have seen some drunken Allied soldiers; I've seen others smashing store shutters and seizing stuff which had to be thrown away because there was nowhere to put it. As soon as it began to get dark the remaining inhabitants crept out, hurrying silently. They went into houses empty-handed and came out with heavy bundles of looted goods. Only the scum of the city is left. The Expiation has begun.

I went to Piazza Cavour to see if I could find P_____. He was not there. An old servant, who had stayed behind to look after her master's belongings, told me that he had left Catania a few days ago to take part in a political meeting. Where? She shrugged her shoulders, "On the mainland."

But I did find D_____, He told me that socialists, communists and former *popolari* (Demo-Christians) had joined in one organization, some national liberation committee, that Badoglio is in serious difficulties on the mainland. "He is trying to be too clever."

That's just it. This cleverness of his will end by putting a noose round his neck, and all other Italian necks too. . . .

Algiers, August 15th, 1943: Colonel Dodds-Parker has sent for me. He asked me to go to Lisbon to see two agents who claim to represent Badoglio and to be authorized to discuss the terms of an armistice. *Badoliani* and pseudo-*badogliani* are turning up everywhere – in Lisbon, Stockholm, Berne and Ankara. I have the impression that most of them are more interested in *imbroglio* than in Badoglio and that their projects are not worth much. It appears that La Malfa is in Lugano, or at least that somebody in Lugano knows where to find him. I told the Colonel that I would rather not go to Lisbon; *badogliani* or no, I would rather let other people have the responsibility of deciding if these agents (a couple of generals) can be trusted. I suggested sending for La Malfa, to know who we were working with. If it is not possible to send for La Malfa, I prefer to go back to Sicily.

The Colonel's lips tightened to a thin line; he said nothing – just like an Englishman! But he has given me to understand that I can go back to Sicily. I do not understand – or rather, I understand only too well – the attitude of Badoglio and the King; they aim to have their cake and eat it too. Once they decided to save themselves by getting rid of the Duce, they should have proclaimed the end of hostilities and a state of absolute neutrality, and should have ordered the troops to defend the Alps. Even if they have not got the eight million bayonets referred to by Mussolini, they must at least have a few divisions. The Germans' first

219

reaction would have been to occupy Italy; if they had met with any resistance they would not have persisted and they might even have come to the conclusion that a neutral Italy would protect them, as Spain protects them in the west and Turkey in the east. The Allies want Sicily and Sardinia. Even if they want Foggia and Capitanata, Italy being out of the war would mean a lot to them, and they would think it over well before attempting a landing on the mainland. Calling an end to hostilities is the one thing that could have saved Italy, but Badoglio is too much of a schemer to think of simple things. Who knows what macchiavellian plans he is hatching? The Allies have no confidence in the new Italian government... how different things would be if there were a complete break with the past, and people like Croce and Bonomi were to form a new Cabinet, joined by those who have spent long years in prison. I am sure that Bauer and Rossi would make first-rate Cabinet ministers.

Palermo, September 4th, 1943: It seems we are going to the Italian mainland.

At Piazza Armerina, on my way across the island, I asked who was bishop now: "Don Luigi's brother."

Now Don Luigi Sturzo would not be at all a bad person to bring here at this juncture. Sforza should be sent for too. The Allies are slow in the uptake. Fortunately our General has authorized Tarchiani and Cianca to come to Sicily. I found them in good spirits and full of energy in Syracuse. If they come with us they will be able to get to the mainland, and perhaps to Rome. The situation in Italy is becoming more and more fluid. Just one person with clear ideas would make for stability and guidance in the right direction. At a time like this two men could do a great deal.

Yesterday evening, at Enna, I was told that the armistice has been signed. Too late: not for the Allies (actually it is just the right moment for them) but too late for Italy. The possibility of Italian neutrality is past, the Allies will fight through the length and breadth of Italy. It is agonizing to think of it.

I have met Graffeo, whom I knew in Syracuse. I have also seen some of his friends. Why do they call themselves socialists when they are really communists? Ingenuous souls ... they must have read quantities of books in recent months. They take one back to the times of the great utopian socialists; they have a child-like conviction that collectivism leads to the abolition of the state, of crime and of poverty, to liberty, happiness and so on. So simple! As simple as believing in paradise.

Here in Sicily autonomists and separatists are suddenly in evidence. The latter, wined, dined and encouraged by the Sicilian Americans who are numerous in the American side of the military administration, have illusions about support from the United States. They dream of Sicily becoming the forty-ninth state of America. I should like to see Sicily autonomous, but within the Italian State, not outside it. Neither autonomists nor separatists inspire me with confidence; they are mainly people who are afraid of revolution on the Italian mainland and want to keep their estates.

The Sicilian Americans seem to have been coached by those who believe that Britain is the real enemy. Fascism, Germany ... these are side issues. The arch-enemy is British imperialism, from which the United States will protect all good Sicilians: Lord Bentinck is not going to return. Since Palermo is in the American occupation zone, we have been instructed not to make ourselves too conspicuous.

— ⌛ —

At sea, September 6ᵗʰ, 1943: We started from Termini soon after midday and are sailing towards the mainland. Our small unit includes four officers: we are an odd assortment! Munthe is the son of a Swede, Gallegos is a Spaniard and Boutigny is French-Levantine. I am the fourth. Altogether we make one and a half Britishers! The NCOs, however are all English (except those who are Scots). Tarchiani and Cianca are with us, also a friend of a friend of Graffeo, who we hope will be useful if ever we are in his part of the country. (He comes from Brindisi.) Our unit has been transferred from the Eighth Army (Montgomery), which has already landed in Calabria, to the Fifth (Clark). Optimism is in the air. The Divisional Command is convinced that the armistice will cause the Germans to withdraw to the Alps at once. I have my doubts: since the Germans have met with no resistance at all from the Italians, they will defend themselves wherever possible with a minimum of troops. At the same time they will hold us in a bottleneck: the mountains that separate Calabria from the rest of Italy are just the place, so are the Abruzzi – one has only to think of the mountains and the narrow strip of land between the Gulfs of Gaeta and Termoli. Failing that, there are the Apennines between Tuscany and Emilia. Hitler knows as much about strategy as I do, which is nil. So he will act as I would, not as his generals would like him to. At all events, it is to be war in Italy.

The Allied fleet is impressive. In the centre sail the LSTs, loaded with guns, munitions and transport vehicles, their prows ready to open like enormous jaws. Flanking them are the LCI, smaller than the LST, carrying men and light equipment. A little farther off are torpedo boats and other light craft, and beyond them the cruisers and battleships. Fighter planes fly overhead. There have probably never been so many ships at one time in the Tyrrhenian Sea since the second Punic War. The water is calm, the sky clear. Who knows what lies ahead?

Paestum, September 10th, 1943: Action has begun, and contrary to what the optimists predicted, it is a full scale battle: furthermore things are not going too well – many are praying that Montgomery will arrive quickly to get us out of this mess[14] . . .

At about one o'clock the day before yesterday, German planes flew over our LST. They came back later and machine-gunned us. No losses. Towards evening the radio broadcast news of the armistice. Too late by six weeks! Is it possible that Badoglio did not know that an armistice signed under pressure of defeat in Sicily, the bombardments and the landing on the mainland, could do nothing to save Italy from invasion? He tried to be so subtle, but it has simply led to betrayal.

When night came the beach was lit up by the flashes of exploding shells. The noise was deafening. Ships

14 Montgomery's Eighth Army had landed at Reggio, across the Strait of Messina and more than 300 miles by road from Salerno, on September 3rd.

and planes kept the projected landing points under intense fire. In the morning there was already talk of difficulties, of furious German resistance (apparently no sign of Italian troops), of Clark's misgivings, of disagreement between the American generals who wanted to stay on board, and the British who were impatient to land. We didn't know where we were, whether we were south or north of Naples. There were rumours that perhaps we would land north of Rome. We left the LST around noon. I was driving a civilian car requisitioned in Sicily. I crept gingerly forward on the pontoon, then on to the beach. On the left, where the sand met the dunes, were a dozen or so blankets in a tidy row; a dead man lay under each one of them, young Americans who would never again see Main Street, the drugstore, the home town where their friends and relations were not too sure just where to find Italy on the map. I bowed my head.

When I looked up again I was startled – Greek columns! I had never seen Paestum, except in photographs. The sun blazed mercilessly on the baked earth. Shells were bursting all around. There were several villages on the hills, and I could see battalions and companies of the 45th Division trying to advance towards them.

Salerno, September 12th, 1943: We very soon realized that there was nothing to do at Paestum except wait to be hit by a shell. By some miracle Gallegos was still alive – we were in a farmhouse and he went to an open window; just as he withdrew a shell burst from a low-flying German plane came in. The only thing was to try to reach Salerno and from there make contact with Naples. It was impossible to use the road, which was partially held by Germans

224

who had made Battipaglia into a fortress. Munthe and I decided to drive along the beach in a jeep, taking Tarchiani and Cianca with us. We would have to cross the Sele – not easy, as it was under fire from German guns.

We left in the late afternoon and managed to reach the bank on the other side of the river. We turned left and got to the sea, then drove slowly along the hard sand. There was no sign of life. Gradually the sounds of battle died away. Along the beach we saw quantities of Italian equipment – helmets, old rifles that our grandfathers had used, the modern muskets our fathers used, a few machine-guns, cartridge belts, jackets and rations – all the signs of a sudden departure. One could easily imagine the scene. The defence of that stretch of coast had been entrusted to Italian troops. The evening of September 8th brought news of the armistice; excitement and cries of "home! home!" . . . the first few vanishing into the darkness towards the main road, throwing off their jackets so as not to be quickly recognized as soldiers . . . others rapidly following suit . . . by daybreak not a man left. For them the war was over.

It should not have been like this. Their duty was to fight the Germans; too many of the officers failed them, demoralized as they were by fascism. Now we must make amends. But even if the Italians lacked the will to help the Allies, the armistice has served a useful purpose and it is clear that the Allies will have to bear this in mind when dealing with Badoglio. The Germans, alone and unaided, have almost prevented us landing. If they had been backed up by even a few Italian battalions, if the weapons thrown away on the beach had been used, the Salerno landing would have failed.

On a bridge we saw an Allied armoured car which had been destroyed by a mine. If it had not got there first, we would probably have been blown to bits. The sound of gunfire grew as we neared Salerno in the dusk. There wasn't a soul to be seen; on either side of the road were ruined buildings and fire-blackened walls. We had no idea whether Salerno was still in our hands, whether it had been reoccupied by the Germans, or whether it was No Man's Land. We broke open a door. On the second floor there was a dentist's brass plate. We went in. Nobody there, nobody in that building or in the others nearby. After a few minutes shells began to fall again; they rained down on the street we had come along and sounded very near. We went to the ground floor, lay down in our blankets in a hallway, and listened for some sound that might tell us whether we were in enemy or friendly territory. Some armoured cars drove past. Germans? We relaxed. Those uncouth words that are the mainstay of the military vocabulary could be coming only from the mouths of British soldiers!

At daybreak I went to the Town Hall with Tarchiani and Cianca. Only three of the municipal staff were still there. Cianca recognized an old friend in the Mayor, a Member of Parliament in pre-fascist days and friend of Amendola, who had withdrawn from public life during the twenty years of the dictatorship, and had been appointed Mayor of Salerno by the Badoglio Cabinet. His age would have entitled him to stay away from trouble. Yet there he was, doing everything possible to keep things in some sort of order. He told us that only a tenth of the population were still in Salerno. Many had been killed in the air-raids, the others had taken to the hills. The area by the sea was

226

in ruins. It is the tragic scene of Catania again, but worse. The only people to stay are those who live in the slums of the old town. They have looted everything they could lay hands on. The supplies of flour have gone, and, of course, the public utilities are now non-existent. Unless something is done quickly, hunger and disease will be here in a few days. The Four Horsemen are galloping side by side.

Salerno, September 28th, 1943: Now we can breathe again, but we have been through two weeks of hell. This war is very different from what was described to us at the Officers' Training College in Milan, thirteen years ago. Except for the dead and a few prisoners, I haven't seen any Germans, although they have been very close and far too active for my liking. So as not to be too much exposed to German gunfire, we had installed ourselves in a house half-way up the hill overlooking the town. Every morning, punctually at ten o'clock, the Germans started firing on the town and the surrounding plains. A salvo of about forty shells whistled past every eight or ten minutes to land a little below us. After three hours they stopped, and started up again in the evening. At night the dry thuds of shells exploding three or four hundred yards away got on one's nerves. Our worry was that they might decide to shorten their range. Whenever I noticed symptoms of hysteria in anyone, I began to talk about trivialities, hoping to give the impression of a *sang-froid* I certainly did not feel. I recommend bombardments to all who suffer from constipation. . . .

Given the situation at Salerno and – during those first days – the fear that the town would be reoccupied by the Germans, Munthe was in a hurry to send Tarchiani and Cianca to relative safety in Capri. First Gallegos went to Sorrento to pick up Croce and his family. At Capri they found fascist *frondeurs*, like Malaparte,[15] now eager to please the Allies, also some ex-internees from Ponza and Ventotene. Among them was Zaniboni who has, heaven knows how, survived seventeen years of prison and internment. At Torchiara we found General Pavone, ready to organize a group of volunteers to fight with the Allies. They will constitute the armed forces of a National Committee organized around Croce. The initiative can succeed if the Italians are united, but if leaders here and in Brindisi start to knife each other in the back (as some have done already), it will fail. Officers who want to get back to the war – on the Allied side this time – are turning up continually. One of the most intelligent of them is a lieutenant-colonel of the Italian Air Force, who told me that during these last months underground anti-fascist groups have been organized among the officers of the Air Ministry, attached either to the Action Party – which consists mainly of members of *Giustizia e Libertà* – or to the Communist Party. A lieutenant of paratroops told me of General Morigi's attempt to make a stand against the Germans at the Futa Pass. If only there had been others like him!

During these last two weeks there wasn't much to choose between staying in Salerno or moving about outside. In the southern outskirts of the town, our jeep was hit by splinters from a shell which landed a few yards away, and gave us a bad fright but nothing worse. Two shots (probably

15 Curzio Malaparte; one of the best-known fascist writers, after the liberation a communist fellow-traveller.

from a sniper hiding in an attic) nearly put an end to me while I was inspecting telephone wires which looked as though they had been put there by the Germans, probably to enable their observers to direct artillery fire. As a result of a reconnaissance drive in the hills above Amalfi I ended up in the church of Maiori which has been converted into a hospital; my head was sewn up, and I remained rather dazed for a couple of days. In Salerno, a German shell exploded a petrol dump and blazing cans flew across the road. If I had been alone I would have turned back; as I wasn't alone I went on, cursing the war. The same thing happened crossing a bridge below Cava, where German shells put our third jeep out of action. Once upon a time horses were killed in battle: now we lose jeeps.

The civilians get the worst of it. Much of the city is in ruins, and every day brings new destruction. When I was in the lower part of the city a few days ago, I heard that infernal whistling noise and just had time to jump behind a pillar. The crash of the explosion was followed by the screams of a woman who had been hit by shrapnel. We took her to the hospital but it was too late. On another occasion I was in the No Man's Land near the Picentino looking for a road to Avellino, when I came to a farmhouse. In the yard were two farmers, one dead, the other wounded. They had been hit by a mine which the Germans had laid in the lane the night before. The widow was screaming like a madwoman; she was surrounded by five children, all very young, who could not quite understand what had happened. Passing by Pontecagnano one day I heard cries; shells had exploded there just a few minutes before, killing and wounding a number of people. At Amalfi I came across a Neapolitan workman. He had had two children. Both of them lay buried beneath the ruins of his home.

Munthe and I have gone with Pavone to meet General Donovan, head of the American OSS. We found him encamped in an olive grove below Capaccio. Donovan, who has considerable funds at his disposal as well as Roosevelt's backing, seems to be disposed to help Pavone as long as he accepts American help exclusively. Let him have it that way, if it gives him satisfaction. The important thing is that Pavone should be able to get things done; his chief aide is Craveri, one of the best men I have come across so far. Thank goodness Valiani, Pierleoni and Gentili have arrived; I am hoping that they will let Garosci, who is still in London or Algiers, I don't know which, come back to Italy soon. Working with the Capri group, they will be able to put into effect a plan which, if left in the hands of Pavone (an excellent man, but old) would probably come to nothing. As soon as the news spreads through Italy that there are volunteers siding with the Allies, even if it is only one battalion, those who want to be active will take heart.

A few energetic people have gone to Naples to see if there is any chance of organizing a popular insurrection which would induce the Germans to leave without atttempting to defend the city; defence would mean destruction. Those who have returned say that things are in a state of great agitation, particularly in the working-class districts. There is no lack of arms, since many soldiers and officers bartered them for civilian clothes after the armistice. But the people who ought to lead the revolt have disappeared from circulation. If they haven't left Naples they are in some cellar and can't be found. The remaining

Italian troops are commanded by generals who apparently still believe that the Germans will win and so do not want to compromise themselves. We hear that armed bands, some call them Partisans, are being formed even among the refugees from Naples on the slopes of Vesuvius.

The situation here is a great deal better than it was in Sicily and Sardinia where there was no group representing a non-fascist Italy, such as the one we have in Capri, and where there was little or no popular support for the fight against the Germans. Let's hope that things go on improving. . . .

Brindisi, October 5ᵗʰ, 1943: Yesterday Tarchiani returned to Salerno from Capri. He told us that Croce, Pavone, Cianca and a few others have formed a Committee of National Liberation to bring together here in the south the political groups which, it seems, have been united by similar committees in Rome and the north. The Committee is sending him to Brindisi with Craveri to talk to Badoglio.

The same evening I happened to hear that my sister had crossed the lines on her way from Rome with messages from the Rome Liberation Committee for the Allied Command. Stopped by American troops, she was handed over to the British. British Intelligence, always cautious lest people who cross the lines turn out to be spies, had sent her to Agropoli. I had not seen her since I was in France a few days before the fall of Paris. I was glad she had managed to get back to Italy, and hoped for news of our parents, of whom I had heard nothing for nearly two years. I went to find her early in the morning, and had no difficulty in getting her released. The officer who took me to her room

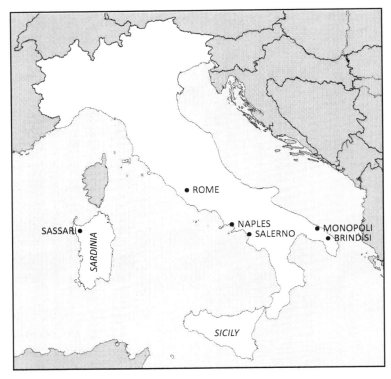

was visibly astonished when she threw her arms around my neck. We have different names, I am in British uniform under an assumed name and she is an Italian who has crossed the lines ... how the hell did we know each other so well? First, we went to Torchiara to see Pavone, who was about to leave for Naples to organize his volunteers there. Then I took her to Salerno to meet members of the Capri group which is now the Naples Liberation Committee, and also Allied representatives who have some influence and knowledge of the situation in Italy.

Apparently things went from bad to worse in

Rome, after the armistice. I suppose it was only to be expected: after twenty years of dictatorship it is difficult to find dynamic people who can keep their heads and handle a crisis. All the same, it is sad. Among all those who might have done something because they had armed forces at their disposition, there wasn't one with the energy and vision to exploit the unexpected opportunity. Carboni, Calvi, Caviglia[16] (the latter an excellent man but much too old): they all waited. . . . But for what? When every hour counted, days went by without anything being done. With a little initiative Italian troops could have kept control of Rome. A provisional government might have been formed; had there been voluntary Italian participation in the war, the past alliance with Germany might have been overlooked, and Italy would have become a belligerent on the Allied side.

My sister uses harsh words: I don't believe that all the Ministers, senior officials and generals were fascists and traitors. Some, yes; the others were simply little men who were unequal to an occasion which called for a measure of greatness. The outcome is that Rome too has been surrendered. The heroism of the hundreds of men who died fighting around Rome under Cadorna, or in Rome itself, rather than let their arms fall into German hands, makes compensation.

It took longer than I expected to get to Brindisi. As we could not use headlights, we spent the first night in a farm near Eboli. The next day we were delayed because the Germans had blown up the bridges across the rivers, and we consequently had to make long detours. At Bari we

16 Two generals and a retired field-marshal who at one moment or another commanded the Rome garrison.

233

spent the night with the Laterzas, friends of Craveri. I was glad to get news of the two Pastena brothers who had done so much for *Giustizia e Libertà* eleven years ago. It seems that after the usual thirteen years in prison and *confino*, Calace, one of the closest friends of Bauer and Rossi, has returned to his home near Bari.

The castle of Brindisi, which houses what remains of the Italian government, is a fine symbol of fascism – an impressive façade which would collapse at the first shots fired. What particularly struck me were the round paunches and gleaming riding-boots of the officers around Badoglio – an army strictly for parade. They find our uniforms very inelegant (they certainly are!). They cannot understand why we have no batmen, and they disapprove of our lack of sharp distinction between officers and other ranks.

Tarchiani and Craveri say that they are satisfied with their conversations. Badoglio told them that he personally only wants collaboration with the Naples Committee and Italian participation in the war against Germany. I think he is just trying to play for time, and Alp, who has arrived in Brindisi, agrees with me. If the King and Badoglio had stayed in Rome, the political scene would have been clear: the Germans would have taken them prisoner, and the Naples Committee would have taken over the government. There would have been one authority. As it is, there are now two governments – Badoglio's, which has associations with the old fascist régime, and the anti-fascist National Liberation Committee. Neither the King nor Badoglio is capable of thinking in terms of the Italian nation, they think only of the monarchy.

Naples, October 10th, 1943: Although Allied troops have been here several days and have reached the Volturno, Naples still seems like a besieged city. The southern zone is just a heap of rubble. The bombardments must have been terrible. Here, as at Catania and Salerno, there is neither water nor electricity, and supplies of food are running short. With a million mouths to feed this is very serious. I passed by Poggioreale; one of these days I will go back and take a look at my cell there.

It is very satisfactory to think that several thousands of volunteers have attacked the Germans.[17] A people's insurrection does more than any speech to show the world where their sympathies lie. The Allied representatives here seem to be beginning to grasp the situation.

Valiani and Renato Pierleoni had left for Rome before I got back to Brindisi. They wanted to get across while the lines were still shifting. Let's hope all goes well. I am certain that they will both render valuable services to the Rome Liberation Committee. My sister has also decided to return to Rome. She has agreed with Munthe on plans to drop arms and explosives near Rome for the use of the Resistance. They need wireless equipment so as to keep in touch with the Allies, arms for the Partisans, and explosives for the underground in the city. They also need money. We are beginning to get a clearer idea of what needs to be done to strengthen the Resistance. Gentili has put himself in charge of a group of young men who are

---

17 In what is known as the Four Days (September 28th to October 1st) thousands of young Neapolitans, without leaders or organization, attacked the troops of the German garrison. The uprising was instrumental in compelling the German command to abandon Naples and to withdraw to the other side of the Volturno river.

eager to cross the lines as soon as possible. They are all first-rate. Italy is beginning to show her worth. Pavone, whose headquarters are besieged by hundreds of enthusiastic volunteers, has organized his own general staff.

We are still waiting for the implementation of General Donovan's promises. I have heard indirectly that Badoglio, in spite of what he said to Tarchiani and Craveri, has informed the Allies that Pavone's efforts are weakening the legitimate government, and that he, Badoglio, could give far greater military aid than Pavone's volunteers. The government versus the nation: it was only to be expected. Munthe has recruited a lot of volunteers too. I haven't much use for small-scale action at the front; the Allied troops are there, and they don't want to be bothered with irregulars. The best thing is to send as many volunteers as possible over the lines into German-occupied territory, to equip the Liberation Committees so that they can take independent action, and not interfere with what the Allied troops are doing at the front.

— ⌛ —

Brindisi, October 25ᵗʰ, 1943: I have been asked to go to Bari to welcome Sforza. He has arrived with his son and Almagià. He wanted to land at Naples, but the brilliant politicians of the Control Commission have decided that before he meets hotheads (!) like Croce, De Nicola and Rodinò,[18] he must have some coaching from Badoglio. They do not understand that it is best to let matters

18   Then the three most distinguished democratic leaders in Naples, two of the Liberals (Croce and De Nicola), the third a Christian Democrat.

develop naturally . . . but I, of course, see things from the liberal point of view. Do they trust Sforza or don't they? If they don't they should not have let him come back to Italy; if they do, they should give him a free hand. This kind of interference only makes for irritation and waste of time. It is absurd to imagine that Sforza wants to make trouble for the Allies. He is probably the most 'Western' of the Italian political leaders, and the one least afflicted with the narrow-minded and selfish nationalism that for generations has poisoned Italy's life.

All I can do is write reports which probably go straight into the wastepaper basket. I have repeated to the Control Commission the suggestions I made to Alp: an embargo on all political activities in the zone of operations immediately behind the front lines – as far back as the military authorities deem necessary; and complete freedom of speech and of political activities throughout the rest of southern Italy. Italian volunteers should be given the training they need for modern warfare. (The experts say that it takes nine months to make a soldier; that is certainly time enough for screening the reliable volunteers from the rest.) The members of the Control Commission are worrying about revolutionary movements which are in my opinion completely out of the question. There are also, of course, unpractical people here and among the exiles who want immediate elections, a Constitution and a new government. Before holding elections, the people of Italy must be in a position to assess various possibilities objectively. This will take at least two or three years of free political activity. It is hard to act rationally the moment one wakes from a deep sleep. Italian minds have slept for twenty years. It will be some time before they think clearly again.

At the Control Commission, the two Americans, Taylor[19] and Stone, know little about Italy. One is a professional soldier who longs to be on active service and the other has a typical business man's political short-sightedness. The British General MacFarlane, whose position at the Control Commission is rather insecure, understands more, but he only knows Italy through the books he read in his youth. To help Rieber of the State Department and Caccia[20] of the Foreign Office, I sketched out a diagram illustrating the distribution of political forces in Italy during and after fascist rule. In fascist days there were:

Active fascists: probably no more than two per cent of the adult population – some of them fanatical enthusiasts, the others mere opportunists.

Supporters of fascism, or those who acted as fascists without being fascists at heart: the Crown and devout monarchists, military and civilian bureaucracy, landed proprietors, big business and the clergy – altogether a very considerable minority.

Active anti-fascists: altogether as numerous as the convinced fascists, two-fifths of them democrats of various shades, three-fifths communists and fellow-travellers.

The rest of the population, shouting *evviva!* but basically apathetic and indifferent to political problems.

As soon as the pressure of the dictatorship was removed,

19 General Maxwell Taylor, later American Chief of Staff.
20 Samuel Rieber; later United States representative in the Allied Commission for Austria. Sir Harold Caccia; later permanent Under-Secretary at the Foreign Office, and British Ambassador in Washington.

there would be:

Irredeemable fascists: not more than one percent of the population.

Devout Catholics: people whose first obedience is to the Vatican and its political instructions; about two-fifths of the nation. (Most of the former supporters of fascism would be found among them.)

Marxists (socialists and communists): approximately another two-fifths (the communists are likely to be more numerous than they were in 1922).

Democrats (liberals, republicans, social democrats and other groups), divided on economic and social questions, divided also on the question of a parliamentarian monarchy versus a parliamentarian republic, but agreeing on the superiority of liberty over authoritarianism, of free institutions over coercive institutions.

It is impossible to say how many of the Catholics and the socialists will prefer liberty to authoritarianism, either for conviction or for opportunism: if there are many, democracy will work, otherwise it is bound to fail.

But to return to the present. . . . The best thing to do is to let the various political forces find their own level and regroup. Violent clashes among them are unlikely because people are tired and because no one will make a move as long as Allied troops are about. I said, in conclusion, that now that some measure of liberty has returned to Italy, it seems absurd to expect the survival of a government of fascist fellow-travellers and and ex-*frondeurs,* as Badoglio's. Caccia listened attentively and said that he would pass my comments on to the right quarter – probably the waste-paper basket under his desk.

As often happens where there are well-meaning people, the Control Commission is now working in two opposite directions simultaneously. On the one hand it is restoring liberty, trying to understand what the majority of Italian people want and (especially where the Americans are concerned) doing all it can to act according to their wishes; at the same time it manages to give the impression (by some of its actions) that it supports only the interests represented by Badoglio and the King. It is true that it would hardly be decent for the Allies to throw out Badoglio and the King, to whom they owe, if only indirectly, the success of the Salerno landing and also the cooperation of the Italian fleet, which has proved to be a valuable asset. But it could be made clear – and is actually true – that their recognition of the Brindisi government is neither absolute nor permanent. Perhaps all this is unimportant as one day there will be free elections; nevertheless the present attitude of the Control Commission does nothing to dispel dislike for the Allies, particularly for the British, which fascist propaganda has succeeded in instilling in the Italian people.

Monopoli, November 10ᵗʰ, 1943: What the higher-ups decide becomes law for their subordinates. Since the Control Commission has decided that the Brindisi set (the King and the Badoglio Cabinet) represents the legitimate government and that the Liberation Committees are run by irresponsible hotheads without much following among the Italian people, Alp and his collaborators have decided that the Resistance in German-occupied territory must be contacted and organized through *badogliani.* There is a practical reason for this decision: since the end of October, members of the Italian military Intelligence have crossed the lines and kept in constant touch with Brindisi by radio. I have tried to explain that Intelligence is not the same thing as Resistance; that the two must be dealt with separately – as the British Army has recognized since the beginning of the war; that the organizers of the Resistance are people very different from those useful as Intelligence agents. As far as one can tell, the Resistance groups are being organized mainly by anti-fascists, who may be willing – to some extent – to work with Badoglio and all that he stands for, but who would certainly never consider themselves *badogliani*. Sending followers of Badoglio as Allied representatives and as liaison officers can only be detrimental to the good relations between the Allies and the Resistance. The Liberation Committees represent the break with the past, and should be approached by people who have no connection with the Brindisi government. Otherwise, instead of encouraging the Resistance, the Allies will run the risk of paralysing it.

Alp and Commander Holdsworth, our CO in Italy, are not convinced by my arguments, but they have allowed Munthe, whose opinions concur with mine, and his group at Naples to try on their own initiative to establish relations with the Rome Committee of National Liberation, and have agreed to make supplies available to him for this purpose.

By piecing together scraps of news from here and there, it is possible to get some idea of the situation in German-occupied Italy. The fascist state has collapsed completely. The Social Republic[21] is just a faction like – perhaps less than – the Brindisi Cabinet. The Germans are in control; in a remarkably short time they have managed to establish their authority over the regions which interest them; the seven divisions they had on July 25th had become seventeen by September 8th; now there are probably over twenty. Anti-German Italians are supporting the Committees of National Liberation (CLN) in the towns, and the partisans in the mountain districts.

Who are the members of the CLNs? It is easy to guess: the core consists of the tens of thousands of active anti-fascists who kept the underground movement alive during the dictatorship. The communists are probably the largest group, but are not the majority; then come the *azionisti*, then the followers of the other political parties; they have been joined by a mass of new anti-fascists, mostly young people, and others who are mainly motivated by their hatred of the Germans. Things are changing. Anti-fascism has generally been anti-nationalist. Today anti-fascism is the skeleton of a movement which has its feet firmly planted in nationalism – or just patriotism.

As for the Partisans, little accurate information is available. At Brindisi, Badoglio claims that they are mostly units which survived the army's disintegration following the

---

21 Freed by the German Major Skorzeny from his imprisonment shortly after the Salerno landing, Mussolini had proclaimed a Social Republic and had organized a puppet government in German-occupied Italy, with HQ at Salò on Lake Garda. Clandestine Committees of National Liberation were organized simultaneously in hundreds of towns and villages; they were composed of representatives of three to seven anti-fascist parties – from Right to Left, Christian Democratic or Catholic Party, Republican Party, Action Party (built largely on what had been *G.L.* and with a similar programme). Labour Party, Socialist Party and Communist Party.

armistice. The names of some of the commanding officers, particularly in Piedmont and Venetia, seem to bear this out. Others, who are less authoritative but closer to the feelings of the people, affirm that the Partisans are the troops of the Committees of National Liberation. It may well be that in some of the Alpine districts, particularly Venetia which is more exposed to German pressure, the Partisans are ex-officers and soldiers of the regular army. Elsewhere, as far as I can make out, they are mostly civilians from the cities, directed by the CLNs. Thus the Partisans above Giaveno are mainly from Turin, those on the Grigna are Milanese, and those at the Scoffera come from Genoa. Also there are bands owing their existence to the initiative of some one man able to muster a number of stragglers eager to escape the German occupation; such bands are unconnected with a central political or military organization; apparently there are several of them in Valdossola.

There is not much Partisan activity in central Italy; until now I have only heard vaguely, through escaped British p.o.w.s, of a few bands in the Sabine Hills, on the Maiella, and on the mountains east of Spoleto. Ex-prisoners of war, who have escaped from the camps in central Italy, are constantly turning up. They talk about the help the peasants gave them. They are never able to give us accurate information about the Partisans, which probably means that there is not much to give. The lack of accurate news and the slowness of our communications with them make it difficult to organize the sending of badly needed supplies.

— ⧗ —

Naples, December 5ᵗʰ, 1943: Munthe's plans to drop supplies by parachute in Rome have failed. For one reason or another the equipment doesn't reach the Military Command of the Committee of National Liberation. It gave me immense satisfaction to learn that in both the Committee and the Command are friends with whom I worked years ago. In Algiers there are several people who want to make parachute landings, but either the weather is bad or the pilot cannot find the exact spot agreed on, so something always prevents their being dropped in occupied Italy. Lack of success is preying on our minds. Clearly the Rome Committee (which acts as the supreme organ of the Liberation movement in German-occupied territory) needs supplies of every sort, and its ability to function depends partly on our ability to furnish them. If we don't succeed in getting supplies to the Committees, the *badogliani* will be the only ones to receive aid. If their influence grows, the chance of the complete change essential for the regeneration of Italy will be jeopardized.

It isn't easy to get through the lines now that the front is stabilized. The attempt made at Mignano, first by Cooper, was a complete fiasco because of continual firing from all directions. The lower Garigliano[22] seemed a likely area: a strong swimmer could reach the farther bank in a few minutes. But when it was tried, German patrols were found to be on the look-out on the other side, and after shivering all day in the undergrowth, the men had no choice but to swim back as soon as if grew dark. Below Castelnuovo in the direction of the Meta mountains, Cooper and I explored the valley between the American

22 During the winter of 1943-44 the German right flank rested on the Garigliano river.

and German lines until two in the morning. It looked as if one could get through, but of the five young men who had been Gentili's trainees during the past weeks, and who tried to get over the mountains that night, four were forced back by German gunfire and the fifth, Pintor, failed to return. We went to search for him in the afternoon. I saw his body lying in a field, but a land-mine which knocked me out made us aware that we were in a mine-field, and prevented us from bringing him back for burial. However, we got a good idea of German defences in that area, so were able to warn the American commanding officer at Castelnuovo not to send out the two patrols which were to have reconnoitred the valley that night. Pintor's death may have saved several other lives. I was lucky again, I got off with slight shock and a spattering of blood on my uniform.

The British Admiral in Naples ordered a Special Operations naval officer to examine enemy defences along the coast near Torre d'Astura. The officer reported that the coastline was undefended. That seemed very odd. (He hadn't gone ashore, so how did he manage to see, in the dark?) Further reconnaissance revealed barbed wire and gun-sites.

Avellino, Benevento, Venafro, Isernia. . . . The farther north I go, the more devastation I see. In one village, the Germans allowed the inhabitants half an hour to get out. As one family was late leaving, they shot the children. Thousands upon thousands of Neapolitans pass along the roads; they walk in single file, most of them barefoot – it is cold in winter here – their clothing in shreds and damp with the rain. It is known as the Black Market, but I call it a people's determination to survive (not to restrict it is

245

probably the wisest thing Poletti has done[23]). They plod through Irpinia and Sannio[24] to barter what few things they can spare for a few kilos of flour, a piece of lard, or a hen. AMG does not know what to do. They have restored the public utilities and cleared some of the rubble from the roads, but they cannot feed a million hungry people. The Allies grumble because their rations are stolen, but what can they expect when people have to watch their own children starving? Even military rations, whether stolen or given, are only a drop in an ocean of misery. Those who can't get rations one way or another are the ones I meet on the road.

— ⌛ —

Sassari, December 8th, 1943: After a month spent travelling to the front and along the coast, I have been sent to Sardinia to see if, among the quarter of a million men stationed on the island by the fascist government, there are any officers and soldiers who would go and join the Partisans in occupied Italy. At our HQ in Monopoli they are beginning to discover that Intelligence officers and agents – British or Italian – do not do much to further Resistance. Apart from General Morigi, who welcomed me very cordially, I have met coldness, if not actual hostility, everywhere. Most officers are out-and-out fascists or nearly so. They belong to another age, with their well-cut uniforms and polished riding-boots. They might have been able to fight well in the Crimean War, but they have not

---

23 Colonel Poletti, who had for a short while been Governor of New York State, was in charge of the administration of Naples.
24 Two mountainous districts in southern Italy.

the slightest understanding of this one. They are obsessed by the idea of French imperialism, and still convinced that Germany will win the war in the end. I would not be surprised if some were surreptitiously in touch with the Social Republic. The best volunteer I have found comes from an Alpine valley. According to him, both officers and soldiers in Sardinia are living in an atmosphere of suspicion and intrigue.

The island is beautiful; the poverty everywhere is heart-breaking.

— ⧗ —

Algiers, December 16th, 1943: I have come here to see some of the young men Gentili and Garosci have assembled, who are waiting for an opportunity to be dropped by parachute in or near Rome. Some consider themselves communist sympathizers (they, too, like most Italian communists I have met who had not been exiles, pin their hopes on the utopian socialism of 1830), while others are *Azionisti*.[25] One mission has been flown to Italy since I arrived here, and everything went well. With the news that reaches here from France and Switzerland, one gets a more complete picture of the CLN and Partisan activities. Evidently the CLN are consolidating, and there are beginnings of some cohesion between what previously were innumerable separate initiatives. Even allowing for exaggerations on the part of the couriers, there are more Partisan groups than we had thought. In Brindisi they are mistaken in asserting that the population of German-

---

25 Members of the Action Party.

occupied territory recognizes Badoglio's authority; most of the underground and the guerillas recognize the authority of the CLN In Italy there are none of the conflicts which weaken (sometimes with bloodshed) the Resistance in France and the Balkans – a sign, this, of seriousness and maturity. Like the one in Naples, the Rome CLN, or CCLN (Central Committee of National Liberation) includes representatives of six political parties, while in the Milan CLN only five parties are represented. I am interested in the renaissance of a Liberal Party, but I wonder whether it will be liberal with a capital 'L' or a small one. I would like to think that liberalism might be the basis of the new Italian state; but if my appreciation of the political picture is correct there are too many marxists and clericals for that.

Naples, December 24ᵗʰ, 1943: Munthe has returned from our HQ on the Adriatic.

"We are obliterated," he told us sadly. Because of the many failures in our attempts to contact the Rome CLN , the autonomy of our group was coming to an end, and we were put under the direct orders of Commander Holdsworth.

We have received orders to move to the Adriatic coast. Contacts with the Rome Resistance (both the CCLN and the *badogliani*) are now entrusted exclusively to the Americans.

Naples, January 20ᵗʰ, 1944: Our stay at Monopoli was short. We have to take part in a new landing. Let's hope it will not be as bad as Salerno. This time we are attached directly to the 15ᵗʰ Army Group. I have brought young Federici here and have put him in the care of Gentili. He was sent to us by the Military Command of the Rome CCLN. The failure of all efforts to send them supplies has been a blow to them, as it has been to us. In Rome, part of the Resistance gravitates round the CCLN, most of the rest round the *badogliani*, who appear to have large sums at their disposal; there are also a few autonomous groups. The Rome CCLN ought to become the provisional government when the day of liberation comes. Naturally at Brindisi they will not hear of this. I hope that the next congress of CLNs in liberated territory, at Bari, will clarify the situation. I have been busy arranging transport for Croce and Sforza, whose presence at Bari is indispensable. The success or failure of the congress depends on Croce and Sforza more than on anyone else. A firm stand by them will encourage the CLNs in occupied territory, and will discourage the Badoglio faction and the Control Commission. Leaving political sympathies aside, I believe that the strengthening of the CLNs in the liberated part of the country would greatly stimulate the whole Resistance in enemy-occupied territory.

At Monopoli I met a great many Greeks and Yugoslavs who are engaged on the same task as we are. They are not too happy. They are fighting among themselves even more than against the Germans. Opinions are divided, even among our officers whose job it is to provide liaison with the Greek and Yugoslav Resistance. Those who have come back are usually enthusiatic about the Partisans with whom they have worked, and refer to the Partisans of other colours as German agents. The worst thing that could happen in Italy would be to have a similar set-up;

that could lead to a very long occupation of the country. I suspect that this is wanted, pehaps unconsiously, by the Brindisi faction who are convinced that they will not be able to hold on to the government if the country is free.

Boatloads of people are constantly arriving on the coast of Puglia, from the German-occupied Marche and Abruzzi. Apparently there are effictive, though few, Resistance groups on the Apennines, the best of them on the Maiella and the Gran Sasso. But there are others on the Sybillines, on San Vicino and father north as far as Monte Catria.

Fenoaltea, one of the 'Young Liberals' I knew in Rome twelve years ago, was to have come to us instead of Federici. It is good to know that there are people who have managed to be active in the underground all these years. Fenoaltea tried to cross the lines, but had to turn back. Federici tried several times, and finally succeeded in Val di Sangro. I hope that when Garosci and Di Ruggiero,[26] who landed by parachute last month on Monte Gennaro, arrive in Rome, it will be possible to establish regular contact once more. Through the OSS a CCLN deputation has arrived here: a communist-inclined Socialist, a Liberal and a Demo-Christian. Their presence will add to the importance of the Bari Congress.

— ⧗ —

Anzio, January 30th, 1944: Instead of the magnificent weather that helped us at Salerno, here we have had to <u>contend with </u>heavy seas, an overcast sky, cold and wind.

26 Corrado Di Ruggiero: son of the philosopher Guido Di Ruggiero, later Minister of Education.

Whenever the sky clears a little, German aircraft are active and there are more of them than there were at Salerno. Our hopes of getting to Rome quickly are still only hopes. Munthe is in command of our detachment; with us are Tarchiani, who chose to come with us instead of going to Bari, and Savini, a Tank Corps officer whose main object, I believe, is to rejoin a sweetheart he has not seen for months. We spent the second night at a *cantoniera*[27] near San Lorenzo, beyond the advanced Allied lines. Next morning I felt certain that for me at least the war was over. The Germans were trying to hit the crossroads less than a hundred yards from the *cantoniera*, and salvos of fifteen to twenty shells fell almost uninterruptedly. Munthe had gone to divisional headquarters. The Germans began to shorten their range, so that each salvo fell closer to us than the one before. Between shell bursts, I was able to send all members of the unit to some fox-holes which offered a little protection. I stayed by the *cantoniera* to blow up our material in case the Germans came even closer. I crouched behind a low wall, while the shell-bursts came nearer and nearer. When a salvo burst no more than fifteen yards away (luckily on the farther side of my little wall), I said to myself: "Here it comes!" There was nothing I could do about it. The next would end my career. . . . But it was the last salvo. Leaving philosophical and theological questions aside, the least I could do was to thank Providence, as I did again two days later, when a solitary shell from Heaven knows where landed a few feet away from me; luckily the earth was soft and muddy, so the shell was deep down when it exploded.

27 Houses for highway maintenance men are to be found at regular intervals on Italian national highways.

At Salerno there was some shelter. Here there is none. The Germans are firing all over the place. Their guns are silent only during the brief spells of fine weather, when our planes can fly. After several days the strain becomes almost unbearable. This morning a couple of young British soldiers, who had obviously not slept for days said to me hopelessly:

"This isn't war. It's suicide."

I saw a flying-bomb today for the first time. It did no damage, and the fragments were carefully collected.

Ischia, February 10th, 1944: Mike, the son of our general, has been killed at Anzio, and Munthe is seriously wounded. I was in the infirmary in Naples when the news reached me and, since I was on my own with no one to take orders from, I left for Anzio at once. Admiral Morse has put an Italian Navy speed-boat at my disposal. I set out in it several times, but always had to come back; either the sea was too rough, or the engine gave out, or it was something else (I got the impression that captain and crew were pro-fascist and had no intention of helping the Allies). Meanwhile I have seen Ponza – we were better off there eleven years ago than we are now at Anzio! – as well as Ventotene and the smaller islands I used to gaze at so longingly when I was interned.

Sorrento, March 18th, 1944: Hospital, then convalescence. If it hadn't been for the war, I should probably never have known this little corner of earthly paradise. I have had the good fortune to be warmly welcomed into the Croce household; I spend practically the whole day

there. Members of the Control Commission call Croce the Sage of Sorrento; they are right, for Croce is something more than a literary critic, philosopher and historian. Now and again are born men who seem to have an intuition of truths that escape our limited minds: Plato, Dante, the great modern prophets, from Mazzini to Marx. To have an insight into a part of the truth does not mean that one never makes mistakes. But what do mistakes matter where there is a clear vision of liberty as a fundamental condition of human existence?

We see the war here, from a distance. There are men in uniform, and the usual shortage of food. But the actual fighting is some way off. The other evening I watched the Germans bombing Naples, the worst punishment it has had. I heard that several hundred people were killed. Then Vesuvius began to erupt. Between man and nature, Naples has no respite.

The officers who are convalescing here critcize Anzio as a useless undertaking. This is not how I see it. Anzio was the first serious attempt to penetrate the Fortress of Europe. At Salerno the Germans were trying to gain time, to allow their divisions to get organized in the Abruzzi; at Anzio they made every effort to drive us back into the sea. But we have been there two months and they have not succeeded yet. This means they never will. Until now there have been ups and downs because, when the weather is bad, our aircraft could not go into action, and the Germans advanced; when the weather was good, we advanced. With the coming of spring, the weather will be on our side. The situation has certainly worsened in Rome. The front is near and the Germans mean business. The firing squads are constantly at work. All this is part of the Expiation. . . .

During a visit to Salerno I saw Jung, who is in charge of public finances (or what remains of them). He remembered speaking rather offensively about me after my arrest. He told me that he had realized years ago that he had been mistaken in his admiration for fascism and his devotion to the Duce; I doubt it; he probably first became aware of the evil in fascism when the laws of 1938 hit him personally. As he had to go to Naples, I offered to drive him there in my car. On the way he told me how we must all help Badoglio, consolidate the King's position and save Italy from ruin: the old arguments. He ended by telling me that he would like to have me join the Badoglio Cabinet as Under-Secretary of the Treasury. I replied that I would stay in the army as long as the war lasted, that he and the other members of the Cabinet should meanwhile persuade the King to abdicate in order to make possible the formation of a CCLN government, that there was no question of a violent revolution because the CLN would probably accept the Crown Prince as Regent until a constituent assembly could be elected. Jung asked me to go see the Crown Prince. I went, and got the impression that he would make a good constitutional monarch, but he is surrounded by remarkably stupid and narrow-minded people. Next day, at Ravello, Macmillan,[28] who is certainly the most intelligent of the Allied political leaders in this part of the world, also hinted that if I would like an Under-Secretaryship he would mention it to Badoglio; apparently the British are not satisfied with the present Under-Secretary for Foreign Affairs, who tries to play one member of the Control Commission against another; now he is friendly to the Russians. I said what I had told Jung: while the war lasts, I will stay in the army. I hoped, from the point of view of Allied military expediency, that the CLNs would be given a free hand as the best way to increase Resistance activity. The chief obstacle to Italian unity is the old King, who thinks himself indispensable: perhaps a British Minister will convince him that he is not. . . .

---

28   Harold Macmillan, then Minister for Mediterranean Affairs, with headquarters in Algiers.

Ortona, March 31ˢᵗ, 1944: Convalescence is over and Commander Holdsworth has recalled me to headquarters. We are in fairly regular contact with the Resistance in the Abruzzi, the Marche and Romagna. GAPs[29] and the Partisans have redoubled their activities. Among the names of their leaders are those of old *Giustizia e Libertà* friends. They are always in the foreground, in spite of persecutions and sufferings. I also heard mention of Renato, Tobia and other relations, whom I should never have expected to take such a firm stand. Crises bring out the best in people.

The Partisans are asking for more supplies. They are exasperated at our slowness. I wish they had been with me during the last ten days, to get an idea of the difficulties we are up against when we try to send supplies by sea. One night we started out in a converted trawler, but the engines gave out. Another night we were forced back by heavy seas. A third time we encountered a German or *repubblichino*[30] torpedo-boat, and again had to turn back. One night we actually reached shore, but it turned out to be the wrong beach – or at any rate there was no one there to receive the cargo we had brought. In the course of another little undertaking, instead of destroying the track to be used by a train bringing German supplies, we mistakenly blew up a disused railway line. It is the same when we try dropping supplies by parachute; it seems child's play until the moment comes of actually delivering the goods to those who desperately need them.

---

29 GAPs were the underground fighters in the cities and towns; nearly all were closely connected with one of the underground political parties, particularly the Action Party, the Socialist Party and the Communist Party.

30 Derogatory corruption of *repubblicano*. It was used by members of the Resistance to designate the supporters of the fascist Social Republic.

Salerno, April 16th, 1944: Caccia and MacFarlane have sent me back to Naples. The Control Commission has come to the conclusion that the equation Badoglio = Italy was a mistake. The Americans and British have agreed on the formation of a government that reflects the country's aspirations and political forces more accurately than Badoglio's does. The King has been induced, apparently by Macmillan, to hand over his authority to his son as soon as Rome is occupied. This decision represents a partial concession to the CLN, and Badoglio has been hard at work integrating the CLN in liberated territory in his own Cabinet. As I see it, *badoglismo* must play a minor role in relation to the CLN. The southern CLN is mostly in favour of collaborating with Badoglio on an equal footing; the only ones against this are the main body of the *Azionisti,* and the socialists.

The most important consideration in this problem ought to be – but is not – the situation in German-occupied Italy. For the morale of the Resistance and to avoid the troubles that are occurring in France, Poland and the Balkans, it is essential that the CLN remain united. To settle the differences between the CLN and Badoglio (which means the differences between a parliamentarian republic and an authoritarian monarchy) the best thing would be to admit the *badogliani* as the seventh party in the CLN Catholics and communists are convinced that if they do not join the Cabinet, Badoglio will influence public opinion – who knows how? – to his advantage. So they have decided to cooperate with him. Liberals and Labour Democrats are honestly concerned with legalizing the revolution; so they will join too. As it is essential that the CLN should stay united, *Azionisti* and socialists will yield eventually and cooperate with Badoglio. This may have unpleasant repercussions in Rome and northern Italy, where the CLN considers Badoglio as a traitor.

At the Control Commission I was told that various exiles either have arrived or will soon do so; London has sent Petroni (Christian Democrat), Washington Pacciardi (Republican), Moscow Togliatti (Communist). Apparently they have been chosen to balance each other, which they will not do. The coming of Togliatti will transform the Communist Party. The Neapolitan communists, like those in Sicily, belong spiritually to Fourier's generation and to the liberal tradition. In spite of their confusion, they are people one can talk with. But Togliatti is a good Leninist, incapable of thinking in terms either of tolerance or of opposition, a firm believer in the gallows as the best instrument of government. Until now we have had only one orthodox Leninist, Spano, who does not count for much and is moreover working for the Allied Intelligence. Togliatti will take the communists in hand. He is as different from the communists of southern Italy as St. Ignatius from St. Francis: it has not usually been the Franciscans who have led the Church. . . .

On my way here, I saw Woditzka at Cosenza. He was one of my best friends at Ponza. He has been interned, here and there, ever since those days. His wife stayed with him. He has not changed at all, and is as enthusiastic and energetic as ever. It was a pleasure to meet this good friend again, loyal, trustworthy, incapable of a mean act. Naturally everyone is against him, the old fascists as well as the new anti-fascists — who are often, in fact, the same.

258

— ⌛ —

Naples, May 10ᵗʰ, 1944: As usual, I am waiting. A wave of optimism has come with the warm weather — a new offensive, pushing the front line to Anzio, Rome liberated, the race to the Alps .... I am not so sanguine. The Germans won't run away. I keep hoping that the front will shift beyond the Adriatic, but the Russians are cagier than ever: they want the Balkans for themselves and for Tito, with no 'westerners' about. The British would not worry about what the Russians think, but the Americans are either pro-Soviet or scared to death that Stalin will take offence and will one day repeat what he did on August 23ʳᵈ, 1939, and sign an armistice with the Germans, which would throw the entire nazi armed strength against the Western Allies.

Thanks chiefly to detailed reports that come through Switzerland, we are beginning to get a clearer idea of the situation in occupied Italy. There are Partisan bands in nearly all the upper valleys of the Apennines and Alps. Military Resistance leaders and the CLN are trying to achieve some kind of organization. There are some internal disagreements, but not many. All who manage to contact the Allies ask for supplies.

Hitherto the Resistance bands have rarely been a serious threat to the Germans. But now that they have been joined by some of our officers, they can get regular supplies, and I should not be surprised if there comes a time when the Resistance will keep more Germans and Social Republic troops engaged than the Allied troops do.

Among the Partisan leaders in the Spezia area is my cousin, Alberto Brofferio. I haven't seen him since I was a child. He never became a fascist, and jeopardized his position as a naval officer by criticizing the fascist government. After September 8th he was one of the first to make a serious effort to organize Partisan groups.

— ⧗ —

Cisterna, June 4th, 1944: Yesterday evening I went beyond the advanced Allied lines between Velletri and Genzano.[31] A hundred yards from the front line a German patrol had barricaded themselves inside a house. We shouted to them to surrender, but the answer was a burst of gunfire; we left them, to die holding the position entrusted to them.

At Cisterna not a single house was left standing. Like Battipaglia, Velletri was a heap of rubble. At a turning on the road to Rome were the bodies of two peasants who had been killed while trying to escape with their cart. In some places the stench of putrefying corpses almost turned us back. Fourteen years ago I came to this beautiful part of the Castelli with Joyce. I never dreamed then under what conditions I would return here.

Rome, June 5th, 1944: We are actually here! It seems like a dream. Last night came the order to start. The column was divided into three groups. We proceeded slowly. As I knew my way in Rome, I led the first group. There was no sound except the hum of our engines; not a shot was

---

31   Two hill towns about twenty or twenty-five miles south of Rome.

fired. At night the Castelli seemed to belong to a ghostly fantastic world. The streets were full of rubble. Through the gaping windows and the doors which had been blown off their hinges, one could imagine the emptiness which the remaining walls were trying to hide. First Genzano, then – the bridge having been blown up by the Germans – a long way round by the valley of Ariccia, then uphill again towards Albano. I thought of the friends with whom I used to come here when we were organizing groups of *Giustizia e Libertà*. This was a land of wine and hard work: today it is a graveyard.

261

Then down along the Appian Way: Ciampino, and the Capannelle. Suddenly Porta San Giovanni came in sight, its wall, piazza and basilica. I was relieved to see that there was no sign here of the devastation and ruins of Catania, Salerno and Naples. There was no one about. Just before we reached the station, an armoured car sped through an intersection: an American one! I wanted to get to Piazza Verbano but lost my way near the station. (In my day the new station had not been built.) It was two o'clock when we finally reached our destination, and there was still not a soul to be seen. The column halted and we got out of our cars. One window opened . . . two minutes later windows were flung open in every building, doors opened, and lights appeared everywhere. Soldiers and officers, invited by the overjoyed inhabitants, vanished into the houses. Why stop them? There was no fighting to do, and it was just as well to forget everything for an hour or two.

At five, I reported to headquarters that everything was under control. I then set off in search of my sister and her husband, Lussu. I had no idea where to look, and went first to De Bosis'[32] flat in Via Due Macelli. I found Fenoaltea there, and at first he did not recognize me; twelve years had gone by since our last meeting. The arrival of the Allies has caught the CCLN unprepared; they have not had time to occupy the Capitol, Quirinal, or Palazzo Venezia. The situation has not been improved by differences of opinion among the leaders of at least three groups, each of which separately had been authorized by the Allies to govern Rome during the interregnum.

---

32 Brother of Lauro De Bosis.

I have seen my old friend Renato Pierleoni, who has been organizing GAPs in Rome for eight months. I have also met friends from the days of conspiracy, and others whom I had known at Ponza. They told me about those who are no longer alive, of Concetti who died while acting as underground courier between the Rome CLN and the Castelli; of Martini and Magri who were interned with me at Ponza in 1933, and Filippini, whom I had sent off from Algiers, who were shot, with 332 others at the Fosse Ardeatine.

Rome, June 10th, 1944: It is twenty years since Matteotti was killed by the fascists. Seven years since Carlo and Nello Rosselli were murdered; four since fascism brought Italy into the war. . . . Rome is still in gala mood. Perhaps because it is June, perhaps because it looks as if military operations are going well, people are optimistic. They all predict that the war will end this autumn. In Normandy, as at Anzio, the Germans are not strong enough to push the Allies back to the sea.

— ⧗ —

'San Tommaso', June 22nd, 1944: I had heard that Polish troops were advancing along the Adriatic coast, so asked leave of the CO to go and see my parents. I stopped a few hours at Bari, where I met Enzo Sereni.[33] He asked to be dropped by parachute in northern Italy, and has been attached to the least effective of the four groups that are

33 Action Party leader and active Zionist. As enthusiastic and convinced a democrat as his brother Emilio was an enthusiastic and convinced communist. Enzo was killed by the Germans in the summer of 1944.

concerned with contacting enemy occupied territory. They have decided to send him to northern Tuscany. It doesn't seem to me to be the right place. Enzo is a first-rate man, I hope he wll be successful in his mission. I heard about him years ago from mutual friends, and never dreamed that the war would bring us together.

We left Bari early in the morning. I have just been promoted to major and was counting on my rank and my uniform to get me to the front line in the shortest possible time. That afternoon I was about to stop at Giulianova when I heard that Polish troops had entered Fermo, seven miles from my home; I pushed on. I relived the past: San Benedetto, Grottamare, Cupramarittima, Pedaso.[34] After Pedaso I knew every inch of the road: Torre di Palma, l'Ete, Santa Maria, Porto San Giorgio. . . . Nothing seemed to have changed, and there was little war damage. The Rio, Capodarco on top of the hill, the Vallato, the pine avenue: I was home. Eleven years away from it all. The light was failing. I got down from the lorry and waited a few minutes before going into the house. Emotion? Why not? Memories and images rushed through my mind: the long years in Switzerland, England, Africa, America; all my experiences before and during the war; efforts both successful and unsuccessful; fallen friends. . . .

Someone was walking along the verandah. I opened the door and went up the dark stairs. I heard muttered words – they did not seem to be directed particularly towards me, but they were – it was my father's voice.

"*Agente straniero!*" – "Foreign agent!"

Wrapped in a familiar black cloak, he passed me

---

34 Small towns and villages along the Adriatic coast.

on the stairs and vanished into the gathering darkness. So that was my welcome home after eleven years! I felt a terribly bitter taste in my mouth. Others might not be so outspoken, but might well have the same thought on seeing me in foreign uniform. Eleven years are long. One becomes a *straniero* (foreigner and stranger) after eleven years. And to think that for all these years I had dreamed of that moment, the moment of seeing my home again...

Porto San Giorgio, June 25th, 1944: I have seen relations, acquaintances, friends, enemies. I have met some of the people who, without any coercion, had taken it upon themselves after I was arrested to inform the police of everything the family was doing. I kept my anger under control, out of respect for my uniform. It is a hard problem. Besides a desire for revenge, I feel certain that it would be right to punish these informers. But if everyone were to punish people as he sees fit, where would it end? Haven't I always protested arbitrariness, irresponsibility and disrespect for the law? Can I now do the things for which I criticized the fascists? This would be just the right moment ... at a time like this no one would stop me, no fascist would find a helping hand. I have decided to go away so as not to see these people with their smooth words: "I really wanted to help you" – "I was forced to do it" – "I didn't actually tell the police anything."

Thank goodness there are decent people here as well. I have seen Silvetti, he hasn't changed at all since he was distributing *Giustizia e Libertà* publications in the province. He gave me news of old friends in Ancona, Falconara, Jesi and Fabriano, who are probably having a hard time, as the Germans have halted at the Chienti river and show no signs of moving on. I have also met Strinati, a retired army officer, who with a few others has been the heart and soul of the Resistance in the district during these last ten months; also Vinci, whose house near the coast has sheltered hundreds of British prisoners on their way south by sea, and Don Marco, who has understood better than some where a priest's duty lies.

Ascoli, June 26th, 1944: Who would have guessed that this sleepy city, a stronghold of clericalism, would be in the vanguard of the Resistance? On September 12th and October 3rd there were big engagements between Italians and Germans, with many killed. This is evidence of Italy's transformation. . . .

At police headquarters I got the files concerning myself and my family. The names of informers were there: uncles, cousins, servants, the gardener, the ex-accountant, the schoolmistress. . . . This was the kind of servility fostered by fascism which caused so many people to lose their lives.

Rome, September 5th, 1944: Two months with the Control Commission are enough. Commander Holdsworth told me that I can finish my parachutist's course and that at the first favourable opportunity I shall be sent north into German-occupied territory. He is in a hurry because he feels sure that the war will be over this autumn.

The members of the Control Commission are all excellent people, but they don't give the impression of being exceptionally bright – chiefly since the departure of General MacFarlane. Of course, it is their duty to control

Max in very bulky British parachute gear.

the Italian Cabinet,[35] but they should also realize that it consists of reliable and intelligent people. If the Allies have no confidence in the CLN, they should not interfere with their activities. Today we have two bureaucracies instead of one. Weeks go by before a decision can be reached. My department (demobilization and re-employment of Partisans in liberated territory) is under a British colonel whose smallest step assumes the dimensions of a decision that will alter the whole outcome of the war. He would have done better in charge of transport, as he was in Bari.

The problems posed by the Partisans are certainly not simple. In the liberated zones near the front during the winter and spring, there were not many Partisans. The further north we go, the more Partisans there are. The bands are bigger and better organized, and there are more of them. But if the real Partisans are increasing, bogus ones are multiplying even faster. There were not more than twelve thousand active partisans in Rome and the rest of central Italy during the nine months of the German occupation, but hundreds of thousands are now claiming to have been Partisans.

We need camps, where the Partisans can be assembled. Large quantities of rations are needed, and clothing too. Intelligent officers are badly needed, to sort out the genuine and the bogus Partisans (an exceedingly difficult job), to decide who can join the regular armed forces, who can be employed in other ways and who ought

35 After the liberation of Rome, Crown Prince Umberto of Savoy had replaced his father as Head of State, Marshal Badoglio had resigned and Signor Bonomi, a moderate socialist, already Prime Minister in 1921 and chairman of the Central Committee of National Liberation(CCLN) during the German occupation, had become Prime Minister. All the Cabinet Ministers belonged to the six political parties affiliated to the CCLN.

to be sent home. It is a terribly complex problem for Colonel McCarthy, who has incessant meetings with the head of the Control Commission, with Fifth and Eighth Army generals and members of the Cabinet. Meanwhile the Partisans (especially the genuine ones) go hungry, and military operations are slowed down because there are not enough troops for the Italian front now that landings have been made in southern France. Fortunately the Fifteenth Army Group gives a fairly free hand to their field commanders, who take the opportunity of recruiting some of the best Partisan bands – the Maiella band, for instance, which has been on the front line ever since it was joined by the Eighth Army, and the bands led by 'Potente' in the lower Arno valley which have made themselves invaluable to the Fifth Army. Not to mention the help given by the Florentine GAP and the *Corpo di Liberazione*, which has been rapidly gaining strength. . . .

I have been able to get away from Rome occasionally. For about a month now the front has been stationary in the Gubbio valley . . . such a quiet peaceful place, as I remember it. Osimo, where German batteries were raining shells on the central piazza, was almost deserted. At Castelfidardo I met old Bocconi,[36] who is still active (I last saw him in Paris seventeen or eighteen years ago), also 'Alberto', who had been sent by the CLN in the north to organize the *Garibaldini* in the region. I don't know who he is, but I have a feeling that I have seen him before, in France perhaps, or in Spain. He explained to me how the partisans and the GAP in the north are organized.[37] Arezzo was

36 Bocconi, a humanitarian socialist, had for a long time been a prominent member of the Socialist Party, in Italy and in exile.
37 In Rome and central Italy most Partisans owed their allegiance either

utter desolation, nothing but débris. Young Treves died in Florence; he had once been an enthusiastic fascist: now a fascist bullet has killed him. . . . In Florence the war of Expiation has acquired new violence. The Allies were on the left bank of the Arno on the southern fringe of the city, the Germans beyond the Mugnone on the northern fringe; between them, Partisans and *repubblichini* fought and died. Civil war: perhaps inevitable, certainly tragic. Florence was once called Fascistopolis. Too many of her citizens had abetted violence twenty years ago. "Kill! Kill! Down with the socialists, the communists, the freemasons; down with liberty, parliamentary government, liberal democracy!" We reap what we sow. A grain of wheat will produce ten more. For every ten fascist assassinations of twenty years ago a hundred fascists are dying today. Violence seemed a fine thing to the fascists when others were being killed; it appears very different now that it is being turned against themselves.

Some of my encounters have not been pleasant. There was the businessman, for instance, who invited me to his home several times and boasted of having given ten million *lire* to the CLN. I knew that the ten million *lire* was part of a sum he had been paid by the Germans for building fortifications along the Gothic Line. At lunch one

---

(cont. from pg. 269) to the Badoglio Cabinet or to the CLN. In Florence and northern Italy few Partisans owed allegiance to Marshal Badoglio or the King (the *Autonomi, Green Flames, Osoppo,* etc.); four fifths of all Partisans in the summer of 1944 recognized the authority of the CLN and were affiliated to the political parties represented in the CLN: The *Rosselli* and *Giustizia e Libertà* formations were affiliated to the democratic Action Party, the *Garibaldi* formations to the Communist Party. Less important were the *Matteotti* bands affiliated to the Socialist Party, the *Popolo* to the Christian Democratic Party, and the *Libertà* or *Italia* to the Liberal Party.

day, General Armellini, highly thought of by the Allies, said that until 1941 he had never considered that there was anything wrong with fascism, and seemed rather pleased with himself on that score. I was unpleasantly surprised by the attitude of an exile who had been helped by the United States government to return to Italy on condition that he join the Partisans – of whom, because of his distinguished record, he would almost certainly have become the leader; he refused to go north.

I have been able to see a little more of my old friends. Thirteen years in prison have not destroyed Bauer's energy and good humour; during the nine months of German occupation he was the Rome CCLN's chief military leader. Thirteen years in prison and *confino* have not changed Fancello, generous and warm-hearted as ever. Giannotti, Bruno, the two Baldazzis and a good many others I found as active and enthusiastic as they had been when I last saw them twelve years ago. For twenty years they have been the conscience of Italy; now at last Italy is listening to the voice of conscience. . . .

I have also seen a number of new faces, people who understand that the war of liberation does not date from the armistice of last September, but goes back to October, 1922. Among them General Cadorna, who was asked by the northern CLN, by Longo and Parri, to join them as 'technical adviser' to the Volunteers for Freedom.[38] He

---

38 *Volontari della Libertà, V.d'L.*, or Volunteers for Freedom, was the general term in northern Italy for all Partisans recognizing the authority of the CLN. Ferruccio Parri: Prime minister, June-December, 1945, was the commander of the *Rosselli* and *G.L.* formations of the Action Party; Luigi Longo, second ranking communist in Italy, led the *Garibaldini*; General Raffaele Cadorna: a regular army officer, had distinguished himself in fighting the Germans after the armistice; later he became Chief of Staff and Senator.

accepted to go north, and was dropped a few days ago near Lake Endine.

Max proudly wore his British army uniform, only changing into civilian clothes as necessary during certain operations.

CHAPTER VII

In Enemy-Occupied Territory

Brindisi, October 30th, 1944: It was Tarchiani who said to me: "War is endless waiting. The moment you stop waiting is often the moment you die." I am still waiting. The parachutists' course lasted only a few days. I did manage to do the jumps without having to be pushed, but it was a damned unpleasant experience. When I arrived, Brindisi and the neighbouring towns were seething with activity: parachutists (Italian and British liaison officers) were being sent north of the lines to pave the way for the forthcoming Allied advance; more parachutists were being dispatched to Balkan and Danubian countries. At HQ they were all convinced that the war would be over in the autumn. Colonel Frank, our new commanding officer, had appointed me to head our missions bound for Lombardy. There were fifteen of us in all, and our main job was to organize the Partisans so that they could intensify their attacks against the Germans and *repubblichini* and occupy the nine provincial capitals of the region at the earliest opportunity. We were to arrange for drops of arms and ammunition, medical supplies and clothing; it would be up to us to maintain public order and to see that industrial plants were not destroyed or damaged. Everything seemed fine. Then the Germans halted, and even the most optimistic (I was not one of them) were forced to realize that there would be another winter to go through.

In view of this delay, we shall have to wait for favourable conditions for the sending of any large mission.

In the meanwhile, as well as being head of the Lombardy missions, I am to act as liaison officer between Fifteenth Army Group and the CLNAI.[1] Captain John Keaney and Sergeant Pickering, a telegraphist, will accompany me. I have also asked for Giordana[2] , whom I met here; his cooperation will be extremely valuable if I ever get to Milan. I was to have made the drop near Lake Endine, where Cadorna, who now heads the *V.d.L.*, made his in August, but we discovered in time that the Germans had occupied the area in the interim. Then a point in the upper Bergamasco was decided on – but the Germans got there first too. Now I am waiting for a favourable moment to be dropped on the Langhe,[3] where I shall probably meet Colonel Stevens, who is commanding officer of our missions in Piedmont and also liaison officer with the Piedmontese CLN.

A good many officers who were parachuted into northern Italy during the summer have returned. Several radios are in contact with SOE headquarters south of Bari. The news is far from good. In the eight provinces of northeastern Italy practically annexed to Germany there have been the fiercest *rastrellamenti* (round-ups of Partisans) to date, with thousands of casualties among both the Partisans and the civilians accused of helping them. What we knew as the Carnia republic no longer exists. The

---

1 After the liberation of Rome, the CCLN had become the Italian government. The CLN organization in German-occupied Italy was directed by the Comitato di Liberazione Nazionale in Alta Italia (CLNAI) or Committee of National Liberation in Upper (northern) Italy. From it depended the Military Command or CMAI. HQ of the CLNAI and the CMAI were in Milan.
2 G.P. Giordana; since 1948 manager of the Italian edition of *Readers Digest*.
3 Mountainous region in southern Piedmont; in 1943-45 a main centre for Partisans.

Germans have used their own troops and two divisions of Vlasov's army (people call them the Mongols). In the thirty-three provinces nominally administered by the *repubblichini*, the Germans have had the valid support of fascist volunteers in their attempts to crush the Partisans. The districts of the Valdossola, the Langhe, the upper Modenese liberated by the Partisans during the summer, have been for the most part reoccupied by the Germans. The 'republics' of Montefiorino, Alba and Domodossola have gone. Several of our officers have been killed in action or taken prisoner. A number of planes have crashed in the mountains while bringing supplies (effective drops mean flying low, often in narrow winding valleys). The CMAI is protesting the lack of supplies. Apart from the usual difficulties caused by bad weather and lack of proper liaison, since the main Allied efforts are now in France, relatively few planes are in Italy, and of those available for Special Operations most have been diverted to Warsaw, to give what help is possible to the Polish insurgents.[4] Since the Russians have refused to help the Warsaw insurgents (to think that they are only a few miles away!) supplies must come from Foggia, 800 miles away. Losses of planes and pilots over Warsaw have been very heavy.

It is reckoned that before the German offensive in October there were about 100,000 fighters in the bands; the largest and best organized were in the mountains of central Emilia, Piedmont and eastern Veneto. How many remain, no one knows. Perhaps not more than twenty thousand. An effort must be made to reorganize them and re-establish their efficiency. The Allies need them for military purposes;

4   August and September, 1944, were the months of the uprising of the underground Polish National Army, led by General Bor, against the Germans.

Italy needs them for her own regeneration. On the other hand the efficiency of GAPs and SAPs in the town has been unimpaired. Their numbers are difficult to estimate but it runs into tens of thousands. In Bologna there was an uprising in which the underground held out for several days.

The Volunteers for Freedom (Partisans, GAPs and SAPs which recognize the authority of the CLN) include *Garibaldini* organized and led by the communists, Action Party *Giellisti* and former *Autonomi* led by officers loyal to the Crown. Communists, democrats and monarchists cannot be easily welded together. The CLNAI attempts it – with more success than many people expected. In the CMAI the dominant figures are the *Azionista* Parri and the communist Longo; to represent the other parties are the socialist Bonfantini, the Christian democrat Mattei and the liberal Argenton.[5]

The Allied Command begins to realize that for perseverance, discipline and military efficiency, the Italian Partisans are probably better than those other countries. Through Expiation comes Regeneration. . . . They have their troubles, of course. In the Fruili near the Yugoslav border there have been several clashes between *Garibaldini,* backed by Tito, and *Autonomi.* There have been excesses here and there which commanders have failed to suppress, forgetting that men who shed blood for the sake of bloodshed are unlikely to be good citizens in peacetime.

— ⌛ —

5 Bonfantini: later a deputy for the Social Democratic Party. Mattei: later a deputy and head of the Italian oil corporation ENI. Major Argenton: a regular army officer.

On the Adriatic coast, November 16th, 1944: Lots of Yugoslavs and Greeks here. I met Tito when I was in Rome with the Control Commission. Our commanding officers are of different opinion, but I am not optimistic about the future of Yugoslavia. On the strength of reports from their liaison officers, to whom the war is a big adventure and politics too puzzling to bother with, the Mediterranean Command of Special Operations see Tito simply as a man who is at war with Germany; so they send arms, ammunition, money rations, uniforms. Planes and supply ships are continually crossing the Adriatic. Actually, Tito is fighting primarily against other Yugoslavs and Italians, and only secondarily against the Germans. He knows perfectly well that he will not win the war, that it is the Allies who will win it; he is interested in being in power in Yugoslavia when the Allies have defeated the Germans. It was a mistake to send to Mihailovitch[6] officers who were brave but politically babes in the wood. I have met several of them. Mihailovitch, a simple man himself, needed guidance and advice and was given the worst of both. Here they say: "What does it matter? When the war is over there will be elections again, the Yugoslav people will decide for themselves," and so on. They probably believe it. The elections will take place under duress. They do not realize that Tito is using the supplies he is sent to strengthen his own position and to get rid of any opposition. He is a fanatical and convinced Leninist. Tito's dictatorship will be worse than that of King Alexander, for Alexander only imprisoned his opponents, he did not kill them. Tito kills <u>his, and by the</u> time he has got rid of several thousand

6 Colonel, later General, Mihailovich, organizer of the *Chetniks*; executed in 1946 by Tito's communists.

Radicals, Agrarians, Socialists and Popular Party members, no internal force will be able to oust him.

I have met Greeks who are enraged by the British attitude. But after all, what do they want? One dictatorship instead of another? Even in ancient times, democracy in Greece often meant the dictatorship of the party that called itself democratic. Odd that such intelligent people have not managed to grasp the idea of freedom – but it is a shortcoming they share with many of our so-called democrats. . . . Were it not for British troops, Greece would share Yugoslavia's fate. Instead, for better or for worse, Greece will be able to have free parliamentary institutions and perhaps in ten years or so the Greeks will achieve really free self-government.

I met Alp in Lyons. Relations between the French and Italian Resistance are a problem. There are influential Frenchmen who want Val d'Aosta, Val di Susa and the Valli Valdesi in northwestern Piedmont annexed to France; some even act on their recollection that in the Middle Ages the whole of Piedmont was more French than Italian and that Napoleon annexed it. When the German front in Italy collapses there may be a very awkward situation if the Allies are slow in getting to Piedmont: De Gaulle's government might – or might not – have the authority (or the wish) to check expansionist tendencies. There is a similar and even tougher problem in relation to Venezia Giulia and Fruili. Tito's Partisans are already refusing to allow Italian Partisans to operate east of Cividale, well inside Italian territory; they are getting ready to pounce on Trieste, Pola and Gorizia as soon as the Germans give up. It is very unpleasant to have to plan defensive measures against invasion by one's allies, but unfortunately this is how things are.

Many of the French are shocked at the summary shooting of a number of Pétainists; others are protesting because the provisional government is trying demobilize the FFL (*Forces Françaises de l'Intérieur*, as the Resistance bands were called): as if privileged armed groups could be allowed inside a free country! It is hardly surprising that French and non-French alike are pessimistic about the future of France. Personally, I think that France will get on her feet again – slowly, perhaps, but more surely than the other occupied countries. The Germans often give the impression of being sensible people – and they behave like lunatics. The French tend to give the impression that they are crazy – yet they can behave with a common sense that is lacking in most other Continental nations.

I tried to find some of my old *Giustizia e Libertà* friends in Lyons and Marseilles, but no luck. The storm has swept them away.

Montreal, December 10ᵗʰ, 1944: In November the Allied Command in Italy decided to suspend further parachute operations in the north. After last autumn's *rastrellamenti* Partisan activity cannot be expected on a large scale before the end of the winter. Colonel Frank gave me a few days' leave to go to America to see Joyce and the children, whom I left nearly two years ago.

I saw very few people in New York. I am told that Italian language newspapers have written about me in most insulting terms. For them I am a traitor, because instead of fighting the war from an armchair or on the radio, as my critics are doing, I chose to disappear among those who have become numbers on identification tags. Fascism had to be overthrown. The stimulus for effective collaboration with the Allies could come only from people who had always fought fascism. In my limited capacity, I have tried to communicate my opinions concerning the regeneration of Italy to responsible Allied representatives. I have tried to obtain all possible help for those on whom the future of democracy in Italy rests.

They tell me not to take any notice of these personal attacks. It is difficult to ignore them entirely. They hurt. The disagreement stems mainly from our evaluation of Great Britain. There are literate and illiterate people, anti-fascists as well as fascists, who see her as an imperialist power. I see her instead as the champion of free institutions. The Italians who are anti-British are relying on the U.S., but I am convinced that it will take a long time before America can replace Great Britain in defending and promoting what liberty mankind can achieve. Americans will help nations to achieve independence, but they will not do what the British have usually done, to insist that there should be constitutional governments. For the Founding Fathers democracy was the organization of liberty; for their descendants it is the will of the people and if the people – as happens in most nations – want a dictator, dictatorship there will be.

– ⧗ –

Rome, December 28ᵗʰ, 1944: Parachute operations are to be stepped up. During their visit to southern Italy, the four

CLNAI representatives, Pizzoni, Parri, Paietta and Sogno,[7] gave the Allied Command and the government a clear and frank picture of the situation in the north. They need large sums of money to finance the central and regional CLNAI commands; they need arms and ammunition, uniforms and rations. Before I went on leave, I had been asked to draft the terms of the agreement on which relations between the CLNAI and the Allied Command would be based. These terms were discussed both with the CLNAI mission and with representatives of the Italian government. They were approved with a few modifications. They define relations between the Allied Command and the CLNAI which is recognized as exercising the functions of the Italian government in occupied territory. The CLNAI is invested with full governing powers during the interval between the surrender or departure of the Germans and the arrival of Allied troops. In some cases the interim period may be quite long, and it is essential that the CLNAI should be able to act as a legitimate government.

I was very moved at meeting Parri. To the Allies and to most Italians, he is one of the leading spirits of the Resistance. To me he is infinitely more – he stands for democracy in its best sense, the expression of a positive desire for freedom. Parri and Rosselli together organized Turati's escape when his life was in danger. He is a friend of Bauer and Rossi, was in *confino* with Bruno, and was one of the founders of *Giustizia e Libertà*. He was a shining example in the dark years of tyranny.

---

7 Alfredo Pizzoni: banker, then a non-party member of the CLNAI, now president of the Credito Italiano, one of Italy's largest banks; Gian Carlo Paietta: Partisan and prominent communist leader; Edgardo Sogno: monarchist, later organizer in Italy of the anti-communist movement Peace and Liberty.

Pizzoni is quite different. A born activist and never idle, patriotism once made him a fascist and now makes him a sincere and reliable anti-fascist. He has brought into the CLNAI the nationalistic element without which the Resistance of the north could never have become a popular movement. Parri and Paietta are fighting a political war, Pizzoni and Sogno are fighting as patriots. Their cooperation is in itself a sign of political maturity and the best thing that could happen to Italy. A hundred years ago liberals fighting for freedom and nationalists fighting for independence found themselves side by side; then they went their separate ways. Now they are together again.

Florence, January 10th, 1945: It will be some time before the city's physical wounds are healed; it will take longer for the scars of fascism to be obliterated.

Contacts with the Partisans in the Apennines are based here and in Viareggio. There are not enough planes for delivering supplies. Crossing the lines means increasing our losses. For front line operations the Fifth Army Command has had the good sense to rely on Partisan brigades whose record has been beyond praise. On the other side of the lines, the fascist Republic of Salò has sent two or three divisions reorganized by the Germans. Their numerical superiority gave the *repubblichini* some success at Christmas, south of Carrara, but they were soon checked, thanks mainly to the courage and initiative of the Partisan brigades. This is civil war, the worst of all wars.

Liaison officers who were with the Partisans at Montefiorino and in Garfagnana, tell of the intrepidity of the Partisans – they know how to fight and how to die.

Though the Expiation is painful, the last eighteen months have seen the emergence of a group which will, I hope, provide the leaders of tomorrow. This war is frightful, but at least it is strengthening the Italian character; without it, the Italians would surely have sunk into a morass of low politics and intrigues – as was already happening with the disgraceful Brindisi government. Perhaps they will still sink into the morass, but there is now a hope of avoiding it.

The shock of the unexpected German offensive in Belgium is beginning to pass. In Florence, Siena and Caserta, the Allied Command has been seriously concerned – partly because of the lack of adequate Allied troops in Italy. If the Germans should be encouraged by their success in Belgium to attack unexpectedly in Italy, things might go badly. Ever since Italy has become a secondary front there has been scarcity of everything.

— ⧗ —

Spoleto, January 15th, 1945: A maddening delay. There were several things to arrange before I leave for northern Italy – which should be in a few days, as soon as weather permits. The car has broken down on the hill above Spoleto, and I am waiting while the mechanics make new parts. (There are no spare parts to be had.) I have been to see the Fonti del Clitunno,[8] the Rocca dell'Albornoz and Monteluco: three different worlds.

---

8 The Fonti del Clitunno (Springs of the Clitumnus) was a place of worship in pre-Christian times; the Rocca dell'Albornoz is a fourteenth century fortress symbolizing the violence of the Middle Ages; Franciscan friars built a monastery at Monteluco.

Terriccio, January 18th, 1945: The airfield we are to take off from is only a few miles away. There are six of us, and everything is ready. Lt.-Col. MacMullen, head of the Ligurian mission, reached his destination by parachute the day we arrived here. Col. Stevens in Piedmont is pessimistic about the prospects of the two Partisan leaders 'Nanni' and 'Mauri' being able to hold what little ground they still have on the Langhe. We must be quick. But we are obliged to wait for the right weather. At ten each morning the RAF officers at the airfield let us know whether there will be parachute operations that day. When there are to be none, we are free till six in the evening, when we have to report, in case there is to be a night flight. This waiting about is wearing. A parachute drop is unpleasant enough; landing in enemy territory is positively loathsome. As ten o'clock and six o'clock approach, our nerves get more and more tense. Then we relax briefly, and it starts all over again. This goes on day after day.

To make waiting even worse, we have had bad news. Major Williams, the head of our paratroop training school, crashed into Monte Argentario and was killed. Only the evening before, he was telling me about his future plans, after the war is over. Several of our officers have been wounded or taken prisoner in the Maritime Alps, and some have been captured in the Biella area. We have no news of others in the Veneto for months; it is doubtful whether they are still alive. Babin, who had been training with me in England, is dead: he was from Verona and longed to see his family again. The Germans captured him soon after he landed, tied him up and drove an armoured car over him. Parri has been arrested and if he stays in the hands of the *repubblichini* he will be shot. We hear of fierce reprisals, of people being shot *en masse*, whole villages destroyed. Even if not all of this is true, it is clear enough that German-occupied Italy is an inferno.

Terriccio, January 25th, 1945: Who would have imagined that I would be spending weeks on end in a farmhouse in Maremma? From ten till six I roam the countryside. On my way up the mountain I saw a house where the Germans shot an entire family because they had sheltered some prisoners of war. Parents, grandmother, children, up against a wall. In a minute it was all over. The house is deserted, no one has touched anything. The fire has gone out but the pan is still there. The bed is unmade as they left it. There are spoons on the table. In a corner of the kitchen is a little wooden horse, and there is a doll on a chair.

Near a pile of shells by the main road, there are eleven crosses for the eleven German artillerymen who were ordered to hold out, and did so until not one was left alive. They might have surrendered, they could have climbed down the cliff and disappeared into the woods. But they stood firm.

. . . I can see the peasants standing against the wall . . . I can see their terrified faces. . . I can hear their cries. . . The Germans are not conscious of the peasants they have killed. What they see and admire are their own soldiers dying for the fatherland. The spirit of sacrifice blinds them to their own cruelty; above and beyond all else is the dream that appeals to the Germans as it does to all other human beings: peace and prosperity. Few do evil for the sake of evil. The Christians burned the heretics to do good; the communists slaughter non-communists to do good. The Germans shot the peasants – to do good. It might be well if people were to concern themselves a little less with what is good for others.

To be sure of not making mistakes when I reach my destination, I have asked Lt.-Col. Hewitt, our second in command, to explain my duties in detail. Combining this information with instructions I have had from Fifteenth Army Group, I have outlined a programme with seven main points:

(1) To coordinate as far as possible the activities of the Partisans and GAPs with the operation of the Allied army.

(2) To see that supplies in sufficient quantities reach the Volunteers for Freedom, irrespective of political colour.

(3) To encourage the CLNAI to set up an organization in each province able to take over all the functions of public administration during an interim period.

(4) To notify the CLNAI and the *V.d.L.* that the local committees and bands must take the necessary steps to protect industrial plants and power stations.

(5) To prevent individuals and groups affiliated to the CLNAI and *V.d.L.* from making any kind of agreement with the Germans.

(6) To keep informed of the situation on both eastern and western fronts so as to prevent Yugoslav or French infiltration.

(7) To do everything possible to maintain harmony among the parties of the CLNAI.

Points (1) to (4) correspond to written instructions I have received. It is essential that point (2) be implemented – many liaison officers have shown a tendency to identify themselves with the Partisan group to which they are attached, and ignore the others, often sending disparaging reports about them. This raises the suspicion that the Allies deliberately play favourites. There certainly has been favouritism, but it has been owing mainly to individual liaison officers. As soon as I learn, in Milan, what the effective strength of the various formations is, my job will be to distribute supplies equally. As to point (5), I must take the responsibility for including this among my functions.

The Germans often make truce proposals locally, which look good. They are always prepared to sell the fascists down the river, if by so doing they can gain the neutrality of the Partisans. Whenever a Resistance leader has asked the Allied Command for advice on such occasions, he has received an evasive answer – seemingly because of Allied unwillingness to interfere with the Resistance, but really, I believe, so as to have no obligations towards the Partisans and a pretext, in case the situation alters, to drop them for having treated with the enemy – as happened with Mihailovitch in Yugoslavia. Apart from purely military activities, my job will be to make suggestions, never to give orders. The CLNAI must act as a sovereign body and not as a puppet.

— ⧖ —

Milan, May 25th, 1945: The War of Expiation is over. My long war against fascism is over too. A chapter of history was ended yesterday. Certainly not a happy chapter: it began twenty-five years ago with the murders the fascists committed to get into power; it has ended in ruins and suffering.

There were six of us at Terriccio waiting to be dropped by parachute. Three in my mission, three in [Major] Hope's, headed for the hill south of the Po. Of the three officers among us I alone remain. Keaney was killed in the lower Monferrato in a clash between Germans and Partisans and Hope was accidentally killed soon after reaching his destination. Both of them contributed to the victory they did not live to see. I have just been luckier.

It must have been about nine in the evening of February 4th when our DC-3 took off. Nobody said anything. Darkness and cold, winter; destination, question mark. Who would feel inclined for conversation? That damned door we had to jump through was open: better look the other way. In the dim light of the one bulb in the plane the faces of my companions were weird and green. My thoughts wandered far. I thought of Joyce, of the children, of the calm peaceful life I had dreamed of. I cursed the war, cursed Hitler, fascism, the human idiocy that had led me to end up in a DC-3 heavy with the stink of burned oil, armed with dagger, revolver and sten-gun as though I were a bandit. And that damned door. Just as years ago, whenever I felt discouraged, I used to think of the many friends who were scattered throughout the prisons of Italy and counting on us to carry on their work, so in that DC-3 I saw in my mind's eye all the people I had known who had given their lives, people whose sacrifice must not be in vain. They were the old and new familiar faces – Ceva, Rosselli, Riccardi, and Lugli; Babin, 'Newton', Fabbri, Pintor, besides countless others who had died in Italy, Spain, France, Africa, and in the Atlantic. I kept my thoughts to myself. The other five were watching me. I was the senior officer. If I kept calm, they would be calm too. It wouldn't do to show any signs of nervousness.

Soon after ten o'clock the pilot called out: "Ready!" We got up. We assembled slowly in single file, and I passed round the flask of brandy. The two RAF NCOs who stood ready to push if any of us were reluctant to jump, smiled; they could afford to, they were staying behind in the plane.

"No lights here. We'll have to go back."

289

We sat down again. The weight that had been growing second by second during the last hour, was lifted – I felt light again.

"Thank Heaven!", I thought, "Nothing today. It will be tomorrow."

The plane was circling once more, to make quite sure that there were no reception committee lights to be seen.

"Ready!"

We sprang to our feet. The green light by the door lit up. I was at the door, fists and teeth clenched, more from fear than determination, looking down into space. "Damnation! Why must I do it? Curse this war."

"Go."

One step forward, a gust of cold air, a drop into the abyss. Then complete calm; I relaxed. There was no more noise. Once one had jumped, there was nothing more to worry about. The parachute had opened and I looked down. I could make out the blurry mass of the mountains, the light patches that were snow-covered pasture, the black patches of woods. I looked up: stars, millions of stars. I was just an atom. . . . I had landed. I had fallen on snow, and with all the extra weight I carried I had sunk deep. But I felt light: the tension of the last long months was over; I was a different man.

I tried to get up. No good, I was too deep in the snow. From somewhere above me came a voice:

"Quick! Germans!"

Quick, hell! Stuck in the snow with all the impedimenta, how could I be quick? Luckily the radio operator, twenty-year-old Sergeant Pickering, had landed only five yards away. He got up, took off his parachute, and came to my rescue. With great difficulty, sinking into the soft snow with every step, we made our way in the direction of the voice. There were a good many people there – Partisans, and farmers who were helping them. Captain Ballard was there too, a South African who had waited with me for weeks in the autumn for an opportunity to make a parachute drop. We were all there, even Keaney who had landed on a tree. We hurried away. Besides the Germans, who were not so very near (two miles away), there was our plane which would circle back to drop supplies without parachutes. A package on your head would end the war for you.

When we got to a farmhouse, Ballard assigned Regis to me as guide; he was to stay with me for several weeks. We had landed in the western part of the Langhe. Monesiglio was more or less the capital of the district controlled by 'Mauri's' Partisans. There was another band farther down the valley. 'Nanni' and his *Garibaldini* were nearby to the east, and brigades of *Giustizia e Libertà* had also grouped to the west. Ballard told me that until I found another guide to take me to the plains and to Turin, I was to stay with the Galiano family at San Luigi, above Monesiglio. Regis and I left the farmhouse soon after our arrival there. At three o'clock in the morning Signora Galiano opened her front door to us.

I had to get to Milan as quickly as possible. It took me more than a month. In peacetime I should have arrived there by car in three or four hours. I went to see the local Partisan commanders to find out if they could provide a guide, transportation and contacts. A doctor who acted as courier for the Piedmontese CLN was expected to come from Turin to get me, but it would be well to prepare to manage without him, in case he couldn't get through. I was warmly received by 'Mauri', 'Nanni' and the commanding officer of *Giustizia e Libertà*, from whom I learned that Venturi[9] was one of the leaders of the Piedmont CLN. (I had had no news of him since 1941, when I had heard that he was in a fascist prison in Spain.) My papers were in order – excellent false documents in my own name. With Ballard and Regis I went to see the local Partisan leaders, cllimbing up and down the frozen Langhe. Ballard took care of settling Keaney and Pickering, with their wireless equipment, at Casa Bianca, a large farmhouse belonging to a family of farmers who for over a year had been a pillar of the Partisans. Above Casa Bianca, hidden by trees and rocks, was the half-ruined shack we had turned into a wireless station.

Stevens, who was in command of our missions in Piedmont, was near Carrù. I went to see him. The news he had from Turin was none too good: many people had been shot, more had been arrested. But there was no doubt that the CLN was better organized, politically and militarily, in Piedmont than in any other part of northern Italy. There was encouraging news from the mission to Liguria. Stevens had his own convictions about the Partisans, and although he thought he acted impartially, there was no doubt that he leant towards the right-wing *Autonomi* and had little contact and less sympathy with either *Giellisti* or the *Garibaldini.*

There were some nasty moments. One evening I

---

9 Franco Venturi, now professor at the University of Genoa.

was passing by Murazzano where a German garrison was stationed and where, I was told, Brosio was interned.[10] Suddenly, we almost ran into an armed patrol: it was night, so we disappeared into the darkness. Below Feisoglio the mist unexpectedly cleared and I found myself within a few yards of of four or five soldiers who were feeling their way carefully: a quick dash down the slope and I was again enveloped in the mist, which I blessed most fervently. To get to Clavesana we had to cross a narrow defile which the Black Brigades[11] were firing on continuously. Regis and I leaped like frogs from a haystack to a ditch and then to a tree. The fascists were a few hundred yards away and were incensed – we were told they had just lost a mule cart bringing supplies, in an encounter with Partisans. They were probably firing because they thought there was some big concentration of Partisans where we were. But it was just we two. And all the time we had to look out for mines along the paths.

One night, before crossing the road on top of the *langa* which the Germans controlled, we stopped for ten minutes to make sure there were no patrols in the area. It was very quiet. The night was clear, and cold as it can be 3,000 feet up on the *langa* in early February. I looked up at the sky, at the brightest shooting star I had ever seen. A good omen! I thought of Joyce and the children. Taking new heart, I decided that we could safely go on. Superstition? I dare say. But when one's life is in the balance, a little superstition can help.

---

10 Lawyer, brother of Manlio Brosio, member of the CCLN, Minister of War after liberation of Rome, Italian Ambassador to Moscow, then London, then Washington.
11 Volunteer troops of the Social Republic.

One Monday I was to have lunch at Monesiglio with Ballard, 'Mauri' and two or three others. On my way there I slipped badly on the ice and hurt my back. We ate to the accompaniment of violent gunfire. "My Partisans can hold out for another quarter of an hour," said 'Mauri', "then they will be out of ammunition." Fifteen minutes later we got up from the table; in the *piazza* we said goodbye and each of us disappeared towards his hideout in the mountains. A few bullets whistled around me as I climbed, as best I could with my painful back; the blackshirts had just reached the *piazza* and could see me – luckily they were not good shots. At five in the afternoon I decided that San Luigi had become too exposed. I left with Regis and Acerbo, another Partisan who had joined me. I had told Keaney to abandon the Casa Bianca and stay with Pickering half-way up the mountain, as soon as he had put the wireless equipment in a safe place. It must have been close to zero (Fahrenheit) with an icy wind blowing. We passed by three villages garrisoned by *Garibaldini*. Their leaders declared that they would make a stand against Germans and fascists. Fortunately they remembered in time that guerrillas are not meant to defend positions, and as the enemy drew nearer they dispersed through farms and woods, and reassembled after dark to attack patrols and sentries.

The local people helped us – without a single exception. One morning at about eight o'clock the three of us came to a farmhouse. We were tired as we had had no sleep and had been walking for several hours in the bitter cold through woods and fields covered with frozen snow. (Mercifully the wind had dropped.) We were aiming to reach the gulleys that would hide us from enemy view. The peasants saw us and asked us in. They invited us to sit by the fire and gave us coffee or some substitute that seemed excellent.

"Don't you know this is dangerous? I said.

"We can only die once, and you need to warm yourselves."

An hour after we left, a German patrol met a group of Partisans just coming out of the woods a few yards from that farmhouse. They assumed the Partisans had been staying there, so burned it to the ground – as they had done to the twelve houses that formed a nearby hamlet.

On another occasion we had stopped in a stable for a few minutes. (We were forced to shelter from the cold from time to time.) A woman, who must have seen us pass, came running to warn us that the 'fascists' were coming down the mountainside (Germans and *repubblichini* were all called fascists.) She hurriedly led us to a farmhouse, near which a large dug-out had been made ready to hide the young men escaping conscription. Regis and Acerbo were starting to go through the narrow tunnel into the dug-out, but I could not do it; sudden and violent claustrophobia made me prefer to be shot where I stood rather than shut myself up in a pit where I would have been entirely safe. When she saw what was happening to me, the woman took the three of us all to her house and we spent the whole day in her attic. The house was not searched. If it had been, nothing much would have happened to me, as I was in uniform; I would have been made a prisoner of war. But the house would probably have been destroyed and its inhabitants shot – like the peasants in the farmhouse in

Maremma.

Late one evening we came to another farmhouse. I saw a faint light in the window. We went into the kitchen. It was not likely that fascists would turn up there at that hour. A woman was there, alone. Her husband and daughter had gone to see neighbours and were late – neighbours can be a long way off in the mountains. We asked if we might stop there for a few hours, until daybreak. She said we might. We went to the stable, where I stretched out on the straw and fell asleep. I was awakened by the light of a hurricane lamp and a voice say, "Good evening". Bending over me was the husband, who had just got back. He had an honest face, rather bandy legs, shoulders bent by too much hard work – a typical Italian peasant.

"Come upstairs. We will give you our bed."

"Thank you, no. I am very comfortable here. Are you sure you don't mind our staying? There are Germans about."

"I know. Stay. Guests are sent by the Lord."

We were the guests of another peasant for two whole days. Not once did he make us feel that our presence was unwelcome. In the daytime we stayed in the woods. We had found a clump of trees growing close together by a stream in a little valley. There we were sheltered from the wind, and we spent hours high up in the branches. The Germans had a nasty habit of throwing grenades into the thickets, but they were unlikely to throw them up into the trees. When it began to grow dark we went back to the farmhouse. There was food waiting for us and (incredible luxury) a bed. The peasant had arranged with his neighbours that they would warn him if there were fascists about.

"Are you sure no one will denounce you?"

"We all know each other. Nobody will say a word."

The priest of the neighbouring parish, a mile or two away, came to visit us. Did he realize the risk he was taking? Certainly, but since there were strangers here, it was his duty to come and see if they were in need of anything.

Days went by. Communications were disrupted. I sent scouts into Val Bormida and Val Belbo. The fascists did not move away, and they did a lot of requisitioning. I would meet Keaney and Pickering every day; they could not send any more messages as their batteries had given out. One morning I reached a mountain top, and from the shelter of a little chapel admired the sea of clouds which covered the plain below, and the white Alps rising superbly above the fog – beyond them lay France, the Allies, safety. Suddenly the four DC-3s which should have come before the *rastrellamento* began, and had been held up by bad weather, appeared; they were bringing tons of supplies. My wireless did not work, and evidently Ballard's was out of action too. Somehow, at our headquarters, they did not know about the *rastrellamenti*; the weather had cleared, and so the planes had been sent. A pilot saw me. I signalled that there was nothing doing. . . . They disappeared towards the mountains and the sea beyond. What a lost opportunity – eight tons of supplies that would probably have been enough to allow the Partisans to take the offensive.

This *rastrellamento* too, came to an end. The blue neckerchiefs of the *Autonomi* and the red stars of the *Garibaldini* were back in circulation, as well as the *Giellisti* red flames. Giordana arrived one night by parachute. I had been waiting impatiently for him for three weeks, as I was counting on him for my stay in Milan. Vigorous and determined, and with a shrewd knowledge of the people we had to deal with, he could circulate more easily than I; in my fifteen years of exile I have developed ways that are perceptibly foreign. Another arrival was the *signorina* who was acting as courier between the CLN Military Command in Turin and the Langhe, and was to take Giordana to Turin.

Keaney and Pickering could not hope to pass for Italian, so it was essential for them to remain in uniform. They were to go to the lower Monferrato, near the river Po. They would set up their wireless equipment in a friend's house and I would keep in touch with them from Milan through couriers. My uniform discarded – "Now you look like a man!" said Signora Galiano – I said goodbye to Regis and Acerbo, and set off with Musso, a lawyer from nearby Ceva. After stopping a night at Clavesana we arrived at Trinità di Benevagienna. Giordana left at once for Turin. I stayed three nights with the parish priest while I waited for Doctor Ré, who had orders from the CLN to come and get me. Not once did the priest ask me who I was or what I was doing. I was not the only one to receive hospitality from him. From time to time others turned up – I recognized them quickly as Partisans. They ate, sometimes spent the night, and were off again.

We had been lucky. The path we had taken on the way down from Clavesana towards the Tanaro river was the only one the fascists did not control. The snow-covered railroad bridge across the river was deserted. The village beyond was also deserted – the Germans had set fire to all the houses. (Shortly afterwards the district was overrun by blackshirts; they caught and shot Acerbo; they also caught and killed the seventeen-year-old son of the people who had given us hospitality at Clavesana.) Once I felt that we were done for; when our guide suddenly stopped at the sight of twenty or so blackshirts advancing towards us. We sighed with relief when we saw that they were prisoners taken to the mountains by Partisans.

When Dr. Ré arrived, I left Trinità. On the way to the river we nearly collided with a German patrol, mostly middle-men, probably territorials. They were proceeding slowly so we had just time to turn off down a lane. At Fossano, where we stayed the night, the innkeeper kept a few rooms in reserve for Partisans. The rest of the inn was occupied by German officers. We went in when one of the Partisans signalled that all was safe. That evening, while the German officers were drinking in the dining-room, we went down to the cellar to listen to the BBC – the Bible of the Resistance in Italy as elsewhere.

Turin was a shock. I had not been there since the winter of 1931-32, when I had gone to meet Piedmontese leaders of *Giustizia e Libertà*. There were ruins everywhere. It looked like a besieged city: few civilians about, most of the shops closed, barbed wire, troops in battle-dress. I walked through the avenues, once tree-lined and gay; every tree had been cut down for fuel. The house of an uncle of mine, where I had stayed a few times, was now used as quarters for German officers. Ré introduced me to 'Creonti', the ADC of General Trabucchi, commander of the Volunteers for Liberty in Piedmont. He and his wife took me and the communist member of the Piedmont CLN to her parents' house, near a strong-point manned by

Germans – this being safer than remaining in the centre of the city. We were most hospitably received. Next day I met Roffi, a liberal and a businessman, who put me up for a few days until a car was found to take me to Milan. Roffi told me of the recent numerous arrests among members of the Piedmont CLN. He also said that the Germans had arrested Sogno (one of the most active underground organizers in Piedmont and Lombardy), while he was trying to rescue Parri. Of the four CLNAI representatives I had met in Rome a few weeks before, two were already in German hands.

I took advantage of my stay to meet members of the Piedmont CCL. Venturi couldn't believe his eyes when he saw me, I gave him news of his parents, whom I had seen in New York in November; he gave me news of Valiani who had crossed the lines in September, 1943, and was now the Action Party representative in CLNAI. It did me good to talk with a friend and to be, for once, not an Allied officer but a citizen counting on the Allied victory to put an end to Italy's dictatorship. I saw Trabucchi, who had been doing excellent work and had increased the efficiency of the Piedmontese Partisans.

I left for Milan early one morning by car with a leader of the reorganized Socialist Party. In Milan the atmosphere was very different from that of Turin. The war didn't seem so close. There were fewer uniforms in sight; German officers and soldiers lounged about in the cafés. The streets were crowded, cinemas and other public places were open and well patronized, the shops fairly well stocked, and the factories working. Life seemed almost normal. There had been considerable damage from Allied bombardments, but with their traditional efficiency the Milanese had put even their ruins in order. There was not the appalling destruction and desolation that I had seen from Palermo to Florence as much as a year after the liberation. We spent half an hour in a friend's flat. The greater risks he was running, as a Jew, did not stop him from acting as head of Sogno's group in Milan. On the morning of my arrival I met Pertini in a café; he was the representative of the Socialist Party in the CLNAI. I had known him by name for years; with Parri and Rosselli he had helped old Turati to escape; instead of staying safely in France he returned to Italy to organize groups for *Giustizia e Libertà*; arrested, he had spent long years in prison and *confino*. Not content with what he had done in Rome and central Italy during the German occupation (he had been a member of Bauer's Military Command in Rome) he insisted on being sent to Milan, which he reached with the help of Allied Intelligence.

In the innocuous-looking office serving as central headquarters of the CLNAI I found Pizzoni, who was responsible for the smooth running of the complex machinery of the CLNAI (an underground government administration and army in enemy occupied territory!) of which he acted informally as non-party chairman. With him was Balzarotti, a socialist, secretary of the CLNAI. An hour after my arrival we were joined by Merzagora, the dynamic and efficient representative of the Liberal Party in the CLNAI during Arpensani's absence. Merzagora took me to lunch in his suite in the Pirelli offices – it was a bit unnerving to share the lift with S.S. officers, whose

headquarters were in the same building! He introduced me
to his friends the Marchesanos,[12] in whose house I spent
the first night.

For security reasons I decided not to tell those with
whom I had to have relations (members of the CLNAI
and the CMAI) where I was going to live. I had seen
Giordana again in Turin, and he had said he would find
me safe lodgings. I knew where to contact him by phone
in Milan. When we met again he introduced me to his
friend Barioli, who very handsomely – knowing only too
well the risks involved – offered to take me in. So for two
months my quarters were mainly at No. 3 Via Visconti
Modrone; there I spent the intervals between my various
appointments. Not only did Barioli give me hospitality, he
also helped me when I had to carry documents. We would
go on bicycles, Barioli riding a hundred yards or so ahead
to make sure there was no unexpected roadblock or patrol.
He always stuffed his pockets with papers so that he would
certainly be stopped, and I would take another road.

Shortly after my arrival I got myself another
lodging of which no one, not even Giordana, knew.[13] I
went to see the son of the cousin who had pushed me out
of his house fifteen years ago. I explained that I was in
Milan clandestinely and needed his flat. Too frightened
to share it with me, he gave me the key and went off to

12 Cesare Merzagora was at that time general manager of Pirelli, one of
the largest Italian corporations. Later he became Member of Parliament and
Speaker of the Senate; in 1955 he was candidate for the Presidency of the
Italian Republic. Giustino Arpesani joined the Italian Cabinet as under-
secretary in 1945; later he was appointed Ambassador to the Argentine and
then to Mexico. Marchesano was a prominent businessman. The three were
members or supporters of the Liberal Party.
13 It was essential to have a number of hide-outs.

join his family in the country. Through Pizzoni, I was able to use the house of an industrialist near Milan. I often spent Saturdays and Sundays there, preparing reports for the couriers (mainly provided by Valiani) to take to our representatives in Switzerland.

Communications with the Allied Command were difficult, but frequent. There were the couriers to Switzerland; Keaney's and Pickering's wireless never reached the lower Monferrato, but there were four transmitting sets, belonging to different Allied services, that I could use to contact headquarters. Through Solari, an engineer and Action Party leader, who had replaced Parri as commander of *G.L.* formations, I sent and received messages by an OSS radio located in Milan. General Masini, whom I met regularly, sent messages through the set in territory east of Milan controlled by the *Fiamme Verdi.* On the mountains south of the Po was MacMullen's wireless station, with which I had occasional contacts by courier. A fourth transmitting station was in Piedmont. After the drop of other Allied missions in Lombardy communications became easier.

In Milan I soon met all members of the CLNAI and the CMAI. I had known about Sereni, Communist Party representative in the CLNAI by reputation, also Longo, commander of the *Garibaldini.* Both of them, but especially Longo, personified the idea I had had for years of communist leaders: admirable in their spirit of self-sacrifice and their devotion to their ideals; ready for any personal sacrifice if it served the Party; inflexible in their dealings with all non-communists. Fascists used the expression 'souls of steel', referring to themselves, but it was the communists who had them. They never showed uncertainty or doubt. Marazza,[14] a lawyer and the Christian Democratic Party member in the CLNAI, was a solid sensible man, energetic and realistic at the same time. Until July 25th, 1943, he had not been an active opponent of fascism; he represented the Catholic Italy whose existence many of my friends had often disregarded, which in obedience to the Pope, had remained aloof during the liberal era, and had made its political reappearance after World War I with the Popular Party. Marazza was clearly conscious of representing the majority party. Valiani, who had replaced Albasini and Parri as the representative of the Action Party, did not get back to Milan until some weeks after my arrival.

To carry out my assignment, I contacted leaders of the regional and provincial Committees and Commands in Lombardy and had evidence of their efficiency as well as their courage. Whenever arrests or shootings disrupted part of the CLN organization, others immediately stepped into the breach. As the CLNAI parties had their headquarters in Milan – the capital of the underground – I made a point of getting to know their leaders. The Liberal Party reflected the division between a majority of conservative liberals who stood for limited constitutional government under a king and the privileges of property owners, and a minority of radical liberals who were against all privileges and for the equal liberty of all, to be achieved through democracy, equality of educational opportunities and maximum diffusion of property. The Socialist Party hadn't changed

---

14 Emilio Sereni and Luigi Longo are prominent Communist Party leaders (Longo is supposed to be No.2 man in the Party and to be considerably tougher than Togliatti). Achille Marazza: deputy and Minister several times since 1945, is a leading member of the Christian Democratic Party.

much since 1922; some of the men were different but the positions identical: a majority of *massimalisti* whose sincere collectivism is in contradiction with their equally sincere attachment to democratic procedure and democratic liberties, and a minority of social democrats ready to revise much of the traditional economic programme in order to enable democratic institutions to function. The Action Party repeated the often-made attempt to bring together reform-minded liberals and non-marxist democratic socialists. It was, with the Communist Party, the main pillar of the organized Resistance, but, while united in action, it was divided in ideas; it was held together by an aspiration but had difficulty in formulating a concrete programme. The Communist Party was the real thing: disciplined, efficient, a hundred percent Stalinist; strong in its cohesion and authoritarian organization as well as in the numbers of Partisans it had in the mountains, and the determination of its leaders. Most of the Christian-Democrats were former *popolari*, but instructions for their activities came from the Archbishop's palace, where there is little sympathy for democracy and none for liberty. *Azionisti*, socialists and communists were convinced that once Italy was liberated a popular front government would govern the country; they tended to underestimate the influence and numbers of political Catholicism. Efforts had been made, chiefly by the communists, to organize a clandestine labour movement which was instrumental in reducing production to a minimum and in devising means to protect industrial plants and power stations; it also played a determining role in the insurrection of April 25th. I met industrialists and bankers who collaborated with the CLN, providing badly needed funds; I found them an unattractive group, largely the same people who financed fascist squads twenty years ago; capitalists in the sense that they own capital, but lacking the drive, initiative and organizing ability which would justify their profits in a capitalistic economy. Fascism made bureaucrats of them. The new Italy will have to take into account their present inefficiency and their unsavoury past.

It did not take long to get a fairly accurate picture of the situation in the north. A revolt throughout the whole area was not easy to achieve on account of German numerical superiority. On the other hand, after the winter's crisis, Partisans and GAPs were rapidly reorganizing. They were more numerous and better disciplined than the Allied Command had expected – but they needed arms. Engaging one-third of the German and fascist troops, the Volunteers for Liberty were the main support of the Allied forces in Italy. Most of the population, irrespective of class, helped the Resistance. In spite of deep differences (on the basis of reports from the various regions I reckoned that the conservative *Autonomi* included about one-fifth of all Partisans, the *Giellisti* over a quarter the *Garibaldini* two-fifths, the rest being composed of independent bands and of bands affiliated to the Socialist, Liberal and Christian Democratic Parties) cooperation prevailed. The instructions to industry to produce as little as possible were followed to the letter. In many districts food was in short supply, but this situation would not become desperate till the summer. The regular troops of the fascist Social Republic (six divisions on paper, four in reality) fought only if compelled to: the rate of desertion was high. The fascist irregulars (Black

Brigades, *Decima Mas*, etc.) consisted of the scum that rises to the surface in times of trouble. This scum, despised by the Germans, was responsible for most of the atrocities which had cost the lives of tens of thousands of civilians.

After a few weeks' interruption due to Parri's arrest and the knowledge that informers had put the Gestapo on their tracks, the CLNAI members reconvened in a seminary. Priests acted as look-outs. Medici Tornaquinci, Liberal Party leader and Under-Secretary of State for enemy-occupied territory, was present; he had come from Rome by parachute. Other meetings followed. Even on the most important questions of policy, and in spite of critical differences, agreement was always reached. I attended the meetings regularly did not take part in discussions except when problems came up concerning, for instance, the coordination of the *V.d.L.* with the Allied armies, the availability and distribution of supplies, the responsibilities of the CLN during the interim period, the protection of industrial plants. (In my reports to HQ I dealt chiefly with the needs of the Partisans, the distribution of Allied missions, relations with Yugoslav and French Partisans.) Warning had to be given against making deals with the Germans, or with fascists trying to save themselves by playing both sides.

I usually met about fifty or sixty people each week. I had to rely on my memory to retain pseudonyms (I refused to know real names) and the time and place of appointments. If I was to meet more than one person at a time the meeting would take place in some building – preferably a religious one. Meetings with just one other person always took place outdoors. I avoided the centre of the city (too closely watched) as well as the periphery (too few people about), and kept as much as possible between the inner ring made by the *Naviglio* canal and what had once been the city walls. Except for the first meeting with Pertini, I never entered a public place; after the first few days I avoided trams. I did not go out at night, and I drank quantities of camomile tea in the evening: not a soldierly drink, but very soothing for the nerves!

How valuable were they, these endless meetings, conferences, discussions, the reports and telegrams sent to the south? There were hundreds of thousands of us, on both sides of the front, each making his contribution to the victory which in northern Italy, as elsewhere, was the result of innumerable individual efforts, all equally necessary, at the front and in the rear, of men and women in uniform and civilians.

In spite of my caution, there were uncomfortable surprises. Soon after I arrived in Milan I came to a road block where none had been a few minutes before. My false papers were scrutinized and found satisfactory, but I did not speak with any regional accent – as nearly every Italian does. I had quite a job convincing the police that I came from the only part of the country where people have no accent! In a tram one day (and it was the last time I went on one) I noticed someone staring at me. I felt quite certain that I had met him before, years ago, and that he came from my parents' home town. But he could not quite make up his mind about me, and while he consulted a friend I jumped off. Another time we had abruptly to interrupt a meeting of the Partisan Regional Command, as the fascists had begun to search the building; while they were going up the main staircase, we went one by one down the service stairs. One day it took me more than an hour to shake off a man, clearly a plains-clothes police agent, who was following me. (As time went on the ring tightened. The secret police knew that there was an Allied officer about in close contact with the central leadership of the the Resistance. By the time the end came unexpectedly on April 25th, I was sure that within two weeks at most they would find me.) On my way back from Bruzzano by bicycle I was overtaken by an Allied fighter which was strafing the road. Flat in a ditch, I ruminated on the absurdity of being finished off by an Allied bullet.

Bad news kept on coming. Giordana was the first to hear that Keaney had been killed in a clash between Partisans and Germans in the Monferrato. He had been with me since October. I was fond of him as a younger brother. During the *rastrellamenti* in the *Langhe* he had always stayed calm and cheerful. Like myself, he was a volunteer. He had wanted to do his bit and complained at never having been in action. The first time he saw action was the last. He was much mourned at the Casa Bianca where he had endeared himself to everyone. A courier from Alexandria reported that Hope was dead, killed accidentally, I was told. The accident didn't sound convincing. In Turin, General Trabucchi was arrested; his predecessor, General Perotti, had been shot by the Germans a few months before. Solari was arrested in Milan. A clandestine radio operator, also in Milan, was caught and shot while trying to get away. Almost every week couriers came from Trieste with stories of atrocities committed by Tito's Partisans against Italians in Venezia Giulia. They urged us to tell the

Allied Command how necessary it was to occupy the city before the Yugoslavs; they begged for a shipload of soldiers to be made available to land on the day, which was bound to come, of the German *débacle*. Besides the usual failures in dropping supplies, equipment that was intended for the Partisans often fell into enemy hands; the pilots were being decoyed by false signals. Early in April the *rastrellamenti* were becoming more frequent and vicious in Piedmont and Venetia. Isolated as northern Italy was, neither we nor the fascists nor the bulk of the Germans realized – in spite of the BBC – how desperate was the situation in Germany, and were convinced that the war would last for months, perhaps until next winter.

Happily, light showed through the clouds now and again. I was glad when Valiani arrived since – as he knew who I really was – I could talk with him more freely than with others. We were elated when we heard that Parri and Sogno were free again; like most people, I had felt dubious when the S.S. commander, to show his sincerity in dealings with Allied representatives in Switzerland, promised to set the two prisoners free. I ran into Cadorna at a street corner, when I least expected to; his absence had been causing us concern and his presence was indispensable now that events were moving quickly – with Parri away and Cadorna absent, Longo was in command of the *V.d.L.* and that meant a free hand for the communists. Giordana returned safely from the mountains where he had gone to meet an Allied mission dropped to the Partisans. Arpesani came back from Rome and at once resumed his work in the CLNAI. Pizzoni returned from a mission with the Allied Command in Caserta (it was he who informed me of my promotion to lieutenant-colonel).

Occasionally the courier from Switzerland brought a very delayed letter from Joyce (who probably guessed that I was behind the lines but hadn't the slightest clue where, or if I was alive at all). The best moment of all was on March 25th, when the BBC announced that Montgomery's troops had crossed the Rhine. It is true that there had been a bridgehead at Remagen since March 9th, but that had been a matter of luck, while on March 25th the Rhine was crossed in spite of vigorous German defence. The end was in sight. There was no more fear of the one thing that might have prolonged the war: an armistice between Germany and Russia which would have enabled the Germans to hold the front on the Rhine and in Italy for months.

The end came more quickly than I expected. It is true that already at the beginning of March there had been signs of disintegration. The German ambassador had had a secret conversation with Milan's cardinal who was in touch with the Allies; the commander of the S.S. in Italy had tried to establish contacts with Allied representatives in Switzerland; fascists were busy looking for friends in the Resistance who could hide them. I had reported that the calibre of German troops in northern Italy was for the most part low; as for the fascists, only the irregulars – only a few tens of thousands – might conceivably make a last stand. Still, there was a hard core of loyal and disciplined German troops, of fanatical nazis and fascists; there were also French militiamen and Vlasov's soldiers for whom surrender was the equivalent of a death sentence. If the Germans, I thought, were to withdraw to the mountainous areas between the Bavarian plateau and the Venetian plains, between Graz and the Swiss frontier, where they could hold out for at least six months and maybe get ready the new weapons Hitler boasted about, there would be enough troops in Italy to hold parts of Lombardy and Venetia and protect the approaches to the Alpine Fortress against the numerically inferior 15ᵗʰ Army Group. News was too scanty, it was not possible to evaluate the situation correctly. Hitler stayed in Berlin and there was no defence of the Alpine Fortress.

On April 21ˢᵗ, the fascist *festa nazionale* and Labour Day, there had been the usual parades, ceremonies and speeches. As late as the morning of April 22ⁿᵈ the ex-dictator – in his residence on Lake Garda – was convinced, according to the rumours, that he would emerge safely from the crisis: it was true, he thought, that the British detested him, but it was the Americans who were now the most influential, and a deal could be made with them – they would surely need him to keep order in Italy: hadn't most Italian-Americans been admirers of his?

It seems that on April 22ⁿᵈ he realized the end was close. The only thing to do was to save himself and, possibly, the few who still remained faithful to him – whom he genuinely believed to be more numerous than they actually were. He came to Milan, where strikes – on orders from the CLNAI – were rapidly increasing. With a Monsignore as intermediary, a meeting was arranged with representatives of the CLNAI and the CMAI. That morning I saw Sereni and Marazza. Valiani was keeping me constantly informed on what was happening. The CLNAI representatives asked for unconditional surrrender of the fascists who could not be considered prisoners of war but would be tried by tribunals which had a legal status as a result of the agreements of the previous year between the CLNAI, the Italian government, and the Allied Command. In the atmosphere of the moment there could be no doubt what the verdict of the tribunal judging the ex-dictator would be: his answer never came, he decided to flee.

On the morning of April 25th, the CLNAI held a meeting. In the large, bare, shuttered room whose approaches were watched by silent black-cassocked figures, there were seven of us. Our hearts were heavy with emotion and a burden had been lifted from our spirits. We knew that this was no ordinary day. The end was at hand; the end of the war, for all men; the end of what we had been fighting against for twenty long years, for us. April 25th meant much more to the Italian nation than the *coup d'etat* of July 25th, 1943, the result of palace intrigues. The order to revolt was given to all the organizations of the CLN. Each group had already prepared a plan of action on the basis of the instructions given during the previous months by the CLNAI. We wanted the new democracy to be born with as little bloodshed as possible. Morandi, the socialist economist who had spent years in prison, having been elected President became in fact the head of a provisional government. Commissions were appointed to take charge of the various branches of the administration. A proclamation was drafted, addressed to the population by the CLNAI acting as the government in liberated territory; there were ten signatures, two for each party; of the ten men none had ever slackened in his opposition to the dictatorship.

On leaving the meeting, I saw groups of bewildered

looking German soldiers wandering about. I was going to lunch and to have meetings with friends of Merzagora, and left my bicycle in a parking lot not far from the Piazza del Duomo. One could feel the tension of an impending crisis, but everything looked normal – people in the streets, trams running, shops open, and the troops about just as usual. Less than two hours later I went to get my bicycle. The young attendant said to me:

"Go home, quick!"

"Why?"

"Everyone's running away."

I got on my bicycle, but not to go home. I wanted to see what was happening. Not a tram in sight, not a shop open. Here and there frightened shopkeepers were hurriedly pulling down their shutters. There was scarcely anyone in the streets, only a few people walking fast, hugging the walls. Life seemed suddenly to have stopped. Only on Corso Sempione was there any traffic, cars going north – only north, towards the frontier. The scum of Italy on the run – running to beg asylum from the Swiss, from the guardians of the liberty which fascists had scathingly called a rotting corpse. I could see the apprehensive faces of drivers and passengers; and I could see that the cars were piled with luggage and furs. I shrugged my shoulders – they would not get very far. As I turned into Via Visconti I saw a lorry full of silent men in shirt-sleeves. They were all standing holding guns and rifles. Above them flew the red flag which to Italians means Mazzini's and Garibaldi's republicanism more than Marx's socialism. It was about five o'clock in the afternoon.

I went back to the flat but did not stay there long.

There were appointments. This time I went on foot. The Germans were no longer circulating; they were mounting guard behind the barbed wire that protected their headquarters. By now all the streets were deserted. There was pandemonium inside the fascist barracks; blackshirts and other volunteers seemed to be frantically getting ready for action. I reached the *prefettura*; people were rushing in and out in a great hurry. The courtyard was crowded. No one seemed to be in charge. Out of control and making a good deal of noise, in a big room on the first floor were the last of the fascist *gerachi*, the last of the ministers, the last of the dictator's personal guard. Silence fell gradually, as the room emptied. I thought I recognized the leader of the *Decima Mas* at a window. He was sneering, perhaps at the sight of the rats deserting the sinking ship. By nightfall only a handful of people remained in the large building.

Next morning I twice saw a few fascists trying to make a last stand. The bullets whistling past my ears were the last I was to hear. In the evening I spoke on the radio. I only said a few words and I do not know how I managed to speak at all. Suddenly I felt terribly tired – as if all the events of the last twenty-two years had just happened: the fascist violence in Florence when I was a child, the clandestine frontier crossings, the years of exile, conspiracy, Regina Coeli, Ponza, the endless journeying on three continents, the landings at Salerno and Anzio, the missions along the Tyrrhenian and Adriatic coasts, the parachute drop and the last months in Milan. I had only one wish – to get away from everything and everyone, to be alone and to forget.

I couldn't leave yet. It was necessary to wait for the

arrival of the Allies. In spite of its leaders' efforts, it was difficult for the CLN to control the situation completely. Excesses, understandable even if unjustifiable, did occur. There were, in the CLN, would-be imitators of Marat and Robespierre. There were Partisans who would have liked to do in 1945 what the fascist *squadristi* had done in 1922. Outside Milan strong German units, well equipped and well armed, were in control of roads and bridges; negotiations for surrender proceeded slowly, partly because nobody knew who was really in command, either on the German or the CLN side. Allied officers who happened to be in the former German-occupied territory as members of missions or as prisoners of war, acted on their own initiative, ignoring the agreement which gave the CLN full powers till AMG took over, and giving contrary instructions. The situation on the eastern and western frontier was becoming tense, through Yugoslav and French infiltration. The CLN had to be strengthened so as to repress abuses and to organize forces capable of defending the city, in case the Germans rallied, while waiting for Allied troops to arrive, something I was urging in my messages as hard as I could.

At one session of the CLNAI it was announced that the ex-dictator and other fascist leaders had been arrested. Orders were given to bring the prisoners to Milan to be tried. To avoid misinterpretations I made it clear once again that during the interim period the CLNAI was, in the eyes of the Allies, the government — that governmental powers, of course, included the administration of justice, but that as soon as the Allied troops arrived, the governing authority would automatically pass to the Allies, to whom all prisoners would have to be surrendered; as an Allied officer I was in a position to accept the surrender of regular troops or others recognized by the Allies; I could not do so in relation to civilians or to irregular formations.

There was no trial in Milan. The fascist leaders had already been executed in Dongo. To many people in Italy and abroad, this was a brutal act of civil war. They were wrong. The Dongo executions were the punishments for crimes which until then had gone unpunished, crimes committed twenty, twenty-five years before by the order of the fascist leaders when thousands of people were assassinated to open the road to power for the fascists. The executions at Dongo were punishments for the greatest crime of all – that of robbing the Italian nation of its liberty. Because Italians had been deprived of their liberty, there had been aggressions in Africa, Spain, and the Balkans – the massacre of hundreds of thousands of people who had never done any harm to Italy or to Italians; there had been the steel pact with German fascism and the consequent deaths of nearly half a million Italians in a war which the great majority of Italians did not want, which had no justification, and which brought ruin and devastation to the entire peninsula.

On Sunday, April 29th, I happened to be in Piazza della Scala at noon, and saw the first American patrol – two armoured cars preceded by two jeeps. At first the crowd paid little attention, and it crossed my mind that perhaps the citizens of Milan were as tired and dazed as I was. Next day General Crittenberger, commander of the American IV Army Corps, arrived. So, too, did Colonel Poletti, who found his work as head of AMG facilitated by the administration set up by the CLNAI and Lt.-Col.

Vincent, entrusted with closing down Special Operations missions in Lombardy. Ernesto Rossi, whom I had not seen since he had been arrested in October, 1930, and who had spent thirteen years between prison and *confino*, came to see me. Old familiar faces from *Giustizia e Libertà* days appeared – as in a dream; I was so numbed with tiredness that I could hardly grasp what was going on.

Yesterday the Mayor of Milan gave me the 'freedom of the city' award. Pertini made a speech. In my reply I recalled that twenty-two years ago to the day I first had direct contact with fascist violence. Twenty-two years are a lifetime. Now it is all over and the past can be left where it belongs – in the past. Those who have the strength can concern themselves with the future. I am very tired. The tragedy has lasted a long time. The curtain has fallen. The actors can go home.

School for Freedom, Hof Oberkirch, Switzerland, August, 1957: The above was written in 1945. What was then the biggest threat to liberty had just been destroyed. There were, and there are, others. The twenty years covered in this book were merely an episode. The unending struggle for liberty, man's right and duty to live his own life, knows no respite.

— ⌛ —

In May of 1945, Lt. Col. Massimo 'Max' Salvadori, DSO, MC (front left), was made an 'honorary citizen' of Milan and awarded 'the freedom of the city' [essentially 'keys to the city'] for his role in helping liberate Milan from the Germans and Italian fascists.

His award was presented by Milan's Mayor Greppi and witnessed by British officers and various members of the CLNAI, including Pertini.

INDEX

Pseudonyms and nicknames are indicated by inverted commas. Those who died fighting fascism, because of their personal convictions or in the line of duty, are marked with a star. An 'f' after a page number means the subject is also mentioned in that page's footnote.

INDEX

INDEX

Made in the USA
San Bernardino, CA
04 January 2017